Amulet

A Charm Restored and Sailed to the Western Isles

By the Same Author

The Best Guide to Ravenglass
The Best Guide to Cumbrian Shows
Around and About Ennerdale
Saddle Tramp in the Lake District
Saddle Tramp in the Highlands
Saddle Tramp on the Isle of Man
Over the Fells
Blowout
The History of Harrison & Hetherington Ltd, Carlisle
Lakeland Monuments

Amulet

A Charm Restored and Sailed to the Western Isles

By Robert Orrell

Illustrated

Seafarer Books

2002

© Robert Orrell

First published in the UK by:-
Seafarer Books
102 Redwald Road
Rendlesham
Woodbridge
Suffolk IP12 2TE

UK ISBN 095 38180 71

Typesetting and design by Julie Beadle
Cover design, map and boat plan by Louis Mackay

Photographs by Robert Orrell

Printed in Finland by W. S. Bookwell OY

This book is for
Mrs Pam Dickinson
with apologies
for depriving her
of her plant pot

Introduction and Acknowledgements

This is a book for sailors whether they travel by boat or by armchair, and I hope that those familiar with nautical terms and parts of a wooden boat will forgive me for sometimes explaining the obvious and for including a brief glossary of terms.

Behind the fulfilment of my ambition there were many people who, at no little sacrifice to themselves, helped to make it possible. Most appear in the text and to them my heartfelt thanks and gratitude.

How, by a remarkable coincidence, *Amulet* was eventually returned to the Cameron family who built her in 1964 gives the story a perfect, happy ending and for that I am indebted to Alan Cameron of Fort William, Graham Cameron, also of Fort William but now living in Cambridgeshire, and Mrs Jean Cameron of Ayrshire.

Amulet

Lead keel

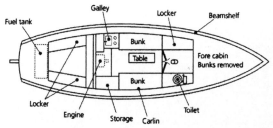

Fuel tank

Galley

Locker

Beamshelf

Bunk

Table

Bunk

Fore cabin
Bunks removed

Locker

Engine

Storage

Carlin

Toilet

Contents

CHAPTER   PAGE

"For a Bottle of Whisky, She's Yours"   9

Mrs Dickinson Loses Her Plant Pot   15

Calming the Bull and Paying the Devil   29

Disaster and the Dawn of a New Millennium   38

Gutless engine, Gale damage and Springing Gunwales   50

Brab's Bitter End and *Amulet*'s Launch   85

To Sea At Last -Exploring Arran - Gateway to The West   102

Old Pals Reunion - Spanish Gold - Skinny Dippers   124

The Anchor Drags - A Dinghy With Legs - Rolling To Canna   150

The Virgin's Infidelity - On Fire - Lassoed By A Lifeboat   174

Gale in the Kyles - Upmarket Urinals - Journey's End   202

About the Author

Glossary of Terms

Map of *Amulet*'s Voyage

"For a Bottle of Whisky, She's Yours."

Thick black smoke poured from the powerful diesel engine of the crane as the wire slings tightened and took the full weight of the old wooden boat, raising it, cautiously, a metre or so above the transporter, then lifting it high into the air and sideways to clear a stone wall and a large glass orchid house. Water streamed from the bilge planking as if the old lady had looked down and wet herself with fright at the thought of what would happen if one of the slings snapped. Looking up from the ground, with similar thoughts running through my own mind, I was close to doing the same; but with practised ease the driver flicked his crane into reverse and gently lowered her onto a waiting steel cradle. The ordeal was over! *Amulet* had arrived.

When the mobile crane and the last of the small band of helpers had gone, I fastened a ladder against the side of the hull, climbed eagerly on board and immediately put both feet through an expanse of rotten wood on the side deck. Trousers torn and bleeding from both shins, I heaved myself out of the hole and crawled onto a cockpit seat. Instantly there was a loud splintering of wood as the locker and the cockpit floor supporting it collapsed and, festooned with an assortment of old paint tins and oily rags, I followed the avalanche of rubble into the bilge and came to rest wedged against the propeller shaft. With so many convenient holes suddenly appearing, giving an almost uninterrupted view from stem to stern, the bilge was as good a place as any from which to take a long look at my newly acquired boat, and it was a depressing sight! Having stood uncovered in a yard in all weathers for over five years, the entire deck, cabin top and cockpit were covered in a thick, green slime. The elegant curved teak deck, once fastened to a plywood base, had sprung apart and split beyond repair, and water had rotted the plywood to a soggy pulp. Rainwater had also caused serious damage to the beams, bulkheads and ribs, on which the boat depended for its strength; and, though the cockpit had looked sound, years of exposure to rain, snow and frost had reduced the whole structure to a crumbling façade held together by a foul-smelling white fungus. As I looked around at the slime, the rapidly-decaying timber, the layers of paint hanging like sheets of paper from the interior of the cabin roof and the alarming shafts of daylight showing through long cracks in the hull planking, my heart sank. I rested my head against the shattered remains of the cockpit lockers and closed my eyes. "Oh God," I groaned, "what have I let myself in for?"

If you live in West Cumbria, anywhere near the ancient harbour towns of Whitehaven or Workington, the quickest way to get to the county's capital, the border city of Carlisle, is along the A595, a rural trunk road that winds through rolling countryside and by picturesque farmhouses and barns built from locally-quarried red sandstone. Occasionally the road crests a high point which opens up stunning panoramic views of the coastal plain and across the tidal waters of the Solway Firth to the hills of southern Scotland. But motorists are seldom able to appreciate the view. On any weekday the road carries an enormous amount of traffic, and during the morning rush hour convoys of upwardly-mobile business types in flashy cars frighten the pants off more sedate motorists by overtaking in crazy situations in their kamikaze attempts to clip another micro-second off their journey time. For much of its length the road is the standard two lane UK trunk road, with just enough room for two vehicles to pass; but from time to time, when governments have acknowledged the urgent problems of their northern outposts and handed over funds for road improvement schemes, the County Council has upgraded and widened a few of the worst sections. Released from the constraints of the bottleneck, the yuppies roar away in a cloud of burning rubber and exhaust smoke; but for ordinary drivers, the new expanses of wide tarmac provide a welcome opportunity to escape from the boredom of staring at the backside of a slow-moving juggernaut or school bus for mile after mile, and they cautiously pull out and overtake.

I had been used to the freedom of the open sea, and the experience of being swept along in this daily tide of aggressive humanity was unbearable; but, desperate for an income after a skippered charter business I operated from Oban foundered in the turbulent waters of the Royal Bank of Scotland, I had returned home to West Cumbria. Job opportunities for someone on the wrong side of sixty were as rare as minke whales on Lake Windermere, and I gladly accepted an invitation to compile and edit a monthly house magazine for a livestock auctioneering company based in Carlisle. It involved an eighty-mile round trip each day along the yuppy-infested, juggernaut-clogged, school-bus-hindered A595, and I loathed it so much I began to explore alternative routes along narrow country lanes. The back roads invariably meandered well away from the direct route and put many more miles on the journey, but they were wonderfully empty of traffic and stress-free, and I discovered parts of Cumbria I had never even heard of. One day I found myself in the tiny hamlet of Curthwaite, nestling in a hollow, complete with a thatched house, old-world cottages and village pub. It was a scene that would have thrilled any landscape painter, but what had me leaping out of my car with excitement was a clinker-built yacht sitting in a rusting steel cradle in the yard of the thatched house. Losing my big ketch to the bank had been very traumatic, and after returning home I had tried to forget the sea; but the sight of this classic wooden yacht brought back all the old yearnings, and I felt that, like me, she longed to feel the movement of the ocean swell and taste salt water. A sign on the wall of the thatched cottage said 'Ian Laval, Furniture Maker' and the yard was stacked with boards of sawn oak. I wanted to knock on the house door and ask if I could climb aboard the boat and nose around, but I knew that, even if it was for sale, there was no possibility of me being able to afford it. I was bankrupt. There was little point in wasting the owner's time, and I crept away.

Whenever I passed through Curthwaite on my way to and from Carlisle, I parked for a short while and sat admiring the boat. It was a great comfort at times of despair and depression. I had no spare money, but dreaming was free and, hoping that villagers out walking their dogs would not suspect I was a burglar and phone the police, I furtively drew rough sketches of the hull and the rig and made lists of what it would probably need to make it seaworthy. About 26' long and clinker-built with a full keel, she had all the appearance of a Stella class, designed by the renowned naval architect Kim Holman in the 1950s, but unlike a conventional Stella she had a raised coach-roof which gave her an extra touch of style. But that was all I could see. The hull resting in a cradle meant that the top of the cabin was about three metres off the ground, and the deck and the interior of the cockpit were hidden from view. Months went by, and I had got no nearer to the boat than the entrance to the yard, but one glorious November day I had been parked, ogling the boat, and was about to drive away when a surge of courage made me leave the car and knock on the house door.

"It's amazing that you should have come today;" said Ian Laval, "it's as though it was meant to happen." A tall, friendly man with a ready smile, Ian had answered my knock and, when I told him of my interest in the boat, he invited me into the house. Over coffee he explained that he was in the process of selling the thatched house and putting his woodworking machinery in store, before leaving for the west coast of Canada to buy a boat and sail it back to the UK via the Panama Canal. "I'd like to find a good home for *Amulet*," he said, staring thoughtfully through the kitchen window at the weathered hull. The sun had gone behind a cloud and a heavy shower of rain was bouncing off the cabin roof and cascading down the planking that had once been painted white, but the protective coating had peeled away exposing areas of bare wood. "It's a lovely name, isn't it? Means 'lucky charm' or something. I haven't got any registration papers for her, but according to a brass plate in the cabin she was built in 1964 by a chap called Cameron, who lived in Fort William in Scotland. The standard of workmanship is very good, but I've no idea whether he was a professional or just a gifted amateur. She's well fitted-out with a diesel engine, a couple of steering compasses, a VHF radio and an autopilot. When I bought her, five years ago, I intended sailing her to Norway and the Baltic, but I've been so busy I haven't had time to work on her, and, as you can see, she's looking a bit neglected." Turning away from the window he said, pointedly, "The mast and spars are in good nick and some of the sails are like new. Even in her present state she must be worth a thousand pounds." "Well, don't get the wrong impression," I laughed. "I get a lot of pleasure from looking at the boat, but I'm not a potential buyer; I'm broke." Undeterred, he said, "Well, if you owned it, what would you do with it?" Reluctant to make myself look foolish by admitting that I had been sitting outside his yard for months, planning voyages and dreaming about the boat like a lovesick lad sighing over a pretty girl, I tried to sound unenthusiastic. "Well, there's absolutely no chance of me raising that sort of money, but I've had a lot of experience with wooden boats, and if I owned *Amulet* I would put what money I could into making her seaworthy and then perhaps sail her round the Western Isles." "Sounds alright to me," said Ian with a big grin. "If you can't afford a thousand pounds, could you manage a bottle of whisky?" I stared at him in disbelief! "A what?" I gasped. "A bottle of whisky," he repeated. "I'm keen to see *Amulet* go to the right person, and for a bottle of whisky, a ten year old MacCallum preferably, she's yours." Outside in the yard the rain had stopped, and *Amulet* was bathed in a glow of sunlight that seemed to melt away the ravages of time and revitalise every piece of her superstructure. She looked magnificent and I was in a daze. I heard my voice say "Done," and we shook hands.

An old friend of mine, Brab Davies, the last of the sailing trawlermen who fished the Duddon Estuary in the south of Cumbria, used to say that if ever he had a grudge against someone he would buy them a wooden boat. "Never buy a wooden boat," he warned in his gruff voice. "Wooden boats is like women. Take one on an' yer 'ands'll never be out of yer pockets; she'll bankrupt yer." After the deal had been sealed I drove away from Ian's house hardly daring to believe my luck, but had barely covered a mile when old Brab's droll advice started to whirl round my head and I felt sick with worry. I had already lost almost everything I owned when my charter enterprise in Scotland had gone bust, and taking on *Amulet* was utterly crazy. I would be pushed to find the money for Ian's bottle of malt whisky, let alone hire a crane and a transporter to get her to my home, and even if I got her home, where was I going to put her? The garden of my rented house might just about take a 26' boat, but what would the owner say? All these problems raced through my head as I drove along, and by the time I reached home the solution was painfully obvious. I would have to phone Ian and tell him it would be impossible for me to take on *Amulet*, and apologise for wasting his time.

But as Ian had said, it was as though it was meant to happen; and a couple of miracles changed everything.

Hearing of my dilemma, a long-standing friend, Patricia Eve, a wooden boat enthusiast and a keen sailor herself, sent me a cheque for £500 with a note that said simply, 'Bring *Amulet* home'. I could hardly contain my excitement, but there was still the matter of permission to put *Amulet* in my garden while I worked on her. Ronald Dickinson, the late owner of the country estate on which my house was situated, had been a naval officer and insisted on having a place for everything and everything in its place, and he liked his tenants to keep their houses neat and tidy. His widow had a reputation for fiercely carrying on the tradition, and when I nervously presented myself at the door of the 'big house' and asked to speak to her, I was uncomfortably aware that a scruffy boat on a rusty cradle was not going to sit unobtrusively amongst tidy flowerbeds and a well-groomed lawn. Mrs Dickinson made it clear she thought so too; but, to my astonishment, she was extremely enthusiastic and very generously suggested I put *Amulet* in the shelter of a barn in her stable yard, and refused to accept rent or payment for the use of electricity.

Events had happened so fast I still had not been able to climb aboard *Amulet* and make a thorough examination of her condition, but now there was no time. With money to move her and a marvellously sheltered and safe place to keep her, there was nothing to hold me back and I hurriedly organised a crane and a transporter. On the crisp sunny morning of January 25th, 1999, I handed over a bottle of MacCallum whisky to Ian Laval and *Amulet* was mine. By an odd coincidence it was the anniversary of the birth of the great Scots poet and philosopher Robert Burns who, a couple of centuries earlier, had warned, "The best laid schemes of mice and men gang aft a-gley." Always a friend of the misguided, Burns may have been dropping a big hint; but I was too excited to notice, and with my car loaded down with wire rigging, sail bags, bunk cushions, anchor chain, and a mass of other vital bits of equipment Ian had unearthed from his sheds, I followed in *Amulet*'s wake as she moved slowly up the hill out of Curthwaite, outward bound on a new adventure.

Mrs Dickinson Loses Her Plant Pot

A damp patch on my hair and the unmistakable smell of diesel stirred me into action as I lay against the wreckage of the cockpit lockers and, opening my eyes, I saw that the collapsing timber had sheared off one of the copper pipes leading from the fuel tank to the engine. Diesel oil was gushing out over the interior planking and running into the bilge. I quickly found the on/off valve and closed it, but it was too late, the tank was almost empty and the cabin floor awash with diesel. A sickening stench overpowered the whole boat and, finding it difficult to breathe, I prised myself out of the rubble and clambered down the ladder to the ground.

It took a couple of days of hard work before I finally mopped up the last of the smelly diesel and was able to take my first good look at *Amulet*, inside and out. Ian said she was a genuine Stella, and the Stella Association's web site on the Internet confirmed her vital statistics, 26' long by 7'9" beam and 3'9" draft. Even the 31' hollow spruce mast had the complicated spreaders of a Stella, but alien to the standard design was the raised coach roof, and I got the impression that perhaps the chap who built her was tall and needed a bit more head room. Another refinement was a completely enclosed self-draining cockpit and a novel 'early warning' system should the boat spring a leak - the automatic bilge pump discharged into the cockpit and sprayed water around the helmsman's ankles. The mahogany cockpit, coamings and cabin sides had originally been varnished, but long exposure to the weather had turned it into a thick green slime, and the teak deck, an unusual feature in a 'low cost' boat, was in a very poor state. The peeling paint on the hull revealed the preferences of successive owners for red, blue, green, white and even a ghastly orange colour, but mercifully the varnish finish in the main and forecabins had been preserved and, though affected by damp, had lost none of its original charm. The layout below was typical of a boat of its size and age; engine under the companionway steps, a tiny galley to port with sink and old fashioned hand pump, copper water tank, and a gimballed two burner gas stove. Two settee/bunks with storage lockers over them in the main cabin, and a forecabin fitted with two small bunks. The interior was similar to a Stella but the builder had made a few improvements, not least a toilet compartment, cleverly concealed with varnished doors which, when open, separated the main and forecabins and gave more room for trouser work. When closed they hid the toilet and gave unrestricted access the length of the boat. The varnished mahogany doors and lockers glowed in the subdued light of the cabin and looked superb, but as old Brab would have said in his gruff, chauvinistic way, "Don't be taken in. Wooden boats is like women, a lick of face paint can hide the ravages of age." When I looked behind the varnish and started poking around *Amulet* with a sharpened screwdriver, I could see what he meant. There was a frightening amount of decay in the sides of the cabin, the beams and bulkheads, and it soon became clear that my dream boat was in a sorry state.

"You're mad," exclaimed my partner, Jean. Hell hath no fury like a woman who is not in favour of her feller buying a boat, and Jean was still suffering from the memory of the hardship of catering for demanding clients in the restricted galley of our ketch and the ignominy of losing all we possessed to the bank. She had a jaundiced view of anything that floated on water, and 'boat' was prominent on her list of unutterable four-letter words. Her enthusiasm for the project had been lukewarm from the start, and my assurances that *Amulet* had 'great potential' and would take 'the minimum amount of money to make her seaworthy' were met with stony silence. She knew to a penny what it cost to maintain even the smallest boat, and when she climbed on board *Amulet* and saw the extent of the neglect she was horrified. I was left in no doubt that, apart from providing me with flasks of tea and sandwiches, she had no intention of helping with the work. Happily, she later changed her mind, but for the present I was on my own and I got on with the depressing task of locating and removing rotting wood.

Not a single one of the strips of teak decking had survived, and the plywood base they were laid on was a mass of soggy pulp that I scooped out by the handful. The short cross-beams supporting the side decks, as well as the carlins and beamshelves they were attached to, which in turn supported the sides of the main cabin and held the hull together, were all completely saturated with water, and the screwdriver plunged into them as if they were soft putty. The cabin top and sides had been beautifully constructed from thick mahogany boards, but fresh water had transformed sections of it into a crumbly sponge which, when scraped away, left gaping holes. Bulkheads separating the cabin from the cockpit fell apart when tapped with the handle of the screwdriver, and water leaking through the deck had completely destroyed several solid oak ribs below the cockpit and one in the toilet compartment. The old Simpson-Lawrence toilet, built mainly of solid bronze castings, had seen better days, but I knew that with a thorough overhaul it would live again. Sadly, this was more than could be said for the Farymann single cylinder 10hp diesel engine. The piston was seized solid, and salt water left in the engine had eaten right through the metal of the cylinder head and ruined it. The once proud example of German engineering excellence was well and truly 'kaput'.

As the days went by, my despair grew in proportion to the rising pile of rotten wood I had ripped out of *Amulet*, and I began to seriously consider abandoning the project. "If you don't want the boat I could find a use for it," offered Mrs Dickinson. She regularly turned up at the barn with a welcome mug of coffee and a plate of biscuits for me, and she arrived one morning when morale had hit rock bottom and I was cursing the day I had lumbered myself with a dream that had become a nightmare. "I could get the chaps at the farm to lift it into the garden with a tractor and I could fill the hull with flowering plants." I was so sick and disillusioned with *Amulet* that I had reached the stage where I was more than willing for Mrs Dickinson to use her as a garden ornament, but first I would have to remove the lead keel and what fittings I could salvage. Patricia had given me £500 to pay for the boat to be moved and I felt obliged to recover the money as best I could. The lead keel, the bronze keel bolts, the deck fittings, the mast, spars, sails and the rest of the equipment would be sold to the highest bidder.

"Don't you even consider it!" thundered Patricia over the telephone when I told her about my plan. "You must be mad." It seemed that no matter what decision I made it was the wrong one. Jean had said I was mad for taking the boat on and now Patricia was saying I was mad for wanting to get rid of it. What was needed was a touch of professional arbitration and I telephoned John Hodgson, a boatbuilder friend who lived at Loch Aline in the west of Scotland. He had served his time at Crossfields of Arnside, renowned in their day for building Morecambe

Bay Prawners, and we had been in partnership in a sailing school in the 1960s. What John didn't know about wooden boats wasn't worth knowing, but to my surprise he didn't seem bothered about the interior and deck when I poured out my horror story, and was only concerned with the hull. "What condition is it in?" he asked. "I'm not sure," I replied. "The beamshelves are knackered and there's one or two longitudinal cracks that let the daylight in, but the planks seem O.K. and I haven't found any sign of rot except where rain water has ruined some of the ribs. It looks to me as if it's been built with European larch planking on oak ribs, with oak deadwoods and a lead keel. Some of the copper fastenings need tightening." There was a long pause while John was obviously considering what I had said. "Well, if the hull is sound at least you've got a project worth considering, but you've let yourself in for one hell of a restoration job and you should get a surveyor to check the hull over before committing yourself."

I didn't like to tell John there was no way I could afford a yacht surveyor, and was wondering what to do when the Gods sent me a free one. As though it was meant to happen, Keith Jones, an ex-marine surveyor, moved into one of the estate houses and, discovering me working on *Amulet* while he was out walking, shot off home for his tools and spent several hours tapping the planking with a small mallet and prodding suspect timber with a penknife. "It's amazing for a boat of this age," he exclaimed, putting his tools away in a box. "I've checked her thoroughly inside and out and the planking is as sound as a drum. You'll have to replace the beamshelves, but the cracks are nothing to worry about, they'll take up when she's in the water. What a shame rainwater has done so much damage to the deck. Anyway, best of luck with the restoration. I don't think you'll be moving very far for a couple of years."

I should have felt pleased that Keith had pronounced the hull sound but standing in a hole that was once the cockpit and looking around at the vast amount of work needed to make the boat seaworthy did nothing to lift my gloom. Never thinking she was anything other than reasonably sound, I had anticipated spending the winter months cleaning *Amulet* up and giving her a coat of paint prior to launching and sailing her in the spring. The last thing I wanted was to be tied to a lengthy restoration project. I already had a full time job editing the magazine and, although I was capable of doing the work myself, I reckoned that the cost of the materials would be in the region of five or six thousand pounds. I didn't have that sort of money.

"If you are prepared to do the work, I'll provide the money." It was Patricia on the phone again. "I've only seen *Amulet* on the photographs you sent me but she's obviously a classic and we can't let a lovely boat like her be broken up." "But," I began. "No buts," she interrupted. "It's unfortunate she's in such a state, but I know you can restore her, so if you are willing, let's get on with it."

Horace, that wise Roman philosopher chap, once said, "We look for happiness in boats." Hoping that happiness was in restoring them as well, I agreed to take on the job, and Mrs Dickinson lost her plant pot.

First I needed a workshop and a store for materials, and once again Mrs Dickinson came to the rescue, and not only offered the use of the barn and benches out of the estate joiner's shop but said I could help myself to anything in the timber store. It was an Aladdin's cave of thick planks of oak, Scots pine and elm, cut from the estate woods in the 1960s and left to season. For someone restoring a wooden boat it was a better gift that a pot of gold. I had plenty of woodworking hand tools but was short of power tools, and from a cut-price machinery store in Carlisle I bought a rise and tilt 10" circular saw bench, a belt sander, an orbital sander and a variable speed electric drill. John Hodgson sent me a large box of different sizes of copper nails and roves and generously loaned me a few specialist tools. I thought it rather extravagant when he also sent about two hundred copies of the American magazine 'Wooden Boat,' but they were packed with practical tips and well-illustrated articles, and when I had a problem I found them easier to understand than many of the boatbuilding books in my collection. The barn was about fifty feet long by twenty feet wide and there was plenty of room for the benches, with storage for the mast and boom and all the paraphernalia that came with the boat. Most important of all, there was electricity. With everything assembled, tools sharpened, materials ordered and Mrs Dickinson bubbling with enthusiasm and arriving at regular intervals with mugs of coffee and biscuits, there was no turning back.

It was a momentous occasion. Not only was a lovely old boat going to be saved from the scrapheap, it was the beginning of the last year of the twentieth century, and halfway through it I would reach the age of sixty five. Everywhere people were planning millennium projects, and I vowed that mine would be to restore *Amulet* and sail her back to Scotland and explore the Western Isles. Well-intentioned relatives muttered that at my age it was time I settled down, but for the first time in months I felt a real sense of purpose and was tremendously elated.

January is a quiet month in the livestock auction industry, and with only a few sales to cover for the company magazine I was able to spend time working on *Amulet* and completely gutted the interior of the hull, leaving only the main bulkheads which divided the toilet compartment from the accommodation and were in good condition. Bunk frames, locker doors, floorboards and anything that could be used again or would make templates for replacements was stacked in the barn, along with the galley sink, water tank, gimballed cooker and the fuel tank. A helpful farming neighbour brought his mechanical hoist and plucked the useless engine from its mountings and swung it to the ground, then saved me a back-breaking struggle by doing the same with the heavy toilet. With the rotten carlins and beamshelves cut away, the carcase of the main cabin was suspended like a bizarre sculpture on temporary spars placed across the boat and held with cramps to stop the hull springing out of shape. Free of clutter, it was much easier to work inside and I was able to pull out the damaged ribs and reach parts of the bilge inaccessible when the engine was in place.

It was now well into February and, with the air temperature hovering around zero, it was fiendishly cold and took a lot of willpower to pull away the frozen tarpaulins covering the boat and start work. One morning I woke to find the countryside and *Amulet* hidden under a thick blanket of snow, and it was a welcome excuse to retreat into the barn and take my first real look at the mast, the boom, and the varnished spinnaker pole and tiller. Having been suspended from the rafters of Ian Laval's workshop for years, they were plastered in a thick layer of fine sawdust, but a vacuum cleaner soon got rid of it and I was highly relieved to find that the beautifully made spruce mast was in superb condition and only needed rubbing down and varnishing. The hollow spruce boom had been made in two halves and looked sound, but when I removed the metal bands from the ends and pushed a knife into the glue seam there was a sharp crack and the two halves fell apart, revealing quite a bit of interior rot. I scooped it out with a wood chisel, then soaked both halves of the boom with Cuprinol. The bone dry wood soaked it up like blotting paper, and I put the boom aside pending a decision on whether it was repairable. The nicely rounded and tapered spinnaker pole had been shaped from a piece of Columbian pine and varnished and, like the mast, only needed a few coats of varnish to restore it. The tiller had been lovingly fashioned from a piece of oak and I tried to imagine how *Amulet* must have looked, varnished and gleaming, on the day she was launched in 1964.

Outside the barn it was snowing heavily, so I kept close to the blast of warm air from an electric fan heater and set about dismantling the Simpson-Lawrence 'Standard' toilet. The company's latest catalogue had arrived by post that morning and, browsing through it over breakfast, I was staggered to read that it would have cost over one thousand pounds to replace the 'Standard' and I wondered who on earth could afford to pamper their backsides with that sort of money. Had the old thunderbox been beyond repair it would have meant going back to the time-honoured system of 'bucket and chuck it'; but the bronze nuts and bolts came apart easily and once the hard scale left by salt water had been chipped out and the parts washed in a bucket of detergent, I could see that all it needed was a new set of gaskets, a coat of white enamel and the seat varnished and it would be like new. Checking through the small stack of cabin and locker doors, I was miffed to find that the varnished finish on almost every one of them had been spoilt by water and would need stripping. It would be a time-consuming job, and it would have to wait. The weatherman on the telly had been promising a rapid thaw and a spell of fine weather, and I was eager to get on with the laborious task of burning the paint off the hull.

The weatherman's prediction was right. A warm sun melted the snow and for the next few days, although there was a hard frost at night, it was warm and sunny during the day and a pleasant change to work outside without the need for sweaters and an anorak. Someone, presumably *Amulet*'s builder, had fitted shaped strips of wood the full length of the planking, starting slightly above and reaching below the waterline. It was a dodge some builders of clinker boats adopted in the belief that it helped to reduce the noise of water lapping against the planking, but it was not a device I was in favour of and, in any case, the strips showed signs of springing away from the hull and water could be trapped behind them. I started to prise them off, but soon wished I hadn't. Some peeled away like a banana skin while others would not budge and had to be chopped off. But, horror of horrors, they had all been screwed on and there were one hundred and fifty tiny screw holes in each plank, some penetrating right through. Forcing waterproof filler into the smaller ones and plugging the larger ones with slivers of larch dipped in glue used up two days and, by the time I had got organised with a gas bottle and torch to start burning the paint off the hull, there was a definite change in the air and I only managed to burn the paint off the port side before the sun dived behind a bank of threatening clouds and rain poured down as if it had every intention of staying around for a while.

In fact it stayed for a week, but I was at the livestock mart for most of it and the tarpaulins on *Amulet* lay undisturbed. I was utterly sick of my job at the mart and longed to be at the barn working on *Amulet*; but with rent and the usual domestic outgoings to meet I needed an income. Like many large organisations, the mart was riddled with intrigue, ambitious ladder-climbers jockeying for position and an unhealthy amount of verbal back-stabbing. The very likeable and popular managing director had fallen foul of the board of directors and it was clear they were out to topple him. Staff morale was low, but it was the time of year when dairy farmers looked for new stock and sales had to go on. Having sat through one particularly tedious sale of four hundred dairy cattle, I was so weary of the endless parade of massive udders I resolved never to drink milk again and in the mart café at lunchtime I ordered black coffee. "Aye, I know what you mean," laughed an old farmer friend when I explained why I had opted for black coffee. "For a hot-blooded feller, two nipples can be exciting but four of them, clustered together and about three inches long at that, take some getting used to." It was a two-day sale and on the second day I went well prepared. In between photographing gargantuan prize udders, I nipped out to my car and studied the sail and rigging plans of a Stella.

February gave way to March and I was overjoyed, though a bit apprehensive, when John Hodgson phoned to say he was driving down to visit relations in the Lake District and would call and have a look at

Amulet. I valued his opinion, but I knew he was a perfectionist and would never accept anything but the highest standard of workmanship. As far as I was concerned *Amulet* was a workboat, a means of fulfilling a dream, and as long as she was sound and seaworthy her appearance was of secondary importance. Not a man who wasted words, John climbed out of his car, put his glasses on and walked slowly round the outside of the hull, tapping it at regular intervals and muttering with disapproval when he sighted along the planking and spotted one plank on the port side a fraction out of line with its mate on the starboard side. He whistled through his teeth when he climbed on board and saw the extent of the devastation, but when he eventually spoke it was cheering news. "The hull's sound, but you'll have to rake out all that sealing compound in the lands. You were right, she's built of larch on oak. It won't take a lot of work to replace the ribs, but don't use anything but English oak. Build a steaming box and you'll find the strips will bend easily. About twenty minutes steaming for inch-thick oak will do. Don't use anything but best quality timber for the beamshelves and carlins; get well-seasoned Columbian pine. Use it for the cockpit frames as well. I'd rather see a teak deck, but it will be too expensive so you'll have to fit a plywood deck and sheathe it with fibreglass cloth. She's a nice little boat! Reminds me of the Folkboats we used to build at Shepherds on Windermere." And that was it. He poked at the mast in the barn and grunted his approval, then climbed into his car and drove off back to the West of Scotland. I yearned for the day when *Amulet* would be afloat and I could follow him.

In between trips to the mart and bouts of rain, I managed to burn off the rest of the hull and give the bare wood a coat of primer. I was puzzled by a round object, about two inches in diameter, embedded low down on the stem; and carefully chipping away the layers of old paint I was surprised to find it was a transducer for an old type of echo sounder. I stuck a strip of tape over it and hoped that when the time came to install an echo sounder it would work and save me fitting a new one.

Having to remove the tarpaulins every time I wanted to work on *Amulet* was tedious so, with Mrs Dickinson's permission, I cut a few long poles out of the estate wood and made a frame to drape the tarpaulins over *Amulet* like a tent. There was very little headroom to work on the deck or in the cockpit, but it meant I could climb on board or work on the outside of the hull and not be held up by rain or snow. What I had not bargained for was that the tent was a perfect target for a bored wind-god sitting on a cloud with nothing better to do than cause trouble, and a few days later he unleashed a fierce south westerly gale that screeched up the Cumbrian coast and reduced the tent to a tangle of broken poles and ripped tarpaulins. Torrential rain followed the gale, soaking every scrap of the hull inside and out and filling the bilge almost to the level of the floor beams. Water spewed out of the garboard planks like a fountain and, helpless to do anything about recovering the tent until the weather improved, I took refuge in the barn. Basking in the warmth of the electric heater, I finished repairing the boom and made a start on scraping the varnish off the mast with my trusty bent file scraper. I learnt later I could have removed the varnish in half the time with a hot air gun which, unlike a gas torch, does not mark varnished wood, but at the time I was unaware of this handy gadget, and old habits die hard. The varnished finish certainly looked as if it only needed rubbing down and a few coats of varnish applying, but I was concerned that the mast had been lying in the rafters of Ian Laval's workshop for five years or more and it was an ideal breeding ground for woodworm. I was ~~leathe~~ to pile on more work than was necessary, but I reasoned that I would rather satisfy myself that the mast was sound than have it collapse in a cloud of dust while clawing off a lea shore in the teeth of a Hebridean gale. It took a couple of days of hard scraping before the lovely straight-grain of the wood was revealed in its true glory, but there was little time to spend gazing at it. The rain clouds had cleared away and outside a weak sun was doing its best to soak up the damp. Brushing a few quick coats of Cuprinol onto the bare wood and squirting a litre or so up the hollow centre with the aid of a garden weed-killer spray, I left if to dry and went to resurrect the tent. It was a Saturday and, in response to my pleas for help, a few friends arrived to give me a hand to untangle the wreckage of the tent and rebuild it over *Amulet*. They were clearly jittery that they might get press-ganged into helping with other jobs, and talked loudly of urgent family commitments. By an incredible coincidence several aged aunts had died that week and funerals had to be organised, there were family weddings at the other end of the country and even abroad, and there was the alarming case of the pregnant Siamese moggy, renowned for multiple births, who had the unsavoury habit of firing out her newborn like machine gun bullets all over her owner's bed and needing round the clock surveillance.

Once *Amulet* was safely under the tent the helpers shot away down the estate drive with the speed of rabbits pursued by a ferret, but my partner, Jean, stayed behind to assist with the rigging up of a cable between the barn and the boat to provide electric light and power. A hefty hand-operated pump made short work of the water in the bilge and then Jean began the back-breaking task of raking out the accumulated rubbish wedged in the planking joints and under the ribs. In the process she discovered a cable attached to the transducer I had found in the stem and I tied it to a rib ready for the day when it would be needed. When Jean left to prepare our evening meal, I made a list of the timber I would need to replace the deck beams, the beamshelves and the carlins. By some miracle, all the foredeck beams in front of the cabin had survived, and I worked out what I hoped would be a fairly easy way of splicing the new supporting beams into them. For an amateur, the work involved in fitting the new timber and attaching the carcase of the cabin securely to it was complex and the problems associated with designing and building a new watertight self-draining cockpit were frightening; but, as John Hodgson was unlikely to be breathing 'perfection' down my neck, I felt I could get away with what he used to scathingly dismiss as 'fishing boat standard'. First though I had to make sure the hull was completely tight before moving on to anything else, and that meant painstakingly checking every nail and fastening. I estimated there were about two thousand five hundred of them. It was clear that if *Amulet* was to be finished and ready to sail to Scotland early in 2000 I was going to need regular help, but from where?

There are no better volunteers than innocents who are not aware of what they are letting themselves in for, and I called to see Margaret Vincent, a friend who lived nearby. "I'm going to start tightening the nails in *Amulet*'s planking tomorrow," I said casually, "and wonder if you would like to help me. There's nothing to it. All you have to do is hold a metal bar against the nail on the outside of the hull while I tap it with a hammer from the inside." To be persuasive it is sometimes necessary to be economical with the truth, and it seemed prudent not to mention that nail-tightening sessions in the many wooden boats I have owned had probably lost me more friends than if I had suffered from chronic halitosis. Seasoned nail-knockers know only too well that tightening existing copper nails in clinker planking can be strenuous and requires the use of a heavy iron rod, or in my case the handle of a large Stillson wrench, ground to a point similar in diameter to the head of the nail. The helper holds the device as best they can against the nail, utilising whatever frontal parts of the body can comfortably absorb the shock of the hammering. Meanwhile the 'expert' inside the hull places a hollow metal tube against the rove, belts the top of the tube with a light hammer to draw the nail through the planking then, having removed the tube, hammers the end of the nail flat against the rove or, if he's a real expert, to a dome. Two taps on the inside planking with a hammer is the signal to move to the next nail, and so it goes on, hour after relentless hour, until, at the end of the day, lady helpers go home with bruised and battered boobs and men helpers go home using vile language. "Sounds fun," said Margaret. "I'll be round in the morning." I gulped and said nothing.

True to her word, Margaret turned up the following morning and, having demonstrated what was required of her, I climbed aboard and we started at the bow on the port side. With a mountaineer's headtorch clamped to my head, and sometimes bent almost double, I was certain that in the process of tightening nails high in the forepeak I had reached places no other human had been before. Pulling myself backwards or crawling along on my hands and knees, I was able to advance a nail at a time towards the stern but had barely got the length of the top plank when groans and yelps of pain on the outside of the hull indicated that Margaret's initiation into the nail-knockers art was well advanced. In the interest of wooden boat restoration, and remembering that I had to have *Amulet* finished as quickly as possible, I ignored the sounds and, with two taps on the hull, signalled her to move to the next nail. There was a gasp and what sounded like a muffled curse, but she moved and by a slow but anguished progression back and forth along *Amulet*'s side we managed to complete three planks. When I climbed down the ladder for a lunch break, Margaret had downed tools and was sitting on a wall. "It's a tiring job, isn't it?" I ventured, handing her a cup of coffee from a thermos flask. She did not answer but stared at me with a glazed expression. Margaret was a Buddist and would not hurt a fly, or any other living creature, but the way she looked at me over the rim of her coffee cup I had the feeling that had I been a fly she would have gladly flattened me with her woolly hat and thought nothing of it. She was utterly worn out and complained of having a painful shoulder, but after resting for a while she perked up and bowled me over by offering to help again if I needed it. I gladly accepted, but made a mental note to keep future nail-knocking sessions as short as possible.

Falling over the rusting remains of the Farymann engine in the barn one morning jogged me into giving some thought to replacing it, though browsing through the glossy catalogues of marine engine manufacturers only confirmed what I knew already, their idea of 'affordable' was way beyond my pocket. With the help of an electrician who had inadvertently strayed into the barn while tracing a fault at the 'big house' I lifted the old engine onto a bench, but even when cleaned up with a can of paraffin and a brush it was obvious from the daylight showing through the jagged holes in the cylinder head that its seagoing days were over. The price quoted by the Farymann UK agent for a new cylinder head was laughable and, even if I had bought it, there was no way of knowing whether the engine was in running order, so I placed an advertisement in the yachting press for a second-hand diesel engine, preferably a Farymann which would match up to the existing propeller and shaft. Several hopefuls tried to offload assorted mechanical nightmares that sounded as if they might have powered Noah's Ark, then one evening a chap from Dursley, near Gloucester, phoned to say he had a brand new Farymann that had been a display model at the London Boat Show. He explained that he had been an engineer with Lister Marine Engines when Lister and Farymann combined forces in a joint venture, and after the show he had acquired the surplus engines. "It's brand new," he assured me, "and it's immaculate. All the metal fittings have been chromed for display purposes and it's complete with a two to one reduction gearbox. I want seven fifty for it." I knew that if I bought a new Farymann from the manufacturer there would not be much change left out of four thousand pounds, and being offered a new one for a fraction of the price sounded decidedly fishy. He must have read my thoughts. "Believe me, it's genuine!" he said confidently. "I've had it lying around my garage for a couple of years and it's in the way. Farymann engines are not well known in this country and I'm keen to sell it. Why not come and see it for yourself?" My brother-in-law, Owen, had just bought himself a smart new car and, keen to give it a long run, he generously offered to run me to Dursley. We set off from Cumbria at the crack of dawn one bleak, windswept morning and, bog-eyed and longing for a hot drink, we followed directions provided by the engineer and eventually pulled up outside his house on a smart suburban estate of lookalike houses. He was very welcoming and, though his wife was busy with their children, she took time to cook us a breakfast. Having enjoyed a plate of bacon and eggs and a few cups of coffee, we went out to inspect the engine. It was all he said it was. Sprayed an attractive blue and with the fuel lines and other metal parts chrome- plated, it was pristine and certainly looked worth every penny of the asking price. It loaded surprisingly easily into the trunk of Owen's car and, leaving behind our thanks for the breakfast and a wad of notes for the engine, we headed north for Cumbria. Back at the barn, the engine was carefully lifted onto a wooden pallet and stowed in a dry corner. Before covering it with plastic sheets to protect it from damp and dust until I was ready to install it, I gave it a rub with a cloth and smeared the gleaming chrome with grease. As the engineer had said, it was brand new and I imagined it humming smoothly as *Amulet* threaded her way through the Scottish Isles. Little did I realise I had bought a whole lot of trouble!

Calming the Bull and Paying the Devil

Pick up any yachting magazine and it is a sure bet there will be pages of yacht chandlers offering 'cut price' equipment and clothing, with tempting carrots like 'exclusive offer', 'sensational reductions' or 'we will not be beaten in price'. Put to the test, give or take a pound or two, there is not a lot between them; and even when a giant who by massive bulk buying, can offer price tags that have sailing types leaping for the phone or e-mail, it has been my experience with these companies that the left hand does not seem to know what the right hand is doing. I have had urgently-needed equipment sent to the wrong address, and on one occasion, having hung about in a harbour for weeks waiting for a part supposedly sent 'express delivery', it never arrived at all. Staff can be unhelpful to the point of being abusive and mention wooden boats and they react as if you had just arrived from Mars.

Like anyone else short of cash, I was keen to keep the cost of restoring *Amulet* to a minimum; but having typed out a list of equipment and fittings so long it could have been mistaken for the prototype of a new brand of toilet roll, and with the estimated cash total curiously reminiscent of the Olympic Games' insignia, my priority was an efficient service from a supplier I could rely on. On the edge of Derwentwater in the Lake District, Nick Newby runs Nichol End Marine, a boatyard cum sailing school, cum chandlers, cum café; cum in anyone who enjoys talking and can let an hour go by even if all they wanted was to buy a small shackle. Though twenty miles inland from the coast, Nichol End probably has the best-stocked chandlery in the area and according to Nick, "If we haven't got what you want in stock, it soon will be." He is a time-served boatbuilder and, like John Hodgson, had worked at Shepherd's yard on Lake Windermere in the 1950s, building wooden Folkboats. He has an incredible knowledge of boats and boat fittings and when I showed him my list all he said was, "That'll be no problem. I'll give you ten per cent off everything you buy and I'll deliver it when I'm down your way." Cut-price promises are no substitute for personal service, and Nick's knowledge and ready advice was to become invaluable as the work on *Amulet* slowly progressed.

The only problem was the availability of specialist wooden boat items such as long galvanised bolts and traditional fittings. With real ships' chandlers like the old established firms of Simpson-Lawrence of Glasgow and Davey & Co of London having to adapt to the demands of the market for stainless steel clad fibreglass boats, anything 'non standard' was not easy to find. Fortunately, despite the demise of so many revered UK yards, the art of wooden boat building is still alive and kicking, and another Scottish boatbuilder friend came to my aid. Based on the Ardnamurchan Peninsula in the Sound of Mull, Sandy Macdonald builds the most magnificent varnished clinker-built sailing craft and he went to considerable trouble to supply me with difficult-to-find galvanised items, bronze screws, caulking cotton and lots more. But fixing myself up with a supplier of chandlery was child's play compared to finding a source of quality timber. In my area of Cumbria, once noted for building wooden ships that were sailing the world from the port of Whitehaven when Southampton was still a muddy backwater, one timber merchant was clearly mystified when I ordered straight grained Columbian pine and sheets of marine plywood. I was sent softwood which could only be classed as 'dog kennel quality', and the imported plywood's only claim to being 'marine' was that it had been transported by ship from the country of origin. A tip from a builder led me to Stanleys Joiners, a very helpful woodworking business in Keswick that had a reputation for high-class workmanship and I was soon on my way home, parting the throngs of visitors in Keswick main street with two long planks of Columbian pine roped to the roof of my car. I ordered various thicknesses of genuine marine ply from another source.

That evening the small circular sawbench paid for itself by sawing 3" x 2" strips off the planks for the beamshelves and carlins and, with the aid of the tilting blade, making short work of cutting a bevel to allow for the camber of the side decks. The surplus pieces of plank provided strips which would eventually be cut to length for the side deck beams. With the aid of an old industrial jigsaw donated by a friend, I shaped two slightly curved beams which would eventually be fitted across the full width of the after deck behind the cockpit. Jean offered to help to fit them and the following morning, with her outside of the hull, balanced on a plank suspended between two stepladders, and me on the inside, we pulled the new beamshelves into place with G-cramps and 'nail-knocked' heavy gauge copper nails at short intervals through the beam and the top plank of the hull. The port side completed, we moved to the starboard side and by late afternoon both beamshelves were secured and Jean dropped the 'nail-knocking' tool to the ground with a sigh of relief. The job of rebuilding *Amulet* had begun, and the clean new timber and the gleaming copper nails seemed to bring her alive.

By now May had given way to June, and I was kept so busy attending sales and putting the newspaper together that the work on *Amulet* had to be put on hold. The crisis at the mart had worsened, with the managing director being finally ousted by the board and replaced by an ex-banker whose number one priority was reorganising the company, and staff morale hit the floor. The only spark of light relief was at an important sale of continental Limousin bulls. At most major livestock marts, bulls are paraded round in a hall so that prospective buyers can satisfy themselves that the animal's essential bits are hanging where they ought to hang; and since Limousin bulls are unpredictable creatures and given to making for the door at the first whiff of a cow, the handlers have a fool-proof technique for soothing their charges and preventing a ton and a half of beefsteak running amok and flattening the onlookers. Each handler, male or female, has a stick and they run the end of it gently up and down the bull's 'willy'. The lucky Limousin stands perfectly still with a glazed expression on its face and, not surprisingly, shows no inclination to move. Bull sales attract the farming press and there was a rather obnoxious photographer who thought he was God's gift to women and was fancying his chances with a very pretty farmer's daughter in charge of a huge Limousin, which she was keeping quiet by the time-honoured method. "Come and do that to me," shouted the photographer, making a lewd gesture with his midriff. The girl smiled at him for a moment and then pointing at the bull said sweetly, "I would if you had one as big as his." The crowd roared with laughter and the photographer made a quick exit.

Being stuck at the mart during a spell of gorgeous weather, ideal for working on *Amulet*, was incredibly frustrating and, when a sympathetic lady who worked with the auctioneers offered to cover a few sales for me, I was so overjoyed I could have hugged her; but instead handed over my cameras and drove as fast as I could for the barn. With the tarpaulins pulled away it was incredibly hot and I was lathered in sweat even stripped down to shorts and tee shirt, but the conditions were perfect for drying glue and I soon had the curved after-deck beams fastened into place. Manoeuvring the long carlins and lining them up with the sides of the cabin was a bit tricky on my own, but with the aid of G-cramps to hold them, lengths of string to pull the ends into tenon joints chiselled into the after-deck beams, and a few swear words when the cramps fell off and I had to start all over again, I fixed them into position, and it was thrilling to see the cockpit area and the decks taking shape. The next step required the use of a 'nail-knocker's' mate to help attach the carlins to the sides of the cabin with copper nails and roves and, desperately anxious not to waste the perfect weather I went to look for a 'volunteer'. Jean was away tending to her horse and, after letting her phone ring continuously, I managed to drag Margaret away from painting her bungalow. "What do you want?" she said irritably when she recognised my voice. "Sorry to trouble you," I said, "but I'm desperate to get a couple of beams fixed onto the cabin and I need a nail-knocker, can you help?" "Oh well," she sighed, "I've nothing planned for tomorrow. When do you want me to come?" "Now!" I said. "The forecast says it's going to pour with rain tomorrow." The urgency to get jobs finished turns boat restorers into incurable liars. The forecast was for continuing hot weather but, fortunately, Margaret did not stop to check and, with her leaning wearily on the handle of the old Stillson wrench, I hammered the last nail onto the rove just as it was going dark. The carlins and the cabin were rock solid and ready for the side deck beams.

I had not bothered to cover *Amulet* after nailing the carlins and there was a fat tawny owl perched on the edge of the hull when I arrived at the barn very early the following morning. He was so intent on watching for a mouse to appear from under the barn door he completely ignored me, and I had climbed the ladder and was in the cockpit before he glared at me with his fierce eyes and let out a loud screech. I had deprived him of his breakfast and, as he launched himself into the air he showed his displeasure by leaving a mess on the cabin roof. The sun was still struggling to climb above the rim of the Lakeland fells, but in the estate woods the dawn chorus of bird song was already in full swing, heralding another beautiful day. By eight o'clock I had measured and cut to size all the short side-deck beams and, while waiting for the air to warm sufficiently to start gluing them into place, I set about making a steaming box, about eight feet long by six inches square, to have it ready for the day when I could get around to fitting the new ribs. It was a simple design based on a principle employed by builders of wooden boats in ancient times. A long, four sided box blocked off at one end but with a hole bored into it to take a pipe from a boiler – in my case it was to be a two gallon petrol can heated with camping stoves. The strips of oak for the ribs are placed in the box, and the open end blocked off with rags. When whatever source of heat used is applied to the boiler, steam fills the box and softens the oak strips so that they will bend to fit the curve of the hull without snapping. Old Brab Davies used to say, "Git it right and they'll bend like tripe," but that is easier said than done. His favourite method was to use a cast iron rainwater pipe instead of a wooden box, but in these days of plastic everything, try asking a builders' merchant for a cast iron pipe!

By the time I had finished making the steaming box, the sun had risen well above the fells, and I put it aside and got on with the job of fitting the side beams. At measured intervals I chiselled notches out of the beamshelves and carlins, dropped a splodge of epoxy resin in, pushed the deck beams into the notches and hammered a galvanised nail into each end. When Jean arrived at lunchtime with flasks of coffee and sandwiches, I had just finished fitting the last beam. Her timing was perfect; I needed a helper for the next job, fitting the lodging knees. I have no knowledge of how fibreglass hulls are held together, but to strengthen the stern of a wooden boat thick triangular pieces of oak, lodging knees, are fastened in the port and starboard corners where the top plank and beamshelf meet the transom. To give it a pleasing shape, a curve is cut out of the longest side of the triangle and the edges rounded off and it is then held in position with galvanised bolts or lengths of round copper rod, the ends hammered over a rove like a planking nail. Contrary to what some writers of books about building wooden boats would have us believe, fitting lodging knees to complex angles can be an absolute pig of a job, but my powerful industrial jigsaw sliced through the pieces of 40mm thick oak as if they were butter, and its tilting table mechanism made light work of the tricky job of accurately bevelling one edge to fit the slight angle of the beamshelf and the other edge to sit neatly against the acute angle of the transom. With a dab of glue on the edges to hold them in place and make it easier to drill holes for the fasteners, I left them to dry held by G cramps, and joined Jean for lunch. Within half an hour the hot sun had set the glue and, having bored the necessary holes through the hull and lodging knees with a long drill, the eight 6mm copper rods were pushed through. With gritted teeth, Jean endured the painful vibrations through the old wrench handle when I had to use extra force with a hammer to flatten the ends of the thick copper then, pleading a sore shoulder and ribs, she made a dash for freedom.

Amulet was beginning to look like a boat again instead of a forlorn hulk. Except for a hatch in the after deck to accommodate the fuel tank, the entire deck frame was finished and work could start on building the cockpit. The only eyesores were the sides and front of the cabin. The thick green slime had dried to a rock-hard coating and, though I tried all sizes of hand scrapers it refused to budge and I was forced to resort to a tactic that would have had a perfectionist tearing his hair. It yielded instantly to the scouring action of a circular wire brush on the end of an electric drill. It put paid to any hope of re-varnishing the mahogany, but in any case the surface had been so badly pitted by the action of rainwater it needed repairing with epoxy resin and then, as old Brab would have said, given a lick of paint to conceal the ravages of age. Cleaned off, the cabin was bone dry and, taking advantage of the ideal conditions, I thoroughly soused the exterior and all the newly-installed wood in Cuprinol preserver. Any bugs lurking about in the bilge and fancying a timber-burger were in for a nasty shock and severe bellyache.

During his flying visit John Hodgson had said I should rake out the garboard seams and re-caulk them with cotton, but first I should remove the existing brass screws from the garboard planks above the keel and replace them with bronze screws. A simple enough job for someone in the flush of youth but for a wrinkly like me, whose midriff had extended to conceal his toe caps, the act of crawling under the hull was a contortion of aching limbs and the inspiration of new expressions that would not have been welcomed at a vicar's tea party.

To make matters worse, the heads of some of the screws snapped off as soon as pressure was put on them with a screwdriver and though I tried to drill them out, it was hopeless, so I filled the holes with epoxy resin and fixed new bronze screws alongside them. Amongst the many thousands of books written about boats there must be one that explains the origins of nautical expressions; though anyone who has crawled under a wooden boat, mallet in one hand, caulking chisels and cotton in the other, to work on the garboard seam will be very familiar with the meaning of 'There's the devil to pay'. Yachts must be a lot easier to work on than the flat-bottomed sailing ships of the nineteenth century, but caulking the garboard seam is a job that can only be relished by a masochist and I was heartily relieved when I had belted the last twist of cotton home with the mallet, sealed the seams with a water-curing flexible compound and heaved myself out into the sun.

One fault in the hull 'Eagle Eye' Hodgson had discovered was at the base of the curved stem. At some time in her life *Amulet* had hit an obstruction that had torn off the shaped piece of 'deadwood' which neatly filled the gap between the keelson, the hefty length of oak forming the backbone of the boat and to which the stem is attached, and the front of the lead keel. It had been replaced with a chunk of 'dog kennel' grade spruce, crudely fastened to the keelson with two six-inch wire nails and saved me a lot of bending and grunting by falling off when I clouted it with a heavy hammer.

A hunt round the estate timber store uncovered a fine piece of English elm which, when trimmed with the circular saw and sculptured with a very coarse-grade disk attached to a heavy duty electric sander, fitted the gap perfectly. Plastered with a layer of water-curing compound on the joints, bolted to the keelson with three long galvanised coach screws, and given a final light finishing with the sander and a coat of primer, it merged so well into the curve of the stem I was very proud of my handiwork. It was my lucky day. The hunt round the timber store had also revealed a magnificent oak plank about eight feet long by ten inches wide and planed to three quarters of an inch, the exact thickness I required for the new ribs. I cut five one inch wide strips out of it, and rounded one face of each to give a touch of professionalism when the ribs were fitted in the hull. It was late in the evening when I managed to drag myself away from *Amulet* and go home, and the tawny owl was sitting patiently on a nearby branch waiting to flit over to his perch on the deck. I was so tired I could only manage a cup of tea and a sandwich before I crashed into bed, but I was extremely happy. It had been one of the most productive days yet and the following day, helpers willing and weather permitting, I would raise steam and get the new ribs in.

I overslept and the sun was already burning a hole in the sky when I reached the barn and hurriedly carried the steaming box into the open and set it up with the blocked end resting on a pile of bricks about two feet high and the open end raised a foot or so higher. Jean was suffering from a painful shoulder and said she would help all she could, but nail-knocking was definitely out. On the phone it took a lot of persuasive talking to coax Margaret away from enjoying her garden, but I promised not to work her too hard and half an hour later she arrived in her car.

Way back in the 1970s a friend gave me a smartly-painted British Petroleum 2 gallon petrol can, complete with polished brass cap and a flexible brass spout. "Vintage car enthusiasts go mad for these," he said. "Keep it safe, one of them is bound to offer you a lot of money for it." So I kept it, but though I advertised it no one offered me a lot of money for it, in fact nobody offered me anything for it and it lay gathering dust in my shed until one day I fell over it and realised it was the perfect boiler for a steaming box. Filled with water it was balanced on three paraffin pressure stoves belching out flames and the end of the flexible brass spout was rammed into the hole bored in the base of the steaming box. While Jean and Margaret got the nail-knocking gear and the electric drill together and hunted round the wood shed for props to hold the freshly steamed ribs into place in the hull, I stood by the boiler and waited confidently for results; but Mrs Dickinson, who was in her garden and had been alarmed by the roar of the paraffin stoves, was not happy with my assurances that all was well. She was worried that the contraption might explode and annihilate the barn. With perfect timing a wisp of steam spiralled out of the top of the box and, when I pushed the strips of oak in and bunged the hole up with an old towel, it helped to convince her that it really was a steaming box and not a missile launcher.

I left the strips in the box for nearly half an hour, then spurred the team into action. The shortest rib to be fitted was in the toilet compartment, and Jean swiftly passed the hot strip up to Margaret in the cockpit, who handed it down to me in the cabin, and I pushed one end into place against the keelson and forced it to bend to the curve of the hull by jamming a timber prop against it. I drilled holes through the rib at every plank joint, Margaret pushed nails through from the outside and held the wrench handle against the heads while inside the hull I cut each nail to size and hammered the heads over roves. The prop was knocked away, the surplus length cut off just below deck level and in a twinkling the job was done and a perfect fit. Actually, the twinkling took about an hour but the time passed so quickly and the rib went in so trouble-free, I felt I had mastered the technique and the other three would, as old Brab had said 'bend like tripe'. I was wrong. The next one was a long brute that started on the port side just behind the cabin, snaked round the concave curve of the hull and under a stringer, a long piece of flat timber running the whole length of the boat on both sides to strengthen the hull, and finally curved in the opposite direction and dived into the deepest part of the bilge. Whoever steamed in the original rib had the advantage of fitting it before the beamshelf and stringer were in place, and had run it in one piece right from the top plank of the hull down into the bilge without any apparent difficulty. I tried to do the same and made a complete mess of it. By the time I had pushed the strip behind the beamshelf and struggled to get it under the stringer it had cooled off, and when I bent it into the bilge it snapped like a twig. In the end I took the easy option and fitted it in two halves, an acceptable repair if not the most professional. The remaining two ribs did not go into the bilge and were bent into place without any trouble and swiftly nailed tight. At last the job was finished and, glancing at my watch, I was amazed to find it was long past noon. The heat of the sun and the frenzied rush to get the hot strips into the hull had drained us and we were all wilting rapidly and in need of a rest. With the roaring paraffin stoves turned off, peace returned and we sat in the shade of a tree and dawdled over lunch.

Disaster and the Dawn of a New Millennium

During August and September I saw very little of *Amulet* apart from the odd Sunday when I managed to slap a coat of primer on the hull or splash Cuprinol wood preserver on the interior, and the few occasions when I had half an hour to spare during the day and drove round to the barn to brush a coat of varnish on the mast, boom and spinnaker poles. It was incredibly frustrating and, even though I had been closely involved in farming during my life as well as having had a long association with the sea, I had lost interest in agriculture. My all-consuming passion was the restoration of *Amulet* and the longing to sail her to Scotland. The autumn sales were keeping me away from my boat and I began to resent the long, wasted hours I spent wedged on hard benches in packed sale rings day after boring day, watching endless processions of pedigree bulls, cows and calves being judged or going under the hammer. If one of them made a record price, I would have to rush out and hang around the pens waiting for an opportunity to photograph the beast and its often very unco-operative and condescending owner. Sheep sales were worse. To have to watch several hundred sheep going through the ring was fatiguing, but to endure fifty thousand or more was an ordeal, particularly on the numerous times when I was jammed for hours in the midst of a solid mass of farmers, absolutely bursting for a pee and gasping for a cup of coffee. By October I had seen enough cows' udders and bovine testicles to last a lifetime and my head was reeling from the noise of bleating sheep and the whingeing of wealthy farmers leaning against their new Range Rovers complaining they were having a hard time making ends meet. The auction mart was no place for a free spirit who longed for the taste of salt water on his lips; and, in any case, the mental stress of editing and producing an expanding newspaper entirely on my own was beginning to take its toll. Sitting in the mart café one lunchtime, I typed out my resignation and felt an enormous weight lift off my head. I would have to work three months notice, but it would pass and at the end of the year I would be able to devote all my time to *Amulet*.

While I was confined at the mart Jean was aware of my frustration and, without saying anything, had gone round to *Amulet* and painted one side of the hull with grey undercoat. It was a lovely gesture meant to surprise me, and it did, but not in the way she intended! I had not ordered any undercoat. "I used the grey paint in the large can under the bench," said Jean, in reply to my puzzled inquiry. "It was a bit thick, but it went on alright." My heart missed a beat. The only grey paint under the bench was a can a friend had given me for painting galvanised surfaces; it was a type that normally contained a high percentage of zinc, and I was horrified when I realised that, immersed in saltwater, the chemical reaction would be the death knell for anything made of copper, like the fastenings in *Amulet*'s planking! Jean was terribly upset and wanted to get the gas torch and burn it off, but I thought the fumes might be dangerous if they were inhaled, so I called the paint manufacturer for advice. When I explained the problem to a man in the customer services department he reacted as though I was accusing his company of attempting to destroy the world. "We cannot be held responsible in any way," he said. "Our product is not designed for that purpose." "I realise that," I said patiently. "It was put on a wooden boat by accident. All I want to know is whether it will be detrimental to copper fastenings." It was like listening to a tape recorder. "We cannot be held responsible in any way. Our product is not designed for that purpose." I had visions of his product already hungrily devouring every bit of copper in sight, and *Amulet*'s planking dropping to the ground like autumn leaves. "O.K.," I said, trying not to let him see I was getting angry. "I understand that, but what's in it? Is it zinc based?" There was a strangled cry at the other end of the phone. "What's in it?" he choked. "I can't tell you that. It's a trade secret." "For Christ's sake," I exploded. "I'm not interested in your damned secrets. The paint was put on the boat by mistake! All I want to know is will it affect the copper fastenings when immersed in sea water?" His voice dropped almost to a whisper. "I'll tell you this much, it's not zinc based." Then, as if someone had turned the volume up, the disclaimer boomed through again. "We cannot be held responsible in any way. Our product is not designed for..." His voice trailed away as I put the phone down. I had got rid of his voice but he had another means of ensuring that I would not use his company's paint for a purpose for which it was not designed. When I went into the barn my foot touched the paint can and as if it had activated a self-destruct mechanism it fell over, the lid came off and the contents spilled out all over the floor.

Although the man was not very forthcoming with his advice, I was at least re-assured that the paint was not zinc based and I decided to leave it on and rub it down slightly to flatten the rough surface, then paint over it with a good quality marine undercoat. Having known boat owners who used nothing else but house-quality exterior gloss on their wooden boats for years without any adverse effects, I have always been sceptical about the claims of marine paint manufacturers but, when it comes to decision time, I always weaken and pay the outrageous prices demanded for a paint with the prefix 'marine'. Fortunately my boatbuilder friend, Sandy Macdonald, eased the pain by offering a substantial discount on the price of a top-grade undercoat, and I bought gloss for the final finish at the same time.

With the agonies of the 'nail-knocking' sessions now only a distant memory, Jean and Margaret actually volunteered to take on the task of rubbing down the hull primer, covering screw-heads and any minor imperfections with waterproof filler, and brushing on grey undercoat as a base for the final coats of Royal Blue gloss, a job to be left until the work on the deck and cockpit was finished. The weather was unusually warm and sunny for early October and, stealing a day off from the mart, I was frantically trying to catch up on a long list of neglected jobs when I did something incredibly stupid, that not only set the work on *Amulet* back several weeks but nearly caused an accident which, but for a stroke of good fortune, I might have had on my conscience for the rest of my life. During the morning, Jean had been busy painting the hull with undercoat and, having finished the starboard side, she went off to attend to her horse. I had rolled back the tarpaulins to let the heat of the sun dry the wood preserver I had sloshed onto the new wood and squirted into dark inaccessible corners, and was sitting on the cabin roof engrossed in working out how many sheets of 15mm plywood would be required for the decks when Margaret drove up and offered to start painting the port side. Unlike the highly-popular bilge keel yachts, which can be seen in any drying harbour sitting upright on the shingle like rows of fat ducks waiting to be fed, keel boats have to be supported when out of the water and owners devise all sorts of ingenious devices to keep their boats upright. In *Amulet*'s case she was held in a conventional rectangular steel cradle, the four corners of which were adjustable legs which clamped against the hull. Undercoat goes on very easily and Margaret, having finished painting the top planks, was working her way round the turn of the bilge and wanted to paint the areas hidden under the leg clamps. Nobody but a complete idiot would remove all the supports from the side of a keelboat; but on that day, with my mind trying to cope with several problems at the same time, I was a complete idiot and removed the two detachable pads attached to the legs on the port side and hammered a single temporary prop under the hull. Margaret continued painting and I went into the barn to draw a plan of the decks. The story might have ended there had I not left my tape measure on the cabin roof. Forgetting all about the temporary prop, I clambered up a ladder and as I stood on the cabin top I heard something hit the ground with a thud. In an instant I realised that the vibrations of the ladder against the hull had dislodged the prop, but it was too late. As if in slow motion *Amulet* began to fall over to port, and shouting to Margaret to get from under I jumped off the cabin and landed heavily in a clump of bushes. As I lay gasping for breath I watched *Amulet* topple over, and there was a sickening crash of splintering timber as one of the steel legs of the cradle smashed through the planking. I was so shocked I could hardly take it in, but was incredibly relieved when I saw that Margaret had escaped uninjured. Luckily, the forward leg of the cradle had jammed against the hull instead of smashing through it, and she had managed to scramble to safety. When I saw the full extent of the damage I felt physically sick. *Amulet* was lying at an angle of about forty five degrees, and there was a large hole where the after leg of the cradle had punched through the planking and ribs below the galley. "How on earth will you get her upright?" Margaret queried. "It will need a crane!" I was thinking along the same lines. Lifting a boat that weighed over three tons, was lying at an awkward angle and impaled on a steel cradle, was not going to be easy, but hiring a crane was a luxury way beyond my resources. Patricia had pledged money to restore a classic boat and I was not going to ask for more to underwrite the misadventures of an idiot.

Old Brab Davies use to say, "If yer've got a wooden boat thou's not likely to have many friends, and if summat goes wrang with it thou's got to imagine yer livin' on a desert island on yer own. Thou's got to fix it theeself." Financially I was very much on a desert island, and with no other options open to me it was time to take old Brab's advice. At least I had a Girl Friday, and sending Margaret into the timber store with instructions to bring out various lengths of timber, I hunted round the barn for a hydraulic jack. The tricky job was lifting the hull in a way that would get the cradle leg out of the hole without it damaging more planks in the process. After carefully sizing the job up, I placed a short fence post between the jack and the planking and raised it until it took the weight of the hull. Very gently, moving only a few inches at a time and trying to ignore the ominous creaks and groans from the shattered timber pressing against the cradle leg, I continued to raise the hull until I could chock it firmly and remove the jack. Margaret held a longer fence post between the jack and the hull and the operation was repeated. Slowly but surely *Amulet* rose higher and higher, and the nervous tension was electrifying. But then we hit a snag. With only a few inches to go to be clear of the hole in the hull, the top of the cradle leg became firmly wedged against the edge of a plank. For half an hour we wrestled with it to no avail, and it seemed the only way I was going to free the leg would be by cutting the undamaged planking away. I was loath to destroy any more of the original larch and, wedging a line of props under the dangerously listing hull, I called a halt in the hope that a cup of coffee would provide new inspiration. When it came I was not sure if it was due to the efficacy of Nestlé's Gold Blend or just sheer exasperation, but I picked up a heavy sledgehammer lying on the ground and gave the cradle leg a couple of mighty swipes. It bent it a mere fraction of an inch, but that was all it needed. Hardly daring to breathe, I gingerly cranked the jack handle, checking every move as the plank edge scraped ominously against the rough steel leg but, at the end of what seemed like an eternity, though was probably only a few minutes, the hull lifted clear and the planking was saved. But there was no time for cheering. Whenever the boat was raised, the line of props fell away with a frightening clatter, and Margaret very bravely knocked them back into place while the whole weight of the boat was taken by the fence post balanced precariously on the jack. It was a great relief to see the hull clear of the cradle leg, but it was still lying at a crazy angle and the task of lifting it became increasingly hazardous. As the boat rose higher, a longer piece of timber was needed on the jack and I was worried that if it slipped before the props were wedged in place the hull would fall heavily onto the cradle again, and what further carnage it would cause did not bear thinking about. With a chainsaw I cut a hefty piece of timber about eight inches diameter from a fallen tree in the estate grounds and, though it was an awkward brute to manoeuvre, there was little chance of it sliding off the jack and it wedged so firmly against the planking under the turn of the bilge I confidently cranked the jack to the full extent of the hydraulic ram. *Amulet* was now almost vertical and we were within a few inches of being able to bolt the detachable pads back onto the cradle legs; but the jack was fully extended, and before it could be lowered and moved to make the final lift we had to go through the wearisome business of wedging the line of props against the hull. Late in the afternoon, after many agonising hours of struggling to achieve what at first had seemed impossible, it needed only two cranks of the jack handle to push the hull upright and allow Margaret to quickly fix the pads onto the cradle legs and push the bolts home. *Amulet* was safely on her feet again and the crisis was over. Soaked in sweat and my shirt clinging to my back like a wet rag, I sank onto a log feeling mentally and physically drained. Equally worn out and shaken by what had happened, Margaret climbed into her car and went home.

After resting for a while, I climbed on board and went below into the cabin to survey the damage. The steel leg had smashed through two planks and left a jagged hole about ten inches long by six inches wide immediately below where the galley sink would normally sit. To make a sound and professional repair to the planking would involve carefully splicing in two new pieces of different lengths, a finicky operation that would use up a lot of time; and where on earth was I going to find lengths of knot-free seasoned larch? I still had a piece of oak but it seemed absurd to have to set up the steaming box to bend one rib. If only I had not been in such a hurry to get the work finished; if only I had put more supports under the hull when I took the pads off the cradle legs; these thoughts churned over in my mind as I stared at the hole, thinking only of the damage to my boat and the setback to my plans. Then the full realisation of what could have happened through my stupidity penetrated my whirling brain, and I went numb with horror. Had it not been for the cradle stopping the fall, *Amulet* would have toppled to the ground and Margaret might have been crushed to death. It was too awful to contemplate and, worn out and in the depths of despair, I lay on the cabin floor and acknowledged to any God who might be listening that I had been extremely lucky, and vowed I would never make the same mistake again.

In contrast to sunny October, the month of November was cold and grey with long periods of icy rain and an air temperature that gave little encouragement to tackle any jobs beyond hand-warming distance from a heater. In between days at the mart I had hoped to get started on building the cockpit, but was reluctant to risk using glue in conditions close to freezing. Like the marine paint moguls, the makers of the new marine glues seemed to have the idea that anyone who owned a boat had money pouring out of their ears and could afford to pay outlandish prices. At £21 for a small carton of epoxy resin, every drop was precious.

The dreary weather was a good excuse to retreat into the comparative warmth of the barn and catch up on minor jobs that had been ignored in the haste to work on the hull, and I was keen to check the condition of the rudder. Made of oak and over six feet high, it was an unwieldy chunk of timber that required two people to move it, and I hijacked a rather startled postman on his way to the 'big house' to deliver Mrs Dickinson's mail and got him to help me lift it onto a bench. He was fascinated with *Amulet* and said he remembered his father owning a sailing boat but, when I asked if he could spare another few minutes to help me turn the mast over, he told me in very unfriendly postman's language where I could stuff it, and made for the door. Despite having hung on *Amulet*'s transom for over five years at the mercy of the weather, the rudder was as sound as a bell, and all it needed was a quick whiz-over with a wire brush on an electric drill to get rid of the dried green slime and reveal the bare wood. I fitted new galvanised bolts in the steel mountings and soused the whole rudder in wood preserver. Leaving it to dry, I turned my attention to the various shapes and sizes of varnished doors that had been taken out of the accommodation. An ancient and cantankerous boatbuilder I was fortunate to have worked with in my youth always drilled into me that the last thing you put near a varnished finish was heat, and he almost foamed at the mouth if he saw anyone stripping varnish with a blowlamp. He would spend hours laboriously removing varnish with nothing more than a broad file, bent over at the end and sharpened to make a scraper; but by the time he had finished working on a badly neglected varnished dinghy or yacht, he had restored it to a mirror finish. This solid training had stayed with me throughout my life and when a friend, who had jeered at my traditional way of stripping varnish off *Amulet*'s mast, arrived one day and demonstrated a hot-air gun, I had an uncomfortable feeling that the ghost of old Eddie was standing behind me about to go berserk and foam at the mouth. But even he would have had to admit that the new-fangled device really worked and removed varnish without marking the wood, and I had bought one ready for use on the interior doors and panelling. Another advantage of the hot air gun was drying out damp wood prior to gluing, and in some instances where joints were coming apart on the doors, rapidly setting the remedial squirt of epoxy resin. It was an incredibly useful tool and I lifted the old varnish off four panelled doors of different sizes in a fraction of the time it would have taken using a dry scraper. Another irksome job made easier by the hot air gun was stripping varnish off the cleats for the mooring warps and main and jib sheets. Beautifully hand carved from pieces of oak, they were works of art. Oddly enough, though an incurable traditionalist, old Brab Davies hated varnish and said it was 'only fit for the sailing-toys of the toffs'. The only thing that glinted in the sun on Brab's elderly boat was water seeping through the inside of the hull planking!

Throughout November the increase of seasonal activity at the mart, the limited hours of daylight and the poor weather played havoc with progress on *Amulet*, and I became increasingly worried that she would not be ready for launching in the spring. The planking damaged when *Amulet* fell over needed repairing, but the most complex and time-consuming job on the list of outstanding work was rebuilding the cockpit. In the timber store I had found a lovely plank of seasoned Scots pine, and filled the barn with the gorgeous aroma of turpentine while I sawed it into suitable pieces for the cockpit frame, but had got no further. The focal point and action centre of most yachts is the cockpit. It has to be built right and it has to look right and, had I been of the religious persuasion where it is necessary to attend a confessional, I would have had to reveal to 'yer man' on the other side of the grill that I had kept putting the job off because I was scared of making a complete cobblers of it. In desperation I contacted John Hodgson for advice, and he suggested I should hire a young boatbuilder he knew who, he said, would build the cockpit quickly and probably fit the new pieces of planking in as well. He lived in the south of the Lake District and sounded very efficient and enthusiastic when I spoke to him on the phone; but, despite repeated promises, he failed to show up and when Patricia got in touch for my regular progress report I was feeling very disillusioned.

"Don't worry about it," she said in her usual laid-back and unruffled way. "There are plenty of good shipwrights in my part of East Anglia who are skilled at working on wooden boats, and if you are prepared to provide food and accommodation, I'll pay his wages. I know a capable lad who is between jobs just now and I'm sure he will come up right away." Passionate in my admiration for the work of Northern and Scottish boatyards, the suggestion of bringing a shipwright all the way from the south of England to work on a type of yacht that Shepherds of Windermere and other renowned yards on the Cumbrian and north Lancashire coast turned out in considerable numbers in their heyday, went very much against the grain; but there was no escaping the fact that the old yards had gone and with them the skilled boatbuilders they employed. And so it was that young David Showell, from Maldon in Essex, arrived at my house at the beginning of December in a car borrowed from his brother, and loaded with tool boxes, portable lamps and an essential piece of equipment without which he could not possibly work, a transistor radio permanently tuned to Radio 1.

He looked so young I wondered how he could possibly have gained any experience of working on wooden boats, but Patricia had assured me he had worked for Arthur Holt at his yard at Heybridge Basin on the river Blackwater. "That's a good enough recommendation for anyone," she said. "Arthur had a reputation for the finest workmanship and he had a high regard for David." There was a slight problem in that I was using the only spare bedroom in the house as an office, and he endeared himself to me when he offered to sleep in my vintage motor caravan, parked in the garden, and join us in the house for meals. When he had stowed his gear I took him to the barn to meet *Amulet*. Allowing someone you have never met before to clamber all over your boat and make scathing remarks about her condition is a bit like inviting them to comment on the inadequacies of the woman you are in love with; but while I could sense that there were things about my workmanship not to his liking, David shrewdly balanced youthful candour with careful diplomacy. Having inspected *Amulet*, he was clearly not happy with my shelter arrangement and immediately set about constructing a number of strong frames which, when bolted to heavy uprights and covered with the tarpaulins, would give him standing headroom in the cockpit area and a tremendous amount of shelter for working on the decks and cabin top. It took him a few days to finish the shelter before he started on the cockpit, and it was time well spent. Over the weeks I worked with David I grew to like him, but I cannot say I ever got to know him. To a wrinkly like me, accustomed to conventional ways and habits, he appeared slightly odd if not eccentric. He ate very little, did not smoke, swear or drink alcohol, in fact he seldom drank anything but cold water or fruit juice even in the coldest weather. Not surprisingly, he was very fit and never seemed to get tired, but making conversation with him was like trying to get money out of a cash point machine when you have left your card at home. Compared with boatbuilders like John Hodgson, who worked flat out and could build a whole boat while others were still unrolling the plans, David could be agonisingly slow, but there was no questioning his almost unceasing energy for work and his meticulous skill as a shipwright. There were many times when, with the temperature well below freezing, I was so cold I had to leave *Amulet* and go home for a hot bath and a large whisky, while David would just smile, take a few slurps from a bottle of spring water, sharpen his chisels and carry on working for several hours. The one habit he had that at times really got on my nerves was his addiction to listening to the caterwauling racket of BBC Radio 1. He could not work without it, and would suffer glazed-eyed withdrawal symptoms if he accidentally strayed out of earshot, which, with the radio blasting full volume, was not easy. The 'big house' had never experienced such an invasion of hideous sounds since hordes of marauding Scottish raiders ravaged Cumbria in the 17th century; and now, not having to worry that the clansmen would run off with her daughter, Mrs Dickinson was concerned that this latter-day transistor tyranny would empty the estate woods of birds and red squirrels. Happily David took the hint and turned the volume down.

At the mart, the programme of December sales was building up to a frenzy and, with all my time taken up with the newspaper, I was highly relieved to have the work on the cockpit in the hands of a capable shipwright. It was now deep into winter with bitterly cold days and severe frost at night but, aided by floodlights and strategically-placed electric heaters, David put in a twelve hour day working under the tarpaulin shelter, and the cockpit framework began to take shape. The edge of every piece of plywood used for the bulkheads between the main cabin and the cockpit, and the end grain of the pieces of Scots pine used for the framing, was painstakingly sealed with epoxy resin to keep out destructive damp, and stainless steel screws were used in preference to brass. I had hoped that much of the work would be finished by the end of December but, with the Christmas merry-making in the offing followed by the millennium celebrations, it was agreed that David would go home and return early in January. I discovered, much to my surprise, that the new managing director at the mart had very generously bought me a bottle of malt whisky and four fine Edinburgh glass tumblers as a farewell present, and planned to present them to me at the office Christmas party; but unfortunately I spoilt everything by going down with a bad dose of 'flu. It laid me up for over a week and Jean was forced to cancel a Christmas dinner we had booked at a local pub, but I was determined I was not going to miss celebrating the end of the twentieth century. I have never been an enthusiastic party-goer and, given the choice, I prefer to climb to the top of a mountain with a few friends on New Year's Eve and 'push the boat out' with a flask of hot coffee and a large dram of whisky. I had celebrated many a Hogmanay on the summit of Ben Nevis but living in Cumbria there was no more appropriate place to witness the end of a thousand years than on the summit of Scafell Pike, 3210ft (988 metres), England's highest mountain, but a warning of snow and high winds scuppered my plans. A painful knee and concern that the noise from the expected firework displays would frighten her dog kept Jean at home, and a couple of hours before midnight I set off with Margaret and her son Howard to climb Gavel, one of the Lake District's lower hills but with a superb panoramic view of the Cumbrian coast and the Isle of Man, thirty miles out in the Irish Sea. For a while there wasn't much sign of either as we trudged uphill through the darkness but, as if in a valiant effort to make the ending of the millennium a memorable event, the Gods blew away the snow clouds and revealed an inky black sky sparkling with millions of stars.

The coastline and the winking lighthouses on the Isle of Man were clearly visible and, as we scrambled onto the summit, revellers eager to get the celebrating under way were letting off fireworks in the ancients harbours of Whitehaven and Ravenglass. I fumbled with my watch to check the time, but there was no need. On the stroke of midnight there was a tremendous explosion and all along the coast a staggering cascade of colour lit up the sky as thousands of rockets, star bombs, Catherine wheels and every firework that was ever invented disintegrated in a shimmering pyrotechnic eruption of reds, blues, pinks, whites and greens. It was an unbelievably beautiful sight, and it was only when the last drop of hot coffee and dram of whisky was finished that were we able to drag ourselves away and head down to the valley. We were frozen to the marrow, but incredibly elated by the once-in-a-lifetime experience. Before going home, I called at the barn to wish *Amulet* "Happy New Year" and give her bow a big kiss. Owners of wooden boats do daft things like that when no one is watching. Wood is alive and sensuous. Kissing fibreglass must be like caressing a tailor's dummy.

In the dim light of my torch, *Amulet* looked finished and ready for the sea, but climbing the ladder and looking down on the half-built cockpit, the gaping hole in her side and the unplanked decks soon shattered the myth, and for a moment the excited anticipation that had accompanied the start of a brand new year gave way to nagging despair. It was clear there was still a long way to go before I would experience 'the wheel's kick and the wind's song and the white sails shaking'.

Gutless engine, Gale damage and Springing Gunwales

During the first week in January, a severe frost and a temperature of minus three inside *Amulet*'s cabin made me very reluctant to leave the warmth of my kitchen fire, but the irritating gnome who lived in my conscience kept up a nagging tirade about the boat not being ready to leave in the spring if I didn't get off my backside and do something; so to keep him quiet I walked round to the barn and tried to keep my hands warm by stripping varnish off small fittings with the hot air gun. The temperature in the large barn was about the same as in the cabin, and even with the hot air gun and an electric fan heater going full blast, it was like trying to warm a walk-in freezer with a candle. The cold penetrated my layers of sweaters and fleecy jacket like a knife and, with chattering teeth, I was on the point of retreating back to the kitchen fire when Margaret arrived to pick up a coat she had left in the barn. "Why don't you fasten one of these nylon sheets to the wall like a tent?" she said, dragging an old tarpaulin out of a heap and spreading it out on the floor. "It'll keep the heat in and you'll be able to work in comfort." Women can be infuriatingly logical at times! Why hadn't I thought of that?

"It's a good idea but I'm far too cold to start messing about with tents," I said unenthusiastically. "Let's leave it for now, I'm away home." The truth was I could not be bothered, but Margaret was not to be put off. "You'll soon get warm if you keep working." There was a hint of sarcasm in her voice. I lifted the end of the tarpaulin half-heartedly with the toe of my boot and let it drop to the ground. "Get some cord," she said, "and we'll lash it to those hooks in the wall. And we'll need some pieces of wood to give it shape." Trying not to think of the ridicule old Brab Davies would have heaped on me for allowing a woman to be 'skipper', I meekly obeyed orders and by the end of the morning we had rigged up a very serviceable lean-to tent inside the barn, with standing headroom, electric light and a small bench. Within minutes of installing the fan heater the interior was like a greenhouse on a summer's day, and though outside the tent the temperature was subzero, inside I could not only remove varnish in comfort, it was warm enough to actually apply it as well. Had it been left to me I would have gone home and kept the kitchen fire stoked up but, thanks to Margaret's persistence, I had a tent that proved to be incredibly useful and enabled me to varnish or paint doors and fittings independent of the weather, and it saved an enormous amount of time. Old Brab would have snorted at the anonymous lines once sent to me by a courageous girl who, much maligned by the old buffers in her local yacht club, had showed them what she was capable of by sailing the Atlantic single-handed:-

> Where is the man who has the power and skill
> To stem the torrent of a woman's will?
> For if she will, she will, you may depend on't;
> And if she won't, she won't; so there's an end on't.

At the end of the week David Showell phoned to say that his return would be delayed owing to family commitments. I guessed that either he had found a new girl friend or things had progressed with the one he had before Christmas. As a token of her undying devotion she had promised to buy him a new wheel for his bike as a Christmas present. The only way a girl can get closer to a man's heart than that is to say she loves his boat! Finally managing to tear himself away from his commitments halfway through the month, he steered his brother's car back to the frozen Lake District; but there was no need to let anyone know he was coming. When Mrs. Dickinson suddenly moved from one wing of her large house to another, birds started to fly higher in the sky and deer and foxes were seen fleeing from the estate wood, it was a sure signal that David and his ear-blasting Radio 1 were back on *Amulet*!

The air temperature was still around zero and the January days short but, with the aid of his arc lights and a couple of electric heaters, David bravely worked from early morning until late in the evening, and within a week the cockpit, except for a few minor details which I was to complete, was finished and looked very handsome. The way he had skilfully combined oak and other hard woods with marine plywood, and his high standard of workmanship, were a true reflection of his professionalism and his feeling for working with wood. Sadly his services were running up a bill faster than a taxi meter and, though I would have liked to have kept him on, the cost of restoring *Amulet* was beginning to compare with the megabucks needed to raise the *Titanic*. It was agreed that David should stay on for a further week to fit the new pieces of planking and repair one or two ribs that had cracked when *Amulet* fell over. The standard practice in wooden boat repair is to fix 'doublers' – short lengths of timber of similar quality to the existing rib – against the damaged rib, but to maintain the strength of the hull the doublers have to fit accurately to the curve of the bilge and be fastened with copper nails and roves to the planking. Because they are often out of sight and out of reach, all sorts of junk timber and short-life fastenings are used for doublers, and that well worn clause 'as far as can be ascertained' beloved by marine surveyors, means that with the best will in the world they cannot always check them either. I could not find any good quality larch planking locally, so the repair to the planks was made with top grade Columbian pine with doublers fashioned from seasoned oak. David made a superb job of the extremely difficult task of tapering the ends of the new pieces and the existing planking, and they mated absolutely perfectly and were quickly glued and nailed into place. It was a tremendous relief to be rid of the gaping hole; it had mocked me for weeks and was a constant reminder of a costly lapse of concentration. On the positive side, clearing away the floors to be able to nail the new planking gave me clear access to the seacock for the engine cooling water and, since it was over thirty years old and looked its age, I cut it out and replaced it with a new one.

Packing his toolboxes and all the paraphernalia of a travelling shipwright into his car, David departed for home at the end of January. He had done a good job and I was sorry to see him go, but I felt I had got my boat back and, for the first time in weeks, free of the semi-hysterical babble of Radio 1 presenters and the discordant onslaught that passed for music, I could hear the birds and low-flying aircraft! After waving goodbye I climbed aboard *Amulet* and, with an electric fan heater rapidly turning the ice on the windows into rivulets of water, I sat in the cabin with a notebook and pen and made a list of outstanding jobs. Having filled both sides of three A4 sheets I felt too depressed to go any further, and decided to start with the most basic job of all, cleaning out the debris which had accumulated in the bilges while the cockpit was being constructed. Shipwrights are like chefs, they produce a magnificent product but they feel it is beneath their dignity to clean up when they have finished. The waste products of David's artistic expression filled a plastic sack and, with the help of a screwdriver and vacuum cleaner, Jean spent several muscle-aching hours laboriously raking out congealed sawdust, discarded screws, glue sticks and copper nails from along the edge of the planking and in the limber holes. Months before I acquired *Amulet*, some passing reveller had flung into my garden one of those walking stick type litter-pickers which urban park keepers use, and it must have been sent from heaven. It was far and away the most useful gadget I have ever used for retrieving fallen screwdrivers, wrenches, and even small nuts and bolts from the often inaccessible depths of a keel boat's deep bilges, and I wouldn't be without it. On one occasion I achieved hero status when I used the litter picker to recover the false teeth of an engineer who sneezed while he was peering into the engine bilge and emerged toothless.

With the cockpit bilge cleaned out, the next step was to slosh Cuprinol wood preserver over all the new wood, including the new planks and doublers, and leave a heater on for a few hours to dry it off prior to applying a coat or two of bilge paint to all surfaces under the cockpit. I prefer every part of a boat to be as accessible as possible and had gone to a lot of trouble to make sure that, through screwed-down floors and inspection hatches, there were no places below the cockpit that could not be reached for maintenance or emergency repair. Likewise, through screw-down hatches bedded in waterproof compound, I had designed the bridge deck and the engine compartment so that it could all be easily dismantled and the engine and gearbox lifted out if necessary. Some of the mass-produced fibreglass cruisers on the market, even very expensive ones, look as though the engine was installed first and the rest of the boat moulded tightly round it.

Given the choice, I would never have bottled gas or a gasoline engine on a boat, and my other aversion is a skin fitting that is not safeguarded with an on/off valve, and *Amulet* had two. The builder had carried the pipes from the self-draining cockpit down to port and starboard skin fittings in the bilge and there was no means of stopping the sea pouring in if one or both of the pipes had sheared. It would not have been possible to have banged a emergency wooden plug in the skin fitting either, because the original cockpit floor had been immovably fastened down. Determined to have the self-draining outlets fitted in the approved manner, I borrowed a selection of valves from Nick Newby of Nichol End Marine to see which would be the best, but though I tried every which way to fit valves on both of the skin fittings I ended up defeated and with a painful crick in my neck from hanging upside down in the cockpit. The skin fittings were so close together in the narrow part of the bilge there was just no room to fit two valves. The only other place wide enough to bore new holes was too close to the gearbox drive for comfort. "Well, the way the existing pipes have not budged for over thirty years at least tells you something," said Nick, when I took the valves back to his chandlery. "If you fit the latest skin fitting that has a very definite serrated edge and push heavy duty hose over it, having given it a touch of heat to soften it up, then finish off with a couple of jubilee clips, it will be an incredibly strong joint. I know you like everything to be right but in this instance I don't think you need have any worries about not having valves on those skin fittings." Despite the assurances I was still unhappy, but in the event Nick was proved right. "By the way," he called as I was leaving, "have you checked your keel bolts. If she's been standing a while you often find that the nuts on the keelson will take up a turn or so." I said it was on my list, but thanked him for reminding me and promised that when I got back to *Amulet* I would check them before I did anything else.

It is strange how things happen. As a gesture of thanks, the engineer whose teeth I retrieved from the bilge had given me a large socket that exactly fitted the keel bolt nuts, and had included a long extension bar to turn it. Altogether there were nine hefty- looking bronze keel bolts holding the lead keel onto the hull, varying from about ten inches in length at the bow to eighteen inches at the stern. With the bunks and floorboards having been removed from the cabin, the bolt heads on the keelson were easy to reach and, starting with the one nearest the bow, I attached the socket and bar and heaved it round carefully. Nick was right, the nut took up a full turn, but when it went round for a second time, then a third and then a fourth, I realised that the bolt was turning as well as the nut. At first I thought that the bolt head embedded in the lead keel had lost its grip, a problem in itself, but when I pulled the socket off the nut my heart sank. Still attached to it was the nut and a short length of highly corroded bronze bolt. Having lain forgotten and neglected throughout three decades, the 16mm diameter bronze had snapped like a twig. When I applied the socket to the rest of the nuts they turned slightly and the bolts appeared to be sound, but I was deeply worried. If one bolt had failed, should all nine of them be replaced? When I phoned John Hodgson for his advice he had no hesitation. "Knock the lot out, it's not worth taking the risk," he replied. "They could be tested by a specialist but you'd have to lift the hull high enough in the air to get the long bolts out. If I were you I'd knock them out as far as they'll go and then keep cutting them off until the last bit is out. I wouldn't bother replacing them with bronze, use marine-grade stainless steel." John had a way of making a job sound straightforward and easy, but I shuddered at the memory of once helping him to remove keel bolts and one jamming. We beat hell out of it for hours with a heavy sledgehammer and a round bar before a large nut, almost eaten away with the corrosive action of seawater, and several lengths of disintegrated metal that had once been a long keel bolt, finally dropped to the ground below the keel, and John considered we were lucky. He told a harrowing story of an occasion when a keel bolt he was removing jammed so badly it had to be drilled out with a very expensive long twist drill and it took several days. When I put the phone down, morale was hovering around zero. Replacing all nine keel bolts was going to use up a lot of time even if there were no complications, and I was already way behind schedule with other work. The possibility of leaving for Scotland in the spring was fading further with every new set back and it was incredibly frustrating. As ever, my long-suffering team were a great help and while Jean painted the bilges with an attractive maroon bilge-paint I had bought through Sandy Macdonald, Margaret slapped several layers of white undercoat on the inside of the cabin roof. One discovery I had made during the months I travelled to Carlisle was a company near the mart that stocked a huge range of steel, and I went to enquire about the availability of marine-grade stainless steel. "Five metres of sixteen millimetre marine-grade stainless steel round bar and eighteen nuts and washers to fit," said the assistant, reading my list. "No problem, are you taking it now?" I could hardly believe it. I was so used to having to order anything 'unusual' from outside the county, wait weeks for it and pay through the nose for carriage, that I was overjoyed. Very few motorists shared my enthusiasm when I weaved in and out of the solid rows of traffic in the centre of Carlisle with a gleaming lance sticking out of the passenger window, but I got it home safely and, with an angle grinder, cut it into the required lengths. It cost five times more than the price of the bar and nuts and washers to have a thread put on each end of the pieces at a local engineering works, and I felt I had been 'done'; but at least I had nine new keel bolts ready to be fitted, and one wet and windy Saturday morning I climbed on board with a heavy sledgehammer and a length of iron bar of similar diameter to the keel bolts, ready to do battle. Jean had her horse to attend to in a stable a few miles from home and Margaret had planned a shopping trip but, fortunately for me, had decided to put it off until the weather improved. When I rang to ask if she would help she was less than enthusiastic about leaving her fire, but I promised it would only take an hour and all she had to do was to watch for the bolt coming out of the keel while I belted it from above. When she drove up to the barn the rain was beating down in icy torrents on the roof of her car, and she showed every sign of being completely fed up with my boat and me, and was in no mood for conversation. I showed her what to look for under the boat and retreated into the cabin. Ignoring the broken bolt, I moved to the next shortest one and, unscrewing the nut to the top of the thread, I thumped it with the sledgehammer. Nothing happened, so I thumped it again a bit harder. John Hodgson had warned that if the bolt head did not dislodge in the keel and you kept on hammering the other end, then the centre of the bolt could buckle slightly and jam. Gritting my teeth I thumped it harder. It did not budge. "What's happening up there?" cried Margaret's voice through the hull. "I'm freezing. Nothing's come out yet." It was time to stop being a wimp. Drastic action was needed. With a shout of 'Geronimo' I swung the sledgehammer down on the nut with all my strength. There was a tremendous crash and *Amulet* shuddered as if every plank was about to fall off. "It's through," shouted Margaret excitedly. "Hit it again." Taking the nut off the thread I whacked the bolt until it sank into the hole then, holding the round iron bar on the top of the bolt I hammered the bar. "It's coming, there's about six inches showing," shouted Margaret. I kept hammering, then suddenly the bar disappeared down the hole. "It's out. Shall I push the bar back?" "Yes please," I called, and when I had pulled it out of the hole I climbed down to inspect the bolt. It looked in perfect condition despite its age, but it could easily have been as far past its sell-by date as its broken mate, and the thought of the rest of them deciding to take early retirement when the keel was under stress in heavy seas convinced me that the trouble and expense of fitting new ones was well worth-while. But there were still eight old ones to coax out and, having led the sort of life that makes me feel nervous when things start to go right, I treated as a fluke the ease with which the first one had been knocked out. But, contrary to my expectations, assisted by determined clouts with the sledgehammer the next bolt slid out without a murmur, though it touched the ground and I had to cut it off with an angle grinder before I could get it all out. I felt badly about destroying what appeared to be a perfectly sound length of expensive bronze, and thought of the times when, as a lad, I had fastened the keels of rickety craft I had built with any rusty old bolts I could scrounge. Bronze bolts were something I had drooled over in Davey's catalogue.

The next three bolts were likewise disposed of and, flushed with success, I turned my attention to the broken one which, to complicate matters, had snapped off deep down in the hole leaving a thin spike instead of a flat. I had to fiddle about to make sure that the spike was in contact with the bar and hoped that it would not bend and bury itself in the side of the hole when I thumped it with the hammer. Just to show that things were not going all my way it did exactly that; and for an hour I cursed and cajoled, heaved and hammered, but the bolt would not move and, to add to the fun, the bar got stuck fast as well. Twisting the bar back and forward with a Stillson wrench eventually managed to free it and, throwing caution to the wind, I lowered it back down the hole onto the bolt and gave it an almighty clout with the sledgehammer. The boat shook like a terrier throwing water off its back, but the bolt stayed put. I tried again and again and again until the sweat poured off me and I was worn out. With barely enough strength left to lift the heavy sledgehammer, I brought it down with all my weight in a last desperate thump on the top of the bar, and nearly followed it down the hole when, without warning, the bolt stump gave up the fight and shot out below the keel taking the bar with it. "It's out!" yelled Margaret, but I was too exhausted to reply and lay on the keelson gasping for breath.

Rather than remove the rest of the old bolts, risking the lead keel slipping sideways and the holes moving out of line, I changed places with Margaret and while she pushed the new bolts, well lubricated with tallow, down the holes from inside the cabin, I lay under the keel, screwed a nut onto the protruding thread and wrapped a few strands of caulking cotton round the bolt before pushing it into a hexagon-shaped recess in the lead. Margaret then placed a washer and nut on the other end and tightened it with the socket. With all five new bolts in place, the remaining four old bolts were soon knocked out and replaced, and the nuts give a final tighten. The wearying slog was over and it was late afternoon. It had been a long 'hour', and Margaret left for home cold, tired and not best pleased.

The following day I gave the keel-bolt nuts another heave with the socket and bar, and sealed in each bolt head under the keel with a wad of waterproof plastic filler before finally finishing off by running a bead of polysulphide mastic into the gap where the lead keel butted up to the keelson. For ordinary mortals, replacing keel bolts is a once-in-a-lifetime job and, glad to see the back of it, I climbed on board to plug a hole in a cover that had been dripping rain water onto the foredeck beams. Like many superstitious fishermen, old Brab used to say that someone was watching over every boat, and whoever was guarding *Amulet* that day certainly had a quaint way of letting me know all was not well. I dropped a wood chisel I was holding and, instead of falling into the forecabin, it hit one of the deck beams, bounced sideways blade first and pierced the thick mahogany of the front of the cabin as if it was hot butter. I was astounded to find a long patch of rot where the front panel was fastened to the deck beam and could not understand how I had missed it. Weeks earlier when I had poked it with a knife I had declared it absolutely sound, but the phantom chisel-thrower knew better and had waited his chance. On closer inspection I found other pockets of rot at the top and sides where it had been fastened into the cabin frame with copper nails and roves, and it was obvious the whole panel would have to come out. I was deeply depressed at finding more rot and being faced with yet another hold up but, by the time I had removed the two glass port lights, the depression had turned to a furious determination that I would not be defeated. Rushing below, I picked up the heavy sledgehammer used for the keel bolts and, going forward in the cabin, I gave the panel a mighty swipe. It shot over the bow and hit the ground with a crash of disintegrating timber and I felt a lot better. As I had planned to paint the topsides rather than struggle to restore the original varnish I had no conscience about replacing the mahogany panel with marine plywood, and with the help of my powerful jigsaw I soon had a piece cut to shape. Within a couple of hours it was ready for fitting into place, but I had no specialist equipment for routing the oval-shaped holes to fit the port lights and, in a hurry to get the job finished I drove to Keswick and pleaded with my friendly joiners. It was dark when I got back, but a single 100 watt bulb gave enough light under the covers and it was an easy job to set the panel in a bed of resorcinol glue and hold it in place for the night with cramps. I left a fan heater running in the hope that the glue would be hard by morning and went home ready for a hot meal and a whisky and to try and persuade one of my 'team' to turn out the next day for a short session of 'nail-knocking'.

I rang Margaret's number several times, but there was no answer and I began to suspect she had invested in one of those gadgets that display a caller's number, and having discovered who it was had dived under a table. At breakfast Jean was feeling the effects of a touch of arthritis in her arms, but valiantly offered to have a go and, as the nails were not particularly heavy gauge, she managed to hold the old wrench handle against the nail heads while I riveted the points over the roves. With remarkable ease the panel was permanently fastened into place, the surplus glue trimmed off and the new wood soused with Cuprinol. The cabin was a lot stronger, and months later in a very hairy situation in heavy seas I was to recognize that the phantom chisel-thrower had done me a great favour.

When February gave way to March and there was still a mass of work to be done, I had to resign myself to the inescapable reality that, barring a miracle - and that meant a posse of skilled shipwrights working round the clock for free - there would be no fond farewells and sailing off into the sunset clutching a bunch of April daffodils. It was all very well for my friend and sponsor, Patricia, to say "Stop pushing yourself, go when you are ready;" and other friends ask, "What's the rush?" How could I get through to them that it was my project for the millennium and I wanted to get as much sailing in Scotland as possible. Couldn't they understand I wouldn't be around for the next one? But in the end I had to accept that they were right and, reluctantly thrusting thoughts of leaving dates to the back of my mind, I concentrated on getting *Amulet* ready for her return to the sea.

During March most of the work effort was focused on varnishing the mast and spars and the locker and companionway doors. I managed ten coats on the mast and the heated tent was a tremendous help in speeding up the drying time between coats on the doors and smaller items. Being less strenuous and more satisfying than the other jobs I had inflicted on them, Jean and Margaret volunteered to help, and with their patience and attention to detail, which I lacked, they had the varnish work gleaming like mirrors. They also painted the bunk frames and mattress bases, the cockpit floors, locker shelves and a multitude of bits and pieces that were spread to dry all over the barn. Job after job was ticked off on the clip-board lists hanging on the wall, and it was when I reached 'fit engine' I realised that the Farymann engine I had bought months before from the chap in Gloucestershire was still lying in a corner of the barn swathed in plastic sheets, and it was time I looked for an engineer capable of installing it.

In response to my telephone call, Ian Smith trundled up to the barn one morning in a rickety van. For years Ian had been chief engineer on the Ravenglass and Eskdale railway, a miniature line that carries thousands of tourists up the Eskdale valley from the Roman harbour of Ravenglass on the Cumbrian coast. He was a boat owner and a keen cruising man, and well acquainted with marine engines. We unwrapped the Farymann and lifted it onto a bench. "You certainly did well," Ian said when I told him what I had paid for it. "A brand new engine for that price must be the bargain of the year."

A high pressure system drifting in from the west had brought a welcome spell of warm, dry weather and, with the covers pulled back and the frames removed from the aft end of the boat, Ken Sharpe, my obliging farming neighbour, was able to lift the engine with his tractor-mounted loader and swing it into the cockpit. It was tremendously exciting as Ian's block and tackle, suspended from a wooden gantry, gently lowered it the rest of the way onto the wooden engine bearers and, with the smart blue paint and chrome-plated pipes gleaming in the sunlight, it looked magnificent. But the huge feeling of relief and pleasure vanished like an ice cream in the Sahara when Ian announced gloomily, "It's not going to fit, it's got different engine mountings and the flange on the gearbox won't match up to the flange on the propeller shaft. Come and have a look." I climbed down into the cabin and could see instantly what the problem was. The engine mountings were wider apart than on the old engine and they would not fit onto the wooden engine bearers, and the bolt holes on the gearbox drive flange would not line up with the holes on the propeller shaft flange. I sank down onto the cabin floor. "I don't believe it," I groaned in despair, "What the hell can we do?" Ian took a few measurements with a steel tape and drew a rough sketch on a piece of paper. "Well, if I bolt a piece of angle iron on the sides of the bearers that will overcome the width problem, but the flange holes are something different. Phone the Farymann agents and see if they can supply an adapter to fit in between the old size flange and the new one." One of the most useful pieces of modern technology is the mobile phone, and I immediately phoned Diesel Power, the Farymann agents based in Surrey, and was put through to the spares department. "Yes sir, we can certainly help you there," said the briskly-efficient storeman when I explained the problem and gave him the serial number of the engine. "Let me see." There was a rattle of keys as he punched the information into a computer. "Ah yes, here we are. It'll cost two hundred pounds plus vat and postage." I nearly fell over with shock. "Thanks very much," I said weakly. "I'll let you know." Ian's eyes opened wide in amazement when I told him. "What a rip off!" he exclaimed. "Look, forget about them. I'll turn an adapter out on the lathe; it'll cost you £60, and I'll be back tomorrow. Let's lift the engine out of the way so I can check my measurements."

True to his word Ian turned up the next morning and, while I drilled holes in the sides of the wooden engine bearers and bolted on pieces of angle iron he had shaped and drilled to accept the engine mountings, Ian fitted the gleaming new adapter onto the gearbox flange. The engine was lowered onto the bearers, and this time the mountings bolted into position without any difficulty and, aided by the new adapter, the two flanges lined up with a precision fit. When the engine sump had been topped up with new oil, the fuel tank temporarily located on its mountings under the after deck and the fuel pipes connected, the control panel wiring and the starter battery connected, and the engine cooling water pump connected to a container of water, we were ready to test the engine, and once again I felt a surge of excitement. Ian pumped fuel through to the injectors, made a final check of the mounting bolts and said, "O.K., press the starter button!" I pressed a large black button on the control panel and the starter motor whined - but nothing happened. "The starter motor isn't engaging with the flywheel," said Ian. "It's probably sticking with having stood for such a long time. Try it again!" I pressed the button and the starter motor whined again. Ian gave the starter a sharp thump with a mallet. "Try again." I pressed the button and once more the starter whined but the engine stayed silent. Ian rummaged about in his tool box and lifted a box of sockets. "I'll take the starter motor off and check it, I'll bet it's just sticking." With the bolts removed, the starter motor pulled away from the engine and Ian examined it carefully. "Can't see anything wrong with it," he said, turning the armature slowly. "Pass me that torch and I'll check the flywheel." I handed him a torch and he shone it into the hole where the starter fitted. He stared at it disbelievingly for a moment, then put the torch down and stuck a finger in the hole. "You're not going to like this," his voice dropped as though he hardly dare tell me what he had found. "There's no flywheel on the engine." For a moment I was dumbstruck, then I realised he must be joking. "Come off it," I said irritably, "I've had enough problems with this boat. Don't scare me with jokes like that." "I'm not joking," he said solemnly. "There's no flywheel on the engine. Stick your finger in the flywheel casing and check for yourself." In a daze I did as he said and it took only seconds to realise he was right; the flywheel, a vital piece of any engine, was missing.

I felt as if someone had kicked me in the stomach, and for a minute or two I was unable to speak. Without a flywheel the engine was useless and it was as if I had stacked seven hundred and fifty pounds into a heap and destroyed it with a match. How on earth was I going to explain it to Patricia? She had provided the money. I was utterly devastated, but I could not believe that the engineer I had bought it from had deliberately sold me a dud, and was sure there was some other explanation. Ian's voice broke through my tangled thoughts. "You still have a bargain even if you have to buy a new flywheel. Give the Farymann agent a ring and see what it will cost." When I phoned I was put through to Steve Barnes, a cheery service engineer who was an authority on Farymann engines. "Depending on the model, it'll set you back anything between three and five hundred quid, but it's rare for anyone to buy a new flywheel; what's the problem?" When I had poured out my horror story there was silence for a few seconds, then he said slowly, "My God! You've sure dropped yourself right in it with that engine. You've got to be very careful about buying ex boat show display engines. On the boat show stands many manufacturers have what look like complete engines on display, but often don't put the pistons or the crankshafts or the flywheels in to reduce the weight, then they tart them up with a lick of enamel paint and chrome-plated fittings and they look eye-catching and tempt potential buyers. The starter motors and the gearboxes can be just empty shells sprayed to look like new. The idea is to get you to order one of the models that's taken your fancy at the show and then they'll deliver a new one that's checked and carries a guarantee. With the Farymann engine you've got, there's no knowing whether the pistons and crankshaft are in and have been fitted properly unless it's stripped down to the last nut and rebuilt by an engineer who knows what he's doing. If I were you I wouldn't put it near a boat unless I knew it was one hundred percent safe." My head was reeling when I switched the mobile phone off. To find the flywheel missing had been a terrible shock, but to be told that the entire engine was, in effect, little more than a heap of brightly painted scrap metal was mind blowing.

Ian looked startled when I told him what Steve Barnes had said, but made no comment and we sat dejectedly looking at the engine. "Tell you what," he said suddenly, breaking the silence. "If we can get the engine into my van I'll take it home and give it a quick check in the workshop. At least it will give us some idea what it's like inside. What do you say?" I felt too miserable to say anything, but there was no point in cluttering up *Amulet* with worthless ballast so I grunted my agreement and, having reversed the installation process, the engine was hoisted into the cockpit, and with Ian sliding it down a metal ladder and me taking the weight on the block and tackle, we managed to get it to the ground and into his van, and he drove away.

I climbed back on board and, absolutely drained mentally and physically, I lay on the cabin floor. The whole project seemed to be pointless and I was worn out with battling against insurmountable odds. With the money sunk into this mound of decaying timber I could easily have chartered a boat for my millennium trip, and could have left in the spring and spent the whole summer enjoying myself sailing in my beloved Western Isles and visiting the places where I used to live. I fell into an exhausted sleep and dreamt that when I tried to start the Farymann engine it exploded and set fire to *Amulet*, but while I cheered and clapped a bird came flying at me in anger, chirping loudly and refusing to leave me alone. At that point I woke up and realised that a blackbird, perched on the branch of a nearby tree, was singing his heart out, and I lay back and let the lovely sound soothe the tension in my head. It was a cheerful song, full of happiness and vitality, and he seemed to be saying that life was great so stop feeling sorry for yourself and get moving; at least you've still got the boat and adventurers sailed round the Western Isles and the world before engines were invented. It was the shot in the arm I needed and, fired with new enthusiasm, I heaved myself to my feet. "You're bloody right," I yelled at the blackbird. "Stuff the engine, I'll go without one." Measuring the engine compartment I was amazed at the amount of extra storage space I would have in the cabin and below the cockpit, and the fuel-tank area under the after deck was a perfect lazarette for stowing mooring warps and fenders. I told myself it was ridiculous to take up so much valuable room in a small boat with a noisy and smelly chunk of metal that was hardly used during a voyage. Good riddance to it. I went home in high spirits, proud that I had joined the ranks of real sailors who sailed their boats engineless, like yachtsmen Joshua Slocum, Harrison Butler, Dixon Kemp and Claude Worth, the incomparable Thames barge master Bob Roberts, and Brab Davies, last of the Duddon estuary sailing trawlermen. They ventured out and sailed the seas according to the vagaries of the wind; not for them was the accursed mechanical topsail.

I reached home still elated with the anticipation of sailing without an engine and reciting aloud Masefield's 'Sea Fever', but was brought rapidly down to earth by the sight of the telephone on the kitchen table and the reminder that I had not yet told Patricia the disastrous news about the engine. I was fortunate in her to have a friend who understood boats and had sailed an old gaff-rigged Essex smack with a clapped-out engine for many years. She could have filled a book with hair-raising stories about boat engines, and when I told her about the Farymann she was remarkably stoical and just said, "Oh well, these things happen. If the man you bought it off was a marine engineer it's difficult to believe he wasn't aware of what he was selling; but you bought it in good faith, it's not your fault." It was typical of her to take it so calmly but, when I said I was prepared to sail without an engine, it was like pulling the fuse on a distress rocket. There was an instant explosion. "Sail *Amulet* in the fierce waters of the west of Scotland without an engine? You must be out of your mind!" she blasted down the phone. "I won't hear of it, and if you persist with this idiotic idea I shall withdraw my support." If a woman tells a man she is leaving him, it can be heart-rending; but when a woman threatens to cut off funds for a man's boat it has the magnitude of a global disaster. "But I haven't time to start looking for a secondhand engine," I cried, "and a new one would cost a bomb." "How much?" she queried. "It's frightening, the Farymann engineer said not much change out of three and a half grand." I thought that would stop her in her tracks, but I should have known better. "Right, order it tomorrow and let me know the full amount. I'll send you a cheque." With that she put the phone down.

Two weeks later a delivery truck backed up to the barn and, with a whirr of an electric hoist, a brand new, yellow-painted, ten-horsepower Farymann single-cylinder, raw water-cooled diesel engine, complete with a two to one reduction gearbox and bolted to a wooden pallet covered in plastic sheets, was lowered to the ground. Never in my life had I been in a position to order, and pay three thousand pounds for, a brand new engine, and I suffered a thousand agonies when Ken, the friendly farmer, shackled on a rusty old chain and nonchalantly lifted it high into the air with his tractor before swinging it sideways into the cockpit. That fright over, I had another scare when Ian Smith lowered it onto the engine bearers with his hoist and announced that the engine mountings had been re-designed and would not fit; but with a touch of judicious repositioning of the pieces of angle iron, the problem was overcome and the engine slid into place and was fastened down. The gearbox and propeller shaft flanges were bolted together, the fuel lines, control panel, starter battery and temporary cooling water supply linked up, the throttle and gearbox control cables clipped on, the engine filled with new oil, and we were ready for a test run. "Press the starter!" ordered Ian, and I pushed the black button firmly home. The starter motor whined and instantly the Farymann burst into life. It was like music to my ears. "Check to see if water is coming out of the exhaust," shouted Ian above the roar of the diesel, and I hurriedly climbed into the cockpit and peered over the stern. Water was spurting out with the exhaust gases. The engine was working perfectly and I gave Ian the thumbs up. Jean had been stationed outside near the stern and when she signalled all was clear, Ian shoved the engine into forward gear and the propeller spun round. With the control pulled back the propeller went astern, then, knocked into neutral, the propeller stopped and the engine was switched off. The test was over and *Amulet* had an engine that would last for years and was capable of pushing her against all but the strongest tides on Scotland's west coast. The sail-only purists were courageous men but, thinking about it later, I wondered whether, had they been fortunate enough to have a sponsor like Patricia, they might also have jumped at the chance of a new engine.

While I had been in a frenzy about engines I could think of little else, but Margaret and Jean had worked steadily away at varnishing and painting the small items in the barn and all the deck beams on *Amulet*; but during the middle of April high pressure was forecast and, as the television met. man promised a spell of warm weather, all hands were mustered for the task of fitting the plywood decks. Free from the confinement of the tarpaulin shelter and the dusty interior of the barn, it was a joy to work in the sun, spreading the sheets of plywood outside between two benches and cutting them to shape with the jigsaw. I cut the two foredeck pieces first and, with the functional weight of the rear ends of the two ladies holding them into position, I went below and pencilled in the shape of the deck beams. Having struggled on many an occasion to paint the underside of decks from inside the cabin and been covered in paint in the process, I have found that, when fitting new decks, it is easier to mark the position of the deck beams on the pieces of ply, mask them off, then paint the panels with the required coats of paint. When they are all ready for fitting, the masking tape is removed and glue applied, and they can then be nailed onto the deck beams. Hey presto, the chore of fighting with a paintbrush inside lockers and awkward places is overcome. When all the deck panels had been cut to shape and the positions of the beams pencilled in and masked off, it took several days to apply the numerous layers of undercoat and white gloss and, while waiting for the paint to dry, it was an opportunity to spread the sails out and air them in the sun. A number of bags bulging with sails, coils of rope and mysterious rolls of canvas had lain untouched in the barn since the day *Amulet* arrived and it was exciting to empty this 'treasure trove' onto Mrs Dickinson's well-trimmed lawn and rummage through it. The sails were all white with the exception of the nylon spinnaker, which had red and yellow vertical stripes and was enclosed in a smart zip-up bag. It had hardly been used and was likely to stay that way. My experience of spinnakers was that they were fiendish sails that behaved unpredictably and provoked crews into calling each other vile names. The genoa and its bag looked brand new but, amazingly, some idiot had stowed it away when it was wet, and a galvanised shackle left on the tack had rusted and permanently stained the terylene with ugly brown blotches. The mainsail and the jib had the tired grey appearance of veteran sails that had flogged through many a sea, but I reckoned that with a few minor repairs there was still a season or two of life in them. What concerned me about the main was the total lack of reefing pennants, and I made a mental note to sew some on. On an old Royal Mail letter sack that doubled as a sail bag, someone had painted in black, 'Storm Sail – hang up and pray.' and inside it was a small storm jib whose well-used condition seemed to confirm that the painter had been unfortunate with his weather and spent much of his sailing time appealing to his maker for deliverance. The coils of rope turned out to be the main sheet, complete with varnished wooden blocks, the jib and spinnaker sheets, and the main and jib halliards. They were all hard three-strand nylon that had seen better days and, having made a note of lengths and diameters, I salvaged the varnished blocks and dumped the rope in the scrap bin. Spread out on the grass, the mysterious rolls of PVC canvas revealed a sail cover, a large awning for draping over the boom, a bosun's chair, cockpit dodgers with the name 'Amulet' sewn on in large blue letters, a large hood with flexible windows and an assortment of faded signal flags. They were all usable, and needed only vigorous attention with hot, soapy water and a brush to remove accumulated grime. The hot weather was set to continue and, with the sails and canvas left out to air and get rid of the musty smell that comes from being stored for too long, the newly-painted deck panels were carried out of the barn and arranged ready for fitting.

To me, fitting the deck is one of the most satisfying stages of building or restoring a wooden boat. It's almost the final bit of the jigsaw puzzle and a welcome sign that the worst jobs are over; but apart from anything else it means that with the narrow beams covered, for the first time in months you can stand on the foredeck or walk round the side decks without giving an impression of a Fakir walking barefoot over a bed of nails. Making a start with the foredeck, a thin layer of resorcinol glue was spread over the beams on the port side, then the plywood sheet carefully lowered into place with the help of Jean and nailed down firmly with galvanised nails. I made a quick dash below to wipe off surplus glue before it dripped onto the planking, and then the starboard piece was glued and nailed into place. Moving slowly down the hull towards the stern, with a break at midday for sandwiches and cold drinks and a session of basking in the sun, we fitted both side decks, and I felt tremendously exhilarated. Over the weeks, as each phase had progressed, *Amulet* had begun to look more like the attractive boat she once was and, with the sun shining on the new deck, I got the feeling she was enormously proud of herself. Before laying the after deck the beams had to be fitted between the transom and the cockpit and they had a pronounced curve which made it tricky to fit short pieces of fifteen millimetre thick plywood and, to make it more of a teaser, a hatchway had to be constructed for access to the fuel tank. Another design fault of modern boats is that there is rarely any means of removing, or even accessing, the fuel tank for cleaning out the water and muck that finds its way in no matter what precautions are taken. By the time the hatch was in place, the cover screwed down on a bed of mastic and the deck pieces joggled to fit round it and glued and nailed into place, it was late in the afternoon, but at last the deck was finished and ready for sheathing with fibreglass cloth.

Years ago, when I was a lighthouse keeper at the Butt of Lewis lighthouse in the Outer Hebrides, I sailed with local fishermen who could forecast the weather by the changing colour of the sea, and they were seldom wrong. Since those days I have tried a more scientific approach to anticipating the weather, but it has always seemed illogical that a nice fat ridge of high pressure allows itself to be bullied and pushed into the North Sea by a malevolent low pressure system that comes snarling in from the Atlantic. Under cover of darkness one such demon blasted across Cumbria and all night a full gale howled around my house and I lay awake listening to the crash of trees being torn from their roots in a nearby wood. The next morning the drive to the 'big house' was blocked with fallen trees and, almost bowled over by the strength of the wind, I battled my way through fields to reach the barn. Mercifully several tall ash trees, which would have flattened *Amulet* had they fallen, were still upright, but the framed 'tent' had taken a severe battering. The wind, gusting under the tarpaulins, had snapped the holding ropes like string and, unable to take the strain, three of the trusses that formed the roof of the tent had fractured, and collapsed onto the roof of the cabin. Encouraged by a tarpaulin flapping furiously in the gale, one of them was battering the top of the cabin like a pile driver and threatening to smash it in. The aluminium ladder had been ripped away from the side of the hull and blown against the barn door, and I dragged it back and climbed up as far as the side deck on the port side, but the tangle of timber and flogging tarpaulins prevented me from climbing any further. Above the roar of the wind I could hear the broken truss battering against the cabin roof and it was only a matter of time before it would have caused serious damage. I had to act fast and thought of cutting through the supporting poles of the tent with my chainsaw and letting the wind carry the trusses and flogging tarpaulins away from the boat, but I realised that, if the combined weight of the tent and the poles crashed onto *Amulet*'s foredeck, it could make matters worse. I had a rapid change of plan, and rushed into the barn for a hydraulic trolley jack I used when putting chocks under the keel. Even if I could reach it, the broken truss threatening the cabin was too awkward to lift without help, and I reckoned that if I could slide the jack under it I could at least raise it clear and maybe make a temporary repair. But the storm had other ideas and, each time I tried to climb the ladder clutching the heavy jack to my chest, it sent a flogging tarpaulin to repel boarders and batter my head until I retreated. I dropped the jack and was trying to grab a short length of frayed rope hanging from a corner of the tarpaulin when, to my relief, Margaret arrived. "Get the roll of thin cord hanging on the barn door," I bellowed above the wind. "I've got to tie this down before it tears itself to shreds." Always quick to weigh up a situation, she found a knife in the barn and came running back with several long lengths of cord she had cut from the roll. They did the trick and the tarpaulin was soon lashed tightly to the steel cradle. In the shelter of the barn I hurriedly explained the problem to Margaret, and back out in the storm I tied a rope to the jack and hauled it up the ladder onto the foredeck while she climbed after it to keep it steady. The collapsed roof-trusses had shunted the whole structure of the frame and the tarpaulin tent at a steep angle towards the bow, and it was being shaken furiously as though it was in the jaws of a giant dog. There was room to kneel on the foredeck, but in the tangle of wood and canvas above the cabin top there was only a few inches of headroom. It was like looking down into a heaving chest in one of those films of operations they show in medical programmes on the telly; only this time, somewhere in the region of the diaphragm, I could see a lump of gyrating timber beating hell out of the rib cage. Helped by Margaret, I eased the long, flat trolley-jack into the 'tunnel' and under the broken truss, and feverishly cranked the handle until the jack had reached its full height. I crawled into the hole and jammed a piece of wood under the truss to support it while the jack was released, then lifted onto a block of wood to give it height, and the truss raised again to the full extent of the jack. All the time we worked the gale continued to rage and the flogging of canvas was deafening, but eventually the truss was lifted out of harms way and propped up securely. I was amazed and highly relieved to find that, apart from a few minor gouges in the Cascover fibreglass sheathing, the coachroof had survived the onslaught without any sign of damage and it was a credit to the builder. The two other trusses that had snapped in the middle were given a quick repair with rope lashings, the flogging tarpaulins tied down wherever possible, and, lowering the jack ahead of us, we beat a hasty retreat down the ladder to the barn. It had taken less than an hour from the time we hoisted the jack on board, but my aching neck, back and leg muscles were arguing that it was longer. Being the quiet type, Margaret said little and took her muscles home for a hot bath.

In Mrs. Dickinson's drive the farm men were busy with chain saws clearing away a huge horse chestnut tree that had succumbed to the storm. It was well over one hundred years old and had a massive girth. I dared not think what would have happened had *Amulet* been underneath it when it fell. Boat owners who dwell on things like that are likely to develop sudden incontinence!

At its height the gale probably touched severe gale force nine, but it was a one-day wonder and disappeared as fast as it came, leaving a trail of fallen trees in its wake throughout Cumbria and a very wobbly tent structure over *Amulet*. Yet when I arrived at the barn the next morning it was as if the gale had never been. The sun was making a brave attempt to push through the clouds; the horse chestnut in the drive had been cleared away; blackbirds and thrushes were competing in the estate song contest; the tawny owl sat impassively on his usual branch and a pair of buzzards 'mewed' to each other as they soared effortlessly over the 'big house'. The only noticeable difference in the tranquil scene from forty eight hours before was that the tent sheltering *Amulet* had a flat roof instead of a sloping one and, if it was touched, the structure supporting it swayed like a Scottish yachtsman at the end of West Highland Week.

Sensing that I was feeling a bit fraught after the ghastly experience with the gale, both Jean and Margaret volunteered to help sort out the mess and the six tarpaulins that covered the frame were dragged off. It revealed a rickety-looking structure about to collapse at any minute, but the two ladies, heaving on a rope, pulled it upright and held it while I strengthened the supports with new timber. Most of the roof trusses needed only simple repair work but rather than waste time trying to repair the badly-damaged truss that had played havoc with the cabin top, it was easier to make a new one. The tarpaulins were heaved back into place and held down with new guy lines and the discarded halliards and jib sheets, and the new tent looked capable of withstanding a hurricane. It had wasted a full day but, thankfully, *Amulet* had survived unscathed and I could move on to the next stage, sheathing the new decks with fibreglass cloth.

I have worked on wooden boats, steel boats, aluminium boats and rubber boats but have always avoided fibreglass. The very smell of it makes me feel sick and when, in the early days of fibreglass boat production, I was shown round a factory that churned out mass-produced hulls like peas out of a pod, the sight of the workers encased in white suits, masks and gloves was so alien to the type of boatbuilding I was familiar with I couldn't stand it and went home. There was absolutely no way I could face plastering the smelly muck on *Amulet*'s decks and I phoned Nichol End Marine at Keswick and pleaded with Nick Newby. "Nick, I'm desperate to get *Amulet* finished and I know nothing about sheathing decks with fibreglass and don't want to make a mess of it. Would you be able to do it for me?" Nick was never one for wasting words. "No," he growled. "I'm too busy. Do it yourself, there's nothing to it. I'll supply the cloth and resin and I'll lend you the rollers. Let me have a sketch of the deck area and I'll work out how much material you'll need." I tried more pleading, but realised I was talking to the dialling tone. "Unhelpful sod," I muttered, and replacing the phone I drew a sketch of the deck and took it over to him.

Yacht chandlers shops flaunting their attractions and drawing in the unwary are more dangerous than any ale house or dockside 'massage parlour' for relieving a sailor of his money, and I had to go through the one at Nichol End Marine in order to seek out the great man to discuss materials for fibreglassing *Amulet*'s decks. A handful of shackles, six expensive rigging screws, a new Suzuki outboard motor and three inflatable fenders later, I managed to escape through the exit and track down Nick in his workshop. He looked at my sketch, grunted, then with a flexible tape measured a length of fibreglass cloth off a large roll. "Have you brought a container to put the resin in?" he asked. "No, you never mentioned that," I said. "What do I do with resin?" He looked at me with one of those expressions of resigned despair marina managers reserve for cocksure customers who attempt to come alongside a pontoon at full speed and end up with their boat in the mating position on the back of a millionaire's gin palace. "I could tell you," he sighed wearily. Nick was not having one of his best days but, ignorant though I was of the art of laying fibreglass cloth, he spent time patiently explaining the procedure and making sure I had all the materials, brushes and rollers I needed, plus a can of hardener for the resin and another of foul-smelling solvent to remove the sticky resin from the tools and me. "And don't forget to wear rubber gloves and a mask when you're using it," Nick shouted as I drove away.

With the end of the restoration of *Amulet* now a distinct light in the distance, the tolerance level of my long-suffering helpers was wearing thin, and my once heart-melting reasons for wanting help had lost their originality. Working with smelly, sticky fibreglass resin that could get on their clothes, on their hands and face or, horror of horrors, in their hair, was definitely a non-starter. They made it clear I was on my own. "Tough," said Margaret. "You know I have a touch of asthma. I daren't breathe that stuff in," said Jean. When I unloaded my dilemma on the phone to a friend who lived safely in London he said, "It's at times like these you discover who your friends are." The discovery time was painfully swift, it took only a few phone calls to realise I hadn't got any. Word had got round.

I tried to employ helpers but I was let down by people who promised to come but never showed up and a few days after visiting Nick I was standing by *Amulet* wondering whether I could tackle the job myself without ending up dropping resin-soaked cloth onto the ground or wrapping it round my head when my mobile phone rang. It was Margaret. "Have you managed to get the fibreglass on the deck yet?" she enquired. I felt that if I said 'no' she would ring off, so I said someone had promised to come but hadn't turned up. "Well, if you want a hand I could come tomorrow. I'll put some old clothes and shoes on and wear a hat, but you'll have to provide gloves and a mask." I was overjoyed and told her so. "Oh well," she said. "I'm not surprised you have so few friends, but I've spent so much time working on your old boat I may as well see it through to the end, then perhaps I'll get some peace!"

Happily the following day was warm and dry, and with Margaret's help I was able to cut the pieces of cloth to shape on a sheet of plywood on the ground. It was the same procedure as for cutting the plywood. Two pieces for the foredeck, long narrow strips for the side decks and measured pieces for the after deck to fit round the fuel tank hatch. Nick had stressed that the ratio of resin to hardener was critical to prevent it from setting too quickly or, if there wasn't enough hardener in, not setting at all; but he said put plenty of the mixture on the decks, so I took him at his word and clarted one half of the foredeck with the thick syrupy mess. Balanced on a plank suspended between two ladders, we stretched the cloth between us and lowered it onto the deck, making sure there was sufficient overlap at the edges, and quickly pressed it in with special fluted rollers. Even through the mask, the acrid smell churned my stomach over, but we kept going, stopping only for a cup of coffee and giving lunch a miss. What would probably have taken an experienced hand less than a morning took us well into the evening, but I had to make sure it was on right. I soon discovered there is no second chance with fibreglass, once it is on, it is on for all time. We were just applying the last mix of resin when Nick Newby arrived. He had driven the thirty miles or so from Keswick just to see how I was getting on, but that was Nick. His only comment was that I could have used more resin, but he was glowing in his praise for our work and I was as happy as a dog with two tails. "There's a lot to be said for mixing old skills with new," said Nick, as he was about to drive away. "Planked decks might be very traditional, but if they leak and your bunk and sleeping bag get soaked every time it rains or a sea washes over the boat, they can soon lose their charm." Having been there, I knew exactly what he meant and later, when *Amulet* sailed to the Western Isles, not a drop of water found its way through the fibreglass-sheathed deck.

April had gone by in a flash, and May looked like doing the same and, though the long list of jobs to be done was well-peppered with ticks, there was a page and a half still untouched and the old nagging worries about completing *Amulet* as fast as possible and leaving for Scotland began to churn through my head. I tried arriving at the barn as soon as it was light and working faster on jobs; but, searching for my sail repair kit at home I had come across a photograph of old Brab Davies standing on the deck of his boat, and I could hear his gruff voice handing out his potted philosophy. "If thou rushes a job on a boat thou'll make a mess of it. Better to tek thee time than have to try and fix summat at sea with a gale howlin' round thee head!" Brab had long set sail for the heavenly fishing grounds but, though I knew he would be appalled that I had a 'toffs' boat, I felt he was still keeping a watchful eye over me and I took his advice. But this divine paternalism stirred up trouble. It angered one of Lucifer's cloven-hoof gang who lived in the bowels of the earth and who seemed devoted to putting every conceivable object in the way of my finishing *Amulet*. He waved his evil wand and the effect was instant. "Bob, have you seen this soft patch in the cabin roof?" shouted Margaret. The 'team' was out in force; I was working in the barn while Jean was brushing another undercoat on the hull and Margaret was painting the top of the cabin. "What's the problem?" I asked, climbing the ladder to the deck. "Look," said Margaret, pressing a corner of the roof with a thumb. "It's spongy." I tried it myself and the plywood went in and sprang out again, a sure sign of water damage. "How the hell have I missed that?" I said irritably. "I hope it's only a patch otherwise the whole damned roof will have to come off." I went below into the cabin and inspected the roof. It had been newly painted but the soft patch was unmistakable and, to my dismay I found that the opposite corner of the roof was soft as well. I was furious with myself for missing them when I first checked the cabin for rot, but being angry wasn't going to solve the problem and I poked the areas again with a knife. The two soft spots were roughly six inches by four inches and, had *Amulet* been destined for use only on an inland lake the condition of the roof would have been no cause for concern; but for the sort of cruising I had in mind I had to consider whether it would withstand the impact of a heavy sea breaking over it. "Will the roof have to come off?" asked Margaret when I went back on deck. "It looks like it," I said dismally. "It's a major job and will take ages. I'll be lucky if I get this bloody boat launched before Christmas." "Could it not be repaired?" she queried. "Well it could," I replied, "but it's a question of whether it would be strong enough, unless... " I suddenly had an idea and climbed rapidly down the ladder, going to the barn where I remembered seeing a piece of thin marine plywood about eighteen inches wide and long enough to fit across the width of the roof. Passing it up to Margaret, I went back to see if there was any fibreglass cloth and resin and hardener left. I was in luck, there was just enough for what I had in mind. "We'll screw and glue this plywood across the roof and over the soft bits, then sheathe it with fibreglass cloth," I explained to Margaret. "I don't want to rip the whole roof off just for the sake of a couple of soft areas, and trying to repair them individually would be more trouble than it's worth." Two ventilators on the roof were removed, holes cut in the plywood to line up with the holes in the roof then, coated on one side with a layer of glue, it was lowered into place and screwed down all round. Surplus glue was wiped off and the edges chamfered to give a smooth finish for the fibreglass and, leaving the glue to set, we spent the rest of the morning helping Jean with the hull painting.

Assisted by an extra squirt of hardener, the glue had set by the time lunch was over and the plywood was daubed with a thick layer of resin and the fibreglass cloth rolled into it. I could never see myself being 'converted' to fibreglass, but I had to admit I was very pleased with the result and when the sheathing had dried and been painted over and the ventilators re-fitted, the 'alien' piece of plywood was not as intrusive as I had feared. Not only did it considerably strengthen the cabin roof, it later proved to be an ideal place for locating the liferaft.

In the days that followed the 'team' got through a prestigious amount of work and, by the end of May, *Amulet* began to look less like an austere convict ship and more like an attractive classic yacht. The hull was ready to be glossed, and the top and outside of the cabin given a last brushing with undercoat and lightly rubbed down with sandpaper. Down below, the teak floorboards were cleaned and slotted into place and the interior varnished until it sparkled. The bunks and the insides of the lockers were given a final coat of white gloss, the varnished doors re-hung and the combined engine cover/companionway steps fitted over the engine. I particularly enjoyed refitting the galley and got a lot of satisfaction out of installing the water tank, the stainless steel sink, a new Optimus two-burner gimballed paraffin stove and building storage bins for the pans and crockery. To give it a more hygienic appearance, the old cream paint in the toilet compartment, the 'heads', was scraped off and brightened up with a fresh covering of white gloss before the mighty Simpson-Lawrence thunderbox, magnificent in a coat of white enamel and with a varnished seat and lid, was lifted on board with due dignity and bolted to a new plinth of English oak. Complemented with a varnished pine toilet-roll holder it looked majestic, and I felt we should have had an installation ceremony but, as neither of my lady helpers was inclined to be photographed putting it to the test, I welcomed it aboard by flushing it through with a bucket of water. To provide extra storage I left the bunks out of the forecabin and although it looked rather bare, the general consensus was that it made the varnished planking all the more attractive. In the 'original' *Amulet*, the anchor chain had been led from the deck down a wooden chute into a small locker between the bunks, but I lashed a ten-gallon plastic drum to the stringers and bored holes in it to let water out. It looked primitive, but it worked. Among the miscellaneous jumble that came with the boat I had been delighted to find a lovely folding saloon table made of mahogany, with a clever device designed by the builder that attached it to the main bulkhead in the cabin, but there was no sign of the tubular leg. A quiet word on the phone with the ever-grateful engineer whose teeth had been rescued from the bilge produced a length of stainless steel pipe that was a perfect fit.

I renewed all the electrical wiring, fitted switched lights in the forecabin, heads, main cabin and in the galley, and made a new varnished control box for the switchgear. The VHF radio and electronic log that had come with *Amulet* had seen better days, and I ditched them and fitted a new Simrad VHF coupled to the latest DSC controller, a new electronic log, an echo sounder to connect to the old transducer discovered in the stem and, for a touch of luxury, a Navtex weather and navigation receiver and a Furuno GPS satellite navigation system. Brought up to navigate with only the aid of a trailing log and a compass, I had treated the new navigation gadgets with sneering contempt until, in the 1970s, as an insurance requirement I was obliged to fit a Decca navigator in my charter ketch. One day, surrounded by reefs and in heavy rain and poor visibility, with the aid of the Decca I was able to thread my way through the dreaded Torran Rocks, south of the Isle of Mull, and I worshipped the magic box thereafter. But only a fool would dismiss basic navigation as an outdated relic. The satellite navigation system is more accurate and more reliable than the now obsolete Decca, but it should never be forgotten that 'he who poketh two fingers at the teachings of the wise navigators and filleth his vessel with 'interfaced' tablets and believeth he hath a celestial homing pigeon which will guideth him on angry waters will surely reacheth for a large toilet roll when the power fails'.

Apart from a few minor jobs the interior was finished, but there was still plenty outside to keep me occupied, not least bolting a new sacrificial anode through the hull near the sternpost and connecting wires from the bolts on the inside of the hull to the engine, gearbox and propeller-shaft in the hope that they would all be spared from the devastating effects of electrolysis. After a final check of the propeller-shaft bolts, the stern-gland greaser, and the self-draining cockpit pipes and skin fittings, the cockpit floor, complete with an inspection hatch, was bedded in mastic and screwed down. Moving about in the cockpit was a lot easier and I was able to fit the hinged seats which gave access to the lockers in which the battery was battened down and warps and fenders and emergency flares and other essential items were to be stored. My all-time favourite steering compass is the Sestrel-Moore and I have owned one for over thirty years and transferred it from boat to boat; but, fearing that it could be clouted by the boom if fitted on the cabin roof, I opted to install *Amulet*'s own compass on its pedestal in the middle of the cockpit floor. The pedestal also served as the mainsheet horse. Accidentally dropping a screwdriver into the cabin while I was working on this job solved a problem I had been mulling over for weeks. I had been undecided about how to conceal an unsightly hole left by the removal of the old speed log in the bulkhead adjacent to the entrance to the cabin, and when I bashed my head on the VHF radio while in pursuit of the screwdriver it gave me an idea. The hole was ideal for that most useful of VHF accessories, a cockpit-mounted waterproof extension speaker.

A light blue paint that contrasted well with the dark blue gloss destined for the hull was chosen for the exterior of the cabin and the interior of the cockpit and the cockpit coamings and, working alternately, Jean and Margaret made a super job of them. When building the cockpit, David had capped the coamings with a lovely piece of iroko that was too nice to cover with paint, so it was masked off and, when the cockpit paint had dried, given several coats of varnish. Human bottoms, especially when encased in shiny waterproof trousers, have a distressing habit of sliding off gloss paint when a boat is heeling, and to provide some grip on the cockpit seats and the bridge deck I used a cheap, though effective, dodge cribbed off John Hodgson. Rectangles with the corners rounded were drawn on the panels; masked off and painted with the dark blue of the hull and covered with fine sand while the paint was wet. When dried it was the perfect 'non-slip' surface. Talking to John on the phone, he suggested I should do the same on the deck, shaking the sand over a coating of resin instead of paint but, though the cost would have been minimal, the actual masking of the many individual panels to give it a touch of professionalism would have been very time- consuming, so I took the easy way out and painted the lot with non-slip deck paint. *Amulet* looked more attractive with each day that passed and I longed to pull the shelter down and reveal her in all her glory, but there was still one fairly major job to be done, and I had been dreading it.

Gunwale is a nautical word that goes back into the depths of time when sailing ships fired cannons at each other, and if it was spelt 'gunnel' the way it is normally pronounced, it would save a lot of confusion. I have known boatbuilders have heated arguments not only about how it should be pronounced but its exact location on a wooden ship. Some say the piece of timber running round the top plank of a hull and extending slightly above the deck is a bulwark, but I have always known it as the gunwale and the Oxford Dictionary's description of a gunwale, 'a piece of timber extending round the topside of the hull,' is good enough for me. When *Amulet* first arrived at the barn she had mahogany gunwales raised three inches or so above deck level, with scuppers cut in at intervals to allow water to run off and brass tracks screwed port and starboard along the top edges for controlling the jib or genoa sheet blocks. A piece shaped to fit the curve of the transom joined the gunwales together at the stern. Sadly, the ravages of time and fresh water had reduced the timber to pulp in many places and it joined the rotten decking on the scrap heap. When *Amulet* was in commission the varnished gunwales must have looked very handsome and I was determined to replace them but, when a timber specialist sent me a price for three long lengths of six inches wide by one and a half inches thick mahogany, it was more than it would have cost me for a week in a nursing home to recover from the shock. I had to forget about mahogany and consider using a less expensive wood, such as pine, but Nick Newby was horrified. "You can't use a softwood for the gunwales," he protested when I phoned to ask if he had any in stock. "It'll look awful and it won't last. I'll tell you what, I've got a bit of iroko stored away, but it's an absolute sod to cut into lengths. If you'll come this evening when we close and help me saw it to size, you can have it for not much more than it would cost you for softwood." It was typical of Nick to want to help out, and I could hardly believe my luck. Similar to teak, iroko is tremendously durable though, like teak, it has to be wiped with a solvent to remove its natural oil before it can be varnished, but that was no problem and I hardly gave Nick time to gulp his tea down before I was parked outside his workshop.

The 'bit of iroko' was in fact a whole tree trunk, about sixteen feet long, that had been cut into boards two inches thick and stacked to dry in the air. The boards were staggeringly heavy and it took the combined strength of both of us to lift one out of the stack onto trestles, and even then the fight wasn't over. Nick's description of iroko being 'an absolute sod to cut into lengths' was no exaggeration. The powerful portable electric saw had barely advanced more than a few inches along the line of the cut before it was brought to a screeching halt by the timber 'binding', trapping the blade fast, and I was given the task of following behind the saw tapping wedges into the cut to keep it as wide as possible. It took ages to cut four lengths but, undeterred, Nick ran them through a planing machine to reduce the thickness to one and a half inches, and then decided he would save me a lot of time and hard work by cutting rebates out so that when the gunwale was fastened in place on the hull, the top three inches overlapped the edge of the deck. I was quite happy, but the small circular saw bench in his workshop took exception to being expected to cut a substantial chunk out of four long lengths of very hard wood and it stopped frequently when the overload button saved the electric motor from going up in smoke. With midnight approaching and Nick's wife storming into the workshop at frequent intervals, angrily demanding to be taken home, I tactfully suggested that perhaps I should come back some other time, but Nick insisted we should carry on until all four pieces were rebated. "You realise you'll have to cut a long scarph to join two pieces together to fit the length of the hull?" queried Nick as he squinted along the rebates to make sure they were clean. "How are you going to do that?" By this time I was too tired to think, and said wearily, "I suppose I'll cut them with a handsaw." "Oh, that's too much like hard work," he said cheerfully, "We'll do them on the bandsaw while we're here; it'll only take a few minutes. Give me a hand to drag it into position." I groaned inwardly, but Nick's wife was less inhibited and, before slamming the workshop door behind her, she launched into a tirade that left no doubt what she thought of him, and me as well. But Nick had already switched the bandsaw on and, while I struggled to hold the length of timber horizontal and at the same time push it forward, Nick guided it slowly through the blade and cut a long scarph joint with more precision than I could ever have dreamed of doing with an ordinary joiners saw. "They're too long to go on your car roof," said Nick, when we had finished all four pieces. "I'll be down your way tomorrow so I'll stick them in a trailer on the back of the Landrover." It was half past one in the morning and I had thirty miles to drive and could hardly keep awake, but I was deeply grateful to Nick for his persistence. There were times when he could be very exasperating, but no one could deny his unflagging enthusiasm and his never-ending concern for his customers. As he drove past me in the dark I could hear a loud voice raised in anger, and I had a feeling it wasn't coming from his car radio!

Nick delivered the timber, and thirty metres of galvanised anchor chain I had ordered, late the following afternoon and, with the benches lined up end to end in the barn, I spread the pieces out and mated up the scarph joints ready for gluing. Bent round the curve of the hull, the gunwale would be under considerable tension and it was critical that the joint was perfect. Another dodge learnt from John Hodgson was to scratch lines on the faces of scarph joints with a wood chisel to give the glue 'something to get its teeth into', and when this was done I mixed what I fervently hoped was the precise ratio of hardener to the resorcinol glue – 'no more, no less' was Nick's dire warning - then spread it evenly on the joints. Juggling with two sixteen foot lengths of wood on my own while trying to line up long scarph joints dripping with glue inspired a few expressions that would not have been welcome in polite company and I wished that Jean or Margaret would suddenly appear, but they were both involved elsewhere. Eventually, with my hands covered in glue, and dripping sweat onto the wood, I succeeded in pulling the joints together with rows of G-cramps and, to give the glue every chance to set thoroughly, I left them unmoved for nearly a week. It paid off. The result was two perfect joints that were tremendously strong and, balanced on the sturdy shoulders of my 'team', the thirty foot lengths of iroko were carried out of the barn without difficulty and pulled slightly round the curve of the hull while I marked off the correct distance from end to end. It was irksome being confined to the barn during a spell of sunny weather, marking out and cutting the slots for the scuppers in the new gunwales, and I envied Jean working outside in shorts and a tee shirt. She had taken the initiative and spread the new anchor chain along the access road to the barn, and was busy marking off the depths in fathoms with different coloured paints. Despite decimalisation and the concerted efforts of the European Club to get me to change my ways, I still prefer to think in fathoms. I reckon that it is better to be able to think quickly in fathoms than go aground while still scratching my head trying to remember how deep a metre is. Sea water is not fussy whether it pours through holes measured in centimetres or inches so, out of respect for *Amulet*'s age and in memory of the days when the UK was an independent country, I made the new scuppers four inches long by three quarters of an inch deep.

Perhaps because it reminded her of the times during the 1939/45 war when she visited her husband Ronald, who was in command of a patrol vessel based at Stornoway on the Island of Lewis, Mrs. Dickinson was intrigued with the anchor chain and photographed it from every angle. Although I had taken over her barn, used her electricity, shattered the tranquillity of her estate, piled up heaps of rubbish and occasionally been reprimanded for commandeering the sacred potting shed or forgetting to turn the lights off in the barn, she had remained a staunch supporter of the project and took an enthusiastic interest in the progress of the restoration. Her house visitors' book read like a copy of 'Who's Who', and she delighted in bringing her guests to see *Amulet*. I was so accustomed to talking about my plans with the 'nobility and gentry', a friend of mine, who had seen me talking to a rather gorgeous countess quipped, "You ought to hang a 'By Royal Appointment' sign up." But it was by hard work, not by royal appointment, that *Amulet* was going to be made ready for the sea; and only when the new gunwales had been well sanded, had screw holes drilled and countersunk for wooden plugs, wiped thoroughly with solvent and given five coats of varnish was I able to request the pleasure of the company of lady Jean and lady Margaret on the occasion of the fitting, dress very definitely informal and bring your own sandwiches!

With aluminium stepladders and scaffolding planks I built a wobbly, but adequate, staging for us to stand on between the hull and the frame of the 'tent' and, with Margaret at the bow, Jean in the middle and me at the stern, we lifted the port side gunwale for a test run. With a G-cramp holding the stern, it took a lot of pushing and shoving, gasping and heaving, to bend the wood round the turn of the hull and force it against the bow, and there were loud sighs of relief when I finally secured it to the stem with a G-cramp. I checked along the gunwale to make sure it was seating correctly on the deck, and had reached the stern when the cramp holding the bow end slipped off. Released with the power of a spring, the gunwale swept Jean and Margaret clean off the staging and pinned them against the side of the tent like two moles in a trap. "Help!" shouted Jean, still clinging onto the gunwale, unable to move. "Get us out of this!" cried Margaret, but for a few minutes I was so convulsed with laughter I could do nothing but lean helplessly against the hull. Realising that the joke was wearing thin and I was in danger of losing my 'team', I rushed to release them, profuse in my apologies; but they were not amused and to mutterings of "Any more tricks like that and you're on your own," and "You've got a typical, twisted male sense of humour," we laid the gunwale on the ground to prepare it for the actual fitting.

No self-respecting termite would risk a stomach ulcer chewing through oily iroko, so the new timber had not been given the usual sousing with Cuprinol but, to prevent moisture gathering between the gunwale and the side of the hull, the rebate was plastered thoroughly with mastic before the gunwale was lifted into position and we had the struggle to cramp it to the bow all over again. This time I was taking no chances and fastened it through the top plank and into the beam shelf with a line of substantial stainless steel screws. Surplus mastic was cleaned off with rags and methylated spirit, the ladders and planks carried round to the other side and the starboard gunwale fixed in place. This time, to spare the 'team' the embarrassment of another incident, we skipped the trial run and screwed the gunwale into position as it was bent round the hull. A piece of flat iroko board was given a gentle camber with the jigsaw then screwed onto the transom to fit neatly between the ends of the gunwales. At the bow, the square ends were cut in a downward curve to give a touch of style and the whole job given a final touch of professionalism with small plugs of iroko cut out of offcuts with a very useful tool provided by John Hodgson. They were coated with glue and tapped into the screw holes with the grain in line with the grain of the gunwale. When dry they were planed flush and, finished off with another two coats of varnish, the gunwales looked superb.

Brab's Bitter End and *Amulet*'s Launch

Browsing through the list of jobs hanging on the barn wall and finding it almost covered in pencilled ticks, I hardly dare believe that the restoration of *Amulet* was almost finished and the only major task left was painting the hull with gloss and, below the waterline, with antifouling. Before burning the paint off the hull I had taken measurements of the waterline and, with the help of a long wooden lath fastened horizontally at right angles to the stem and one fastened likewise to the transom, a long piece of string and a black marker pen, Jean and I drew the waterline on the hull and ran masking tape along it in preparation for the first coat of royal blue gloss. The weather was warm and sunny and perfect for drying paint and, perhaps sensing that at last the end was in sight, the 'team' had two coats on in record time and, whizzing a new run of masking tape round, pressed on with applying the deep red antifouling. I toyed with the idea of having a boot topping of a contrasting colour, but decided there was nothing to be gained and it would use up more time. It was a shock to discover that, having put the antifouling on at the barn, I had committed myself to deciding on a launching date, as the instructions on the can warned that it would lose its effectiveness if the boat was not immersed in seawater within a month. It meant organising a crane and transport for *Amulet*, but first I had to find a suitable harbour to launch her in.

Flying due west from the barn at ten knots, a herring gull could be gorging himself on the fish dock in the ancient harbour of Whitehaven in just under an hour. The jewel in the tourist board's coastal crown, it has been the home of ships and sailors for many centuries and has an incredibly long and fascinating maritime history that includes building ships that circled the world, close ties with the American tobacco trade, and the smuggling of all manner of goods from the Isle of Man and Scotland. The writer of *Gulliver's Travels* had lived there, President George Washington's grandmother was buried in the local churchyard and a special type of stone from a local quarry had been used to build part of the White House in the American capital. Another claim to fame was that the American pirate John Paul Jones attacked the town and destroyed several ships. With the help of enormous grants, the harbour was given a major facelift during the 1990s and all traces of the coal and chemical industries that had saved it from extinction for many years swept away and replaced with upmarket housing, attractive walkways and a marina with a boat hoist capable of lifting forty five tons. It was the perfect starting point for my journey, but there was a snag. Though Whitehaven had once been a tidal harbour, a tidal lock had been constructed at the entrance and, no longer affected by the tide, the rise and fall inside was minimal. *Amulet* had not been in the water for eight years or more and, until her planks had taken up, it was necessary to lean her against a tidal wall or suspend her in the water in a hoist for a day or so. When I enquired about the possibility of launching *Amulet* I hoped there would be someone who understood the situation but regrettably, like so many harbour authorities keen to cash in on the marina boom, their understanding and experience of small boats did not extend beyond allocating a pontoon berth and collecting the money for it. That a piece of maritime history, a classic wooden boat, had been restored almost on their doorstep and could be launched in their harbour raised not the merest flicker of interest or encouragement and, very disheartened by the negative response from my 'home port', I looked elsewhere.

Ten miles to the north, the harbour of Maryport also had an impressive maritime history and boasted a connection with the White Star Line, which owned the *Titanic*, but though once packed with coasting and ocean-going vessels, one of the port's two docks had fallen derelict and were it not for a timely injection of regeneration cash, would have headed in the same direction as the ill-fated ship. With lots of grant money available, the town fathers had followed the fashion and transformed it into a most attractive marina and, even more attractive to me, it was managed by Steve Jackson, a man of all trades and an enthusiastic sailor with an RYA Yachtmaster's ticket, who immediately understood what I needed for *Amulet* and who went out of his way to be as helpful as he could. He offered the use of a slipway where I could lean *Amulet* against the wall and dry out at low water, and said he would provide a portable pump just in case the bilge pumps could not cope, and be on hand if I wanted assistance. Steve was reminiscent of that almost extinct breed of laid-back traditional boatyard proprietors for whom boats and their owners were their life's blood and nothing was too much trouble. Immensely relieved to have found a kindred soul, I arranged to launch *Amulet* on the twenty third of June, which gave me only two weeks in which to get *Amulet* finished.

Sensing the urgency, the weather god cleared away the clouds and left the sun beating down from a clear blue sky and, working almost non-stop to catch up on the remaining jobs, I fitted the stem head roller, the samson post and the anchor chain hause pipe on the foredeck, cleats and winches in the cockpit, the genoa track on the gunwales and mooring cleats. With the help of the 'team' the heavy rudder was hung and the lovely varnished oak tiller slotted into place; then the stainless steel bow and stern pulpits and the stanchions were bolted onto the deck. Nick Newby arrived with a portable press and a roll of stainless steel wire to fit new guard wires on the stanchions and Ian Smith fitted a rope cutter next to the propeller. Margaret gave the chain plates and the mast tabernacle a final coat of paint, Jean put the mattresses on the bunks, and to provide an extra touch of atmosphere in the cabin I fitted two brass, gimballed paraffin lamps to a bulkhead. There was just one important job left to do, getting the anchor chain and the CQR anchor aboard, and *Amulet* would be ready to go back to sea.

Feeding thirty metres of anchor chain through the hause pipe on the deck and down into the plastic tub in the forecabin was an operation that required the 'team' to be strategically placed to avoid scratching the hull and newly-varnished gunwale. Perched on the top of a stepladder at the bow, Margaret hauled up the heavy chain a metre or so at a time from the heap on the ground, passed it to Jean on the foredeck, who lowered it down the hause pipe while I checked that it was falling freely into the tub without snagging. The first link, and the most vital part of any anchor chain to rattle through a hause pipe, is the 'bitter end' and it is secured to the boat with a length of cord. Never was I more reminded of the importance of checking that the 'bitter end' is secure than the time I was out with old Brab Davies in his boat and was ordered to let go the anchor.

A heavily-built man with hands like dinner plates, a battered nose and a face that looked as if it had been sculptured with a blunt marlin spike, Brab had been the terror of his home town of Millom on the south Cumbrian coast and his vicious temper and drinking and fighting exploits were legend. But one night while staggering home drunk from the pub, he fell into the doorway of the local mission hall and was 'saved'. From that day forth not a drop of alcohol touched his lips, nor was he ever heard to raise his voice in anger or utter a blasphemous word. Whatever he said was well-punctuated with cries of 'Hallelujah', "Praise the Lord" or "Jesus lives", and his fishermen pals had long given up taunting him and tempting him to have a drink. I had made him a gaff mainsail out of a cutch-tanned jib that had come off one of the last sailing vessels to carry grain to a flour mill at Silloth, a harbour north of Maryport, and he could hardly contain his excitement. He insisted we put to sea on the next tide and "Tek a run down the Duddon to stretch it," and to the accompaniment of croaky renderings of hymns and shouts of "Hallelujah" and "Praise the Lord", we beat down the estuary into the Irish Sea. For hours we sailed up and down on different tacks while he made adjustments and delighted in hauling in the mainsheet and putting the lee deck under. "She'd leave them toffs' boats standin'!" he bragged, but he was so engrossed in his new sail he forgot about the tide and, when the wind died as we turned to go back up the estuary, it was clear we were not going to make any headway against a lively spring ebb. "Let go the anchor," bellowed Brab. I rushed to the foredeck, grabbed a rusty fisherman anchor half buried under a jumble of trawl nets, lengths of rope and fish boxes, and hurled it over the side. There was a rattle of chain, followed by a 'plop' as the bitter end hit the water and followed the rest of the chain to the bottom, then silence except for the gurgling of the tide carrying the boat stern-first towards the open sea.

With an expression of stunned disbelief on his face, Brab peered over the side of the boat and, as the full realisation of what had happened finally sank home, his battered face twisted and contorted with rage and I could sense that every obscenity and foul word that was ever invented was welling up in his throat, but he could not let them go. He was a born-again Christian! The frustration of not being able to vent his fury in the way he knew best made him writhe in agony and, with a loud groan, he clasped his gnarled hands together, raised them high into the air and sank to his knees on the deck. "Oh Lord," he roared, looking up to the heavens, his whole frame and his voice trembling with emotion. "Oh Lord, I beseech thee, have mercy and forgive thy humble servant for what he is about to say; but the feller with me today is a bloody stupid bastard!"

Engineless and with no wind, we drifted down to the mouth of the estuary until the tide turned and, with the aid of the flood and Brab's skilful manipulation of a long sweep oar, we at length pulled alongside Millom jetty. He jumped ashore and secured the boat and, without a word or even glancing in my direction, went home. I have never forgotten that day, and I made sure that the 'bitter end' on *Amulet* was well secured.

Dismantling the frame tent for the last time was enormously exciting. As, one by one, the tarpaulins were heaved off and fell to the ground, *Amulet* slowly emerged like a beautiful butterfly breaking free from a chrysalis, and with her new coat of paint and varnish glistening in the sunlight she looked, as only a wooden boat can, breathtakingly magnificent. The worries, the heartaches, the stress, the set-backs, the aches and pains, the despair and the tears of the past eighteen months had been worth it, and I shuddered when I remembered that at the beginning I had come close to cutting her into pieces with my chain saw. But *Amulet*'s rebirth was by no means all down to me. Without Patricia's financial backing it would not have started and without the selfless support of Jean and Margaret, whom I often drove unmercifully, it certainly would not have been finished. After commandeering their lives for so long it did not seem sufficient to turn to them and just say 'thanks', but in the eighteen months we had worked together they had come to understand my love for wooden boats and my devotion to *Amulet*, and I felt sure they knew that behind that little word 'thanks' was my undying gratitude.

Probably with some justification, marine insurance underwriters are a very suspicious bunch who appear to have lost all faith in human nature and are not even inclined to believe that a new day has dawned unless the claim is supported by a wad of paperwork signed by an expert. "A classic wooden boat eh?" said a bored voice at the end of the phone when I rang the number of an insurance company advertised in the yachting press. "When was it built and what condition is it in?" I said nineteen sixty four, but it had just been restored and was like new. "Like new eh?" he chortled. "I've heard that one before. I'm afraid you'll have to let us have a surveyor's report, sir, but I must warn you insurers charge a heavy premium on wooden boats; is it really worth me sending you an application form?" His snooty attitude annoyed me and I wanted to tell him where he could put his application form, but I bit my lip, said, "No, thanks," and put the phone down. The launching day was only a week away, and I was worried that I would have to risk transporting and launching *Amulet* without insurance cover, but a friendly boat owner I talked to while visiting Maryport Marina to make final preparations said, "If you want a marine surveyor, give Bert Jackson of Barrow in Furness a ring; if he's not busy he'll help you out at short notice." So I did, and two days later he arrived at the barn and I made myself scarce while he got on with his survey. He spent hours poking and prodding the hull inside and out, and my stomach was churning in knots wondering whether he was going to find fault with her. When he eventually climbed out of the cabin and stood in the cockpit scribbling on a clip board, he seemed to have an expression on his face like a high court judge about to don the black cap and pass the death sentence. "Have you got a minute?" he called. The knots in my stomach tightened as I climbed the ladder and sat in the cockpit waiting for him to speak. He carried on scribbling for a moment or two, then put the pen down and stared at me from behind his glasses. "Well, the first thing I want to say is that you've made a very good job of restoring this boat, it's in excellent condition. The only recommendation I have to make is that you replace the stainless steel bolts holding the rudder with galvanised ones. The rudder fittings are galvanised and I would prefer to see galvanised bolts." Had he handed me a cheque for a thousand pounds he could not have made me any happier, and I was ecstatic that our work had met with such unreserved approval. The following day my morale was boosted even further when I discovered the extent to which his professional opinion was respected. On the phone to one of the UK's largest marine insurers, the underwriter I spoke to insisted on having a written survey report before he would consider insuring *Amulet*; but when I said that Bert Jackson had carried out the survey and was pleased with her condition, he changed abruptly. "Oh, Mr Jackson has surveyed the boat? In that case we'll insure you from midday today and you can send the written report later."

The evening before *Amulet* was due to be transported to Maryport I climbed on board and sat in the cockpit. It was just going dark and the air, still warm after a hot day, was heavy with the scent of rhododendrons. The tawny owl hooted to its mate across the stable yard, and from the depths of the estate wood the sharp bark of a roe deer warned rivals to keep off his patch, then all was blissfully peaceful! There were no lights blazing, no sounds of hammering and sawing, no varnish being scraped or paint burnt off, no Radio 1 blaring, no electric saw-bench whining, no chatter of conversation, nothing but absolute silence. I lay back against the cabin and looked up at the stars shining through the night like a thousand anchor lights. It was hard to believe that the restoration was over and that on the following day *Amulet* would be afloat in Maryport Marina ready to head for the open sea and new adventures. Full of enthusiasm as ever, Mrs Dickinson was thrilled that *Amulet* was at last to be launched, and earlier that day she had called round to the boat with a small rug embroidered with the house flag of her late husband's yacht club, a model yacht made of polished brass, and several little ornaments for the cabin. I hoped that before *Amulet* was lowered into the water there might be time for a little launching ceremony and I could get Mrs Dickinson to splash the bow with something appropriate, but meantime I had to make a final check that Young's, a Whitehaven crane hire firm, would be arriving in the morning to lift *Amulet* up, and that Nick Newby and his Landrover and boat trailer would be waiting underneath when they lowered her down. Leaving *Amulet* in the company of the tawny owls I clambered down the ladder and went home.

The early morning weather forecast on the radio gloomily predicted heavy rain for Cumbria but, when the crane arrived at nine o'clock it was warm and dry and Steven Young, the driver, and his assistant lost no time in reconnoitring hazards such as high trees, electricity cables, telephone wires and the potting shed and glass orchid house before manoeuvring the crane into position and fixing wide nylon slings round the hull. Nick Newby reversed his heavy boat trailer close to the crane, Steven revved his engine, and *Amulet* was slowly lifted out of the steel cradle while Jean and Margaret, Mrs Dickinson and two friends who were staying with her clicked away with cameras, and I held my breath as eighteen months of hard work and many thousands of pounds was raised high into the air and swung over the orchid house before being lowered onto the boat trailer with the skilful precision that crane drivers make look so easy. Mrs Dickinson's friends, Gavin and Jess, helped me to carry the gleaming mast out of the barn and, when Nick had *Amulet* nicely snugged down on the trailer, it was lifted up by the crane and lashed to the bow and stern pulpits, well protected with sponge rubber. The boom, spinnaker pole, sail bags and other gear were stowed in the cabin and, leaving the cradle and an untidy scattering of timber supports to be cleared away some other time, I climbed into Nick's Landrover. With lots of crunching and snapping of low branches that made me wince at the thought of what they might be doing to the varnished mast and new paintwork, *Amulet* was towed down the tree-lined drive and onto the road for the uneventful sixteen-mile journey to Maryport marina.

We arrived just before midday with Mrs Dickinson and Jean in Margaret's car, and Margaret's son, Howard, in his own car close behind. Six foot ex-rugby players can be very useful at boat launchings! I was hoping to get the launching ceremony over and *Amulet* in the water with the least possible delay, and was rather taken aback when Steve Jackson explained that because of a low tide and the marina awaiting major dredging work, there would not be enough water to launch her for a few hours; but he lifted her off Nick's trailer with a boat hoist and parked her ready at the top of he slip. To add to the disappointment, the predicted rain arrived, blasted along by a bitterly cold wind and I was concerned about Mrs Dickinson. She was tough and had boundless energy, but a wet and windswept marina was no place for a lady who was approaching her fourth twenty first birthday and, as diplomatically as I could, I said so. I half expected to have my ears rattled, but she was very gracious and said she was fine, and enjoyed herself enormously when Margaret drove everyone round to a café at the nearby sea life centre for hot tea and cakes. The afternoon ticked by, and to relieve the boredom I pulled on my waterproofs and braved the rain and wind to climb on board *Amulet* and fix mooring warps. Back at the car, I implored Mrs Dickinson to be taken home, but she would have none of it. "I've watched this boat being restored and I shall sit here until I see it in the water," she said firmly, and that was that. I knew from experience she had an iron will and there was no point in arguing with her, so I went away and huddled in the shelter of

Amulet, hoping that Steve would appear and we could get the launch over with.

The water level on the tide gauge had risen steadily during the afternoon, but it was six o' clock in the evening before the deserted marina suddenly became a hive of activity when Steve started up the engine of the boat hoist and began to push *Amulet* towards the water. Having been cooped up in Margaret's small car since the morning, the ladies were clearly showing signs of fatigue and, as it was still pouring with rain and blowing hard, I abandoned the launching ceremony and scrambled aboard *Amulet* to heave fenders over the side. When she floated off the hoist the men on the dockside secured her against the wall and, full of apprehension, I stepped down into the cabin. All the skin fittings had been turned off, but there was an unmistakable gurgling of water coming from under the galley and, when I shone my torch, it revealed an absolute fountain spurting through the new lengths of planking. Within a short space of time the floorboards were awash, and in response to my shouts Steve Jackson lowered a portable fire pump down into the cockpit, but when the automatic electric bilge pump burst into life and squirted water into the cockpit and down the self-draining pipes at over eight gallons a minute, I was highly relieved to see that it was capable of dealing with the leak. Nick Newby had taken his trailer back to Keswick but returned to see how the launch had progressed and, finding a ladder, he climbed down the wall. "Have you got any caulking cotton and mastic sealer on board?" he said briskly when he saw the fountain of water spurting through the planks. By a stroke of luck I had left both in a locker and, twisting several lengths of cotton together to make one thick strand, he rammed it into the seam with a chisel and topped it off with a layer of mastic. The spurt was immediately reduced to hardly a trickle and, taking the torch, Nick inspected the rest of the hull. As expected, the plank seams were weeping almost everywhere below the waterline, and when the hatch in the cockpit floor was opened another fountain was splashing the propeller shaft. "Well, she's been out of the water for so long, she's bound to leak like a sieve for a few weeks," said Nick, unconcerned. "You'll just have to keep pumping at regular intervals and keep a log of how many strokes it takes each time. Enjoy yourself!" and with that he climbed the ladder and was gone.

Howard, Jean, Margaret and Mrs Dickinson stayed only long enough to take a few quick photographs of the launch, and for Jean to hand me a sleeping bag and rucksack full of food and spare clothes, before departing for home; and when Steve and his staff left I had *Amulet* all to myself. I piled the anchor chain and the anchor on the port side to give her a list so she would lean against the wall when the tide went out and, as an extra precaution to prevent her from falling away from the wall, I tied both ends of the main halliard to a ring bolt on the dockside. I was wet and cold when I had finished, but very happy; and flinging my dripping waterproofs into the forecabin, I changed into dry clothes, lit the galley paraffin stove to warm the cabin and boil a kettle for tea, and poured a large whisky. The paraffin lamps cast a cosy glow over the cabin and, having christened the stove and one of the new cooking pans with a pot of tea and a can of stewed steak, I pumped the bilge dry with one hundred and fifty strokes of the manual pump, set an alarm clock for midnight when she should be close to touching the bottom, left the automatic bilge pump switched on and slid into my sleeping bag and fell fast asleep. For three days I never left *Amulet* when she was afloat but, while most of the planking began to take up, the leak under the cockpit floor got worse and I could see it spouting through as if it were a pressure hose. At low water I raked out all the seams around the stern post and hammered in new caulking cotton and, when she floated, the spouting had been reduced to a trickle and the pumping rate dropped to one hundred every two hours. It seemed safe enough to move across to a pontoon berth and, starting the engine, I motored slowly around the marina. Each time I reached the dock gate I was sorely tempted to carry on out to sea for a short trial, but wisdom prevailed. The mast was still lashed between the stern and bow pulpits, and apart from a lifejacket I had no other safety gear on board. As there was every possibility that in a seaway the leaks would open up, I tied alongside to a pontoon and kept a close check on the amount of water coming in. The automatic bilge pump was more efficient than the alarm clock. Every two hours throughout the night it whined into action and woke me up and, to save the battery, I switched it off, pumped the bilge dry with one hundred stokes, then switched the auto pump on again and tried to get back to sleep. Fortunately I could reach everything from the comfort of my sleeping bag but, after nearly a week of broken sleep and not daring to leave *Amulet* for more than a few minutes, I was so exhausted I could hardly think straight and was not in the best of tempers when I found myself at the centre of a dispute about the use of a derrick to raise the mast. In their infinite wisdom, the local authority responsible for Maryport harbour had leased off the workshop side of the marina to a private enterprise, yet granted them the use of marina facilities ostensibly provided for the berth holders. It was a recipe for certain conflict and when Steve, the manager, said yes, I could use the derrick, and the workshop tenant said no, I could not, I was not prepared to become embroiled in local politics and mustered the 'team' plus Margaret's son Howard, and my neighbours, Joe Jackson and his wife Dot. I had raised and lowered many a mast with the aid of a long ladder and a few helpers, and *Amulet*'s mast would have presented no problems. However, with his usual flair for diplomacy, Steve smoothed over the difficulties and I was allowed to use the derrick. With *Amulet* tied firmly against the wall, the helpers heaving on a block and tackle suspended from the derrick, and Margaret on deck brandishing a wrench ready to attach the rigging screws, the mast was raised without any snags and the tabernacle bolts rammed home. There are all sorts of extremely expensive gadgets on the market for measuring the correct tension of standing rigging, but I used the Brab Davies method. "Lie on thee back with thee 'ed agint mast and look up. If it's leanin' for'ard or astern, tek up the forestay or t'backstays. If it's got a list to port or starboard, pull on't opposite shrouds. If it's standin' upright, bouse down thee lanya'ds and leave it alone." Substitute 'lock thee rigging screws' for 'bouse down thee lanya'ds' and it is still sound advice.

To give myself a deadline to work towards, I had made up my mind that I would leave on July the seventeenth, my birthday, but June came and went and instead of showing signs of slowing down, the leaks got worse and the pumping rate increased to nearly one hundred an hour. Three times I dried *Amulet* out against the wall and re-caulked the seams around the stern post, but to no avail; and in desperation I had her lifted out on the boat hoist, and while she was suspended I raked out and re-caulked the garboards on both sides. By this time I had been in the marina long enough to get to know some of the boat owners and Kevin Armstrong, who shared a Macwester with his father Derek, very

generously put his own work aside and took over the messy task of
sealing the caulked seams with mastic. Back in the water there was a
very noticeable improvement and, for the first time since *Amulet* was
launched, I slept through the night without the auto bilge pump
wrecking my sleep. I could not resist the excuse for a sea trial, and as
soon as the lock gates opened the following day I fired the engine into
life and chugged steadily towards the outer harbour. Though happy to
come on board and help get *Amulet* ready, Jean no longer had any
interest in going to sea and Margaret volunteered to crew. She had
never been on the sea in a small boat in her life before and, fortunately
protected by a suit of waterproofs, she had a lively baptism. The wind
strength was only around force three, but it was pushing against a
strong spring tide, and clear of the harbour breakwater *Amulet* was
thrown around like a cork and safely clipped on with a safety harness,
Margaret frequently disappeared under a cloud of spray. The fishing
fleet was heading out at full speed at the same time, and the wake of the
passing trawlers churned the already confused sea into a cauldron
which concentrated my mind on *Amulet*'s leaks, but not a drop came
out of the auto bilge pump outlet. Greatly cheered, I opened the
throttle and the Farymann never missed a beat as, for an hour, we
crashed through the seas giving engine and hull a thorough test and
Margaret and me a thorough soaking. In the calm of the marina it took
only thirty strokes of the pump to empty the bilge and, when I crawled
around inside the hull with a torch, only the new planks were leaking. It
was the tenth of July, only a week to go before the big day. I had a
constant stream of visitors bearing presents and I felt embarrassed in
case they had misunderstood my plans and thought I was about to sail
non-stop round the world, but I was very grateful for the gift of a rare
book about sailing in the Hebrides from George and Dorothy Raven,
who had a boat in the marina, bags of sweets from my grandchildren, a
bottle of whisky from retired farmer friends Angela and Martin Cave, a
whole bag of useful bits and pieces from Jean and a rather beautiful
lode stone in a velvet pouch from Margaret to guide *Amulet* on her way.

    Right from the start it was always my intention to make the journey
alone. In my youth I had sailed small boats around the Scottish west
coast and islands, but they were all open boats and I had suffered so
much at the mercy of the weather I dreamed of having a boat with a

Figure 1. *Amulet* as she was on her arrival

Figure 2. The decaying hull, undecked, from the bow.

Figure 3.   *Amulet* falls over, and the cradle leg smashes through her planking..

Figure 4.   Nocturnal Nick Newby working late to cut iroko gunwales.

Figure 5. 'The team': Jean (left) and Margaret (right).

Figure 6. 'A charm restored'. *Amulet* on her way to the sea.

Figure 7. The launch at Maryport marina.

Figure 8. Could this be it? Kevin Armstrong helping the author to track down a persistent leak.

Figure 9. A breeze arrives off Ailsa Craig

Figure 10. Ardnamurchan lighthouse, the most westerly point on the mainland of Britain.

Figure 11. The most spectacular – and the wettest – anchorage in Europe! Loch na Cuilce, Skye.

Figure 12. Cruise ship *Hebridean Princess* passes *Amulet* at Kyle of Lochalsh..

Figure 13. Canna harbour.

Figure 14. Fingal's Cave, Island of Staffa.

Figure 15. Trying to tow *Sirius* off the rocks at Colonsay.

Figure 16. Under tow by Campbeltown lifeboat.

'lid' on it, where I could sleep snug and dry and eat my meals without having to wear a full suit of oilskins. When I did get one with a lid on I had to make a living with it and put up with some very odd people and their often insufferable children in order to keep the bank off my back, and I promised myself that one day I would get a boat and go where I wanted and at my own pace. By a stroke of good fortune and Patricia's money, *Amulet* was that boat and my dream was about to be realised; but, as Patricia had poured considerable amounts of money into *Amulet* it was natural she would to want to sail her. Half joking, she had said that if I was ever looking for a crew to let her know, and it set me thinking about her coming with me on the first long leg, an eighty mile non-stop sail from Maryport, round the Mull of Galloway to Portpatrick in the North Channel, then another twenty to the Island of Arran in the Clyde, twenty to the entrance of the Crinan Canal and through the canal to Oban. I knew she was a courageous sailor; she had crewed for me when I had a business delivering yachts from the UK to the Mediterranean; but like me she was not a sailing 'fanatic' and enjoyed discovering places beyond a harbour, and climbing mountains. She also shared my preference for quiet anchorages and my loathing of marina hopping. The more I thought about it, the less sailing single-handed appealed to me and, to really convince myself a crew would be desirable, I started to consider the safety aspects. What if I was taken ill when I was alone, had an accident or fell overboard? No adventurer with any guts would ever be deterred by such pathetic reasoning, but I reminded myself I was now a registered wrinkly, had grandchildren, and relatives who were always muttering that it was time I acted my age and settled down. When Jean admitted that she was uneasy about me sailing alone, it was the seal of approval I needed. Agreeing to 'carry out all duties in a respectful and seamanlike manner' and obey the captain, 'master under God', Patricia was signed on.

Thanks to Nick Newby's help, most of the equipment, rope and chain I ordered through his chandlery arrived without any delay, and it was a huge relief. It was almost impossible to get through to some of the large mail order chandleries on the phone and I had given up trying. Patricia sent an old inflatable dinghy for use as a tender, but when I forwarded it to a firm in Glasgow for servicing they rang me up and asked jokingly if it was the one Noah had used to get out to his ark. I

got the message, and ordered a new one. It arrived the following day
and I wished I had ordered a liferaft at the same time. Taken in by the
slick advertising of a liferaft hire company in south-east England, I had
hired a four man raft for three months, paid the hire charge up front
and arranged for it to be delivered to Maryport marina in time for a
departure date of July first. It didn't arrive, and when I phoned the
company I could hardly believe my ears. "It's not been despatched yet,
sir," said a man with an edge to his voice that seemed to say, "What are
you complaining about? Surely you didn't expect to get it on time did
you?" I let fly with a broadside of expletives I afterwards regretted, but
at least the raft arrived by express carrier the next morning. There was
no note of apology with it or an offer of compensation. Just a typed
sheet reminding me that I would be penalised if it was not returned on
time.

A high pressure system hanging around the Irish Sea brought a spell
of gorgeous weather and, with her paint and varnish work sparkling in
the sun, *Amulet* stood out like a jewel amidst the rows of fibreglass hulls
and aluminium masts and scores of people out for a stroll along the
marina side stopped to take her photograph. The dawn on the
seventeenth of July showed every promise of it being another scorching
day and I wanted to celebrate my birthday with a quick run out to sea,
but my conscience reminded me that I still had to rig up some means
of reefing the mainsail and, when Margaret arrived during the morning
we hoisted it and she helped me to attach three rows of reefing
pennants. A sudden and alarming increase in the hourly pumping rate
from thirty to sixty strokes put paid to any hope of a sea trial, and when
Jean arrived at midday to help with last minute jobs I anxiously
motored *Amulet* across the marina just in time to lean her against the
slipway wall on the falling tide. Margaret and Jean had pressing jobs
elsewhere and, not able to hang around until low water, said their
goodbyes and left me searching through lockers for the caulking irons,
ball of caulking cotton, tube of mastic, raking out tools and a mallet. I
had put them all away, confident I would never have to use them again.
When the last dregs of the tide had drained from the slipway and
Amulet was dried out, I was grumpily examining the hull trying to detect
which seam had opened up and caused the worrying leak when Patricia
arrived off the afternoon train, weighed down with bags and seaboots;

having travelled all the way from Suffolk via Derby and Carlisle, she was looking decidedly weary. "When she asked, "Is there anything I can do?" I am sure she was hoping I would say, "Oh no, you look tired. Sit in the cockpit and I'll make you a cup of tea." But, frustrated by the persistent leak, I was feeling tetchy and said, "Yes, there is; put those overalls on and get under the hull on the starboard side and rake out the garboard seam that's dripping water." To add insult to injury, the starboard side was leaning against the wall and the seam was awkward to get at but, without a word, she dropped her luggage on the slipway, pulled on the overalls, slithered under the hull and starting raking the seam out. Crew like her are as hard to find as a fish and chip take-away at the Royal Yacht Squadron.

When *Amulet* was afloat, a considerable amount of water had been seeping in through the area of the stem and running along the keelson beneath the cabin floor, and I had accepted this as normal prior to the planks 'taking up'; but just in case there was a weak spot I had missed I raked out and re-caulked the seams on both sides of the outside of the stem and finished off with a water-curing mastic. The garboard that Patricia had raked out was given the same treatment and, with every visible seam now re-caulked and sealed, there wasn't a lot more that could be done and with several hours to wait before *Amulet* would be afloat we relaxed in the sun-baked cockpit and enjoyed a leisurely chicken salad and a can or two of cool beer. But the hidden gremlins were never keen on leaving me in peace for very long and, late in the evening when the tide came in and I pressed the engine starter button to motor back to the pontoon, nothing happened - the battery was dead flat! It's at times like this that new swear words are invented, but they did nothing to put new life in the battery and I had to start the engine by hand. Completely mystified about why a brand-new battery should suddenly go flat, I checked all the leads and connections, but everything appeared to be in order and back on the pontoon after motoring *Amulet* round the marina I started up a portable generator Nick Newby had supplied and left it charging the batteries while I turned my attention to the leaks. The time spent drying out *Amulet* and caulking the seams had been well worth it and I was very pleased and relieved when the bilges were sucked dry after only thirty strokes of the pump. It had been a nerve-racking day and, aided by a celebratory tot of whisky to mark Patricia's arrival and our success with the leak, I crashed out in my bunk and was asleep as soon as my head touched the pillow.

The eighteenth of July was another blisteringly hot day with a flat calm sea and when I returned to *Amulet*, having been to the marina office to find out what time the gate would be opened and we could leave, I was surprised to find Patricia heaving everything out of *Amulet* and stacking it on the pontoon. I was so eager to be on my way I wanted to fling everything back and cast off, but she declared that no way was she putting to sea until she was ready and that years of sailing a cramped Essex smack with her husband Martin had taught her the importance of knowing where everything was. Looking at the heap of gear stacked on the pontoon I had to back down and agree she was right. Apart from all the usual sailing clothing we had climbing boots, lightweight windproofs, rucksacks and every ordnance survey map of the west of Scotland. That she found places in tiny *Amulet* for the huge heap of gear, food, pans and clothing was nothing short of miraculous, and by the time the sun began to cast long shadows across the marina, the pontoon had been cleared and the galley stove was roaring away preparing the evening meal.

To get the 'feel' of the boat and the sails I would have preferred to put out from Maryport in daylight, with a warm sun on our backs and *Amulet* rolling gently in the swell; but, never designed to make a sailor's life easy, the Admiralty tide table made it clear that the only suitable time to leave was just before the marina tidal gate was closed, three hours after high water, or in my case, one o'clock in the morning. With its many unspoilt harbours the Scottish side of the Solway Firth is a fine cruising area for boats able to take the ground but, exposed to the prevailing southerlies, it is not over-endowed with sheltered anchorages for passage making or with havens for keel boats. As the weather was forecast to remain settled I planned to sail directly for the Mull of Galloway, fifty miles away, hoping to arrive in time to catch the tide flowing up the North Channel between Scotland and Northern Ireland. To use it to the best advantage, the tidal flow between the Scottish coast and the top of the Isle of Man has to be studied carefully because, contrary to the normal pattern, it splits in two at the Mull of Galloway with one ebb flowing north and the other ebb flowing south down the western side of the Isle of Man. Able to interpret a tidal flow chart, there is nothing a stranger to the area cannot work out, though, when the two opposing flood streams meet off the Mull and there is a fresh wind, it can provide very character-building sailing conditions and an opportunity for fervent prayer.

Patricia filled flasks with hot water for tea and coffee and made a pile of sandwiches while I busied myself with sorting charts, working out courses and sharpening my pencils. The navigation and compass lights were checked, the liferaft fixed on the cabin roof with quick-release buckles and the deflated dinghy stowed next to it. Waterproofs and woolly hats were shaken out of storage bags, a large torch left ready for use on the cabin table and, having set the alarm clock, we sank into our sleeping bags hoping that revellers on a nearby gin palace would quickly drink themselves into a stupor and allow us a few hours sleep.

To Sea At Last -Exploring Arran -
Gateway to The West

Coming from the depths of *Amulet*'s hull it was unlikely that the jangling of our alarm clock would have disturbed the slumbering revellers on the nearby gin palace but, amplified by the stainless steel sink where it had been placed, the noise in the cabin was unbearable and dragged from the warm fug of my sleeping bag I scrambled to silence the brute. It was half an hour past midnight, and I dressed and climbed sleepily into the cockpit to check the weather. The surface of the marina was like a mirror and, bathed in the orange glow of the incandescent dockside lamps, the rows of motionless boats, tall masts and petrified rigging and mooring warps were like a surrealist painting. Above the canopy of artificial light, the pale orb of a full moon was suspended in an inky sky and I shivered as the cold morning air penetrated my sweater. In the cabin Patricia had got the paraffin cooker going and a rush of warmth met me when I opened the companionway door. My sleeping bag looked so tempting I could happily have crawled back into it, but a mug of hot tea helped to revive me and drive away the sluggishness and, pulling on an extra sweater and my waterproofs, I started the engine and switched on the GPS, the echo sounder, VHF radio, the Navtex and the compass and navigation lights. Patricia cast off the warps and pulled the fenders aboard and stowed them in the cockpit lockers while I steered for the tidal gate. Outside the marina we were in the darkened outer harbour and Patricia shone the torch on the wall to give me an indication when to make a ninety degree turn to port to get into the main channel and we chugged past the dim shadow of the breakwater, the red light of the echo sounder indicating the depth dropping steadily then climbing rapidly again as we crossed the shingle bar. The harbour entrance light tower gave us a baleful wink as we passed underneath; a playful swell lifted *Amulet* and gave her a shove into the Irish Sea, and we were on our way.

One of the most useful, and yet potentially the most lethal, electronic aids to hassle-free passage-making on yachts and commercial vessels of all sizes is the autopilot. I've had many a fright when a large merchant ship has suddenly appeared over the horizon and charged past so close to my boat I could have scrawled graffiti on the hull, yet there wasn't a sign of life on the bridge. Maritime accident reports involving autopilots make sombre reading but, for a yacht under engine and with only two crew on board, an autopilot is a blessing; and as soon as we had cleared Maryport harbour I set a course on *Amulet*'s tiller-mounted wizardry for a point three miles off the Mull of Galloway, kept an eye on the steering compass until she was holding steady, then sat back in the cockpit to enjoy the night. Patricia had been intently scanning the horizon and announced "There's lights ahead on the port bow." Through binoculars I could make out the familiar green above white masthead lights of a gaggle of trawlers, but they were a long way off and of no immediate interest. What was a real threat, and bang on our course, was an unlit buoy marking a sandbank five miles west of Maryport. It had obviously never occurred to the old sages of Trinity House that anchoring half a ton of unlit floating metal well offshore was more of a hazard than an aid to a small boat not bristling with radar scanners. I plotted the course carefully and though, according to the GPS, we passed close to the buoy, even in bright moonlight and with a powerful torch I never saw as much as a glimpse of it. The fast flowing tide was lifting a lumpy sea that occasionally exploded against the bow in a spray of red and green reflected from the pulpit-mounted bi-colour light, but there was not a breath of wind and the Farymann diesel gurgled along happily as *Amulet* gently rode over the swell and sank into the troughs. To starboard, the flash of the lighthouse on Little Ross Island off the Scottish coast and the two mighty blasts of light from St Bees Head on the Cumbrian coast gave me a fix that tallied near enough with the GPS, and according to my plots we were zipping along over ground at eight knots. As we came close to the trawlers we had a stir of excitement when one of the fleet broke away from the gaggle, and through the binoculars I could see from his navigation lights he was making straight for us, but when he was about a mile off he rounded up and hove to, probably to haul his nets.

About a quarter past four the first streaks of dawn began to penetrate the inky blackness of the eastern horizon and Patricia went below and re-appeared with mugs of tea and a plastic box filled with chicken sandwiches. Whether it is the cold nip in the morning air and the feel of

the wind on the face, the excitement of a breathtaking dawn, or simply
because it is the start of a new adventure I am never quite sure; but to
me there has always been something special about the first mug of tea
and sandwich after putting to sea at night at the beginning of a voyage.
Patricia's tea was pure nectar and the sandwiches could not have been
bettered at the Ritz and, with the autopilot relieving us of the chore of
hanging on to the tiller, we sat mesmerised as the rapidly changing
pattern of light heralded another beautiful summer's day. We were in
the centre of a huge stage and all around us pink, red and gold spotlights
were being switched on with an increasing intensity that dissolved the
blackness of the night and slowly highlighted the spectacular coastline of
Dumfries and Galloway to our right. Behind us the shafts of coloured
light streamed across a vast three-dimensional backdrop of the Lakeland
Fells and magically transformed the wide expanse of grey sea to our left
into shimmering saffron. My boyhood hero, Maurice Griffiths, said in
his book 'The Magic of the Swatchways' that he never enjoyed the
dawn at sea, which is a sad confession from a man whose love for
sailing would be difficult to equal; had he sailed on the west coast he
might have changed his mind!

We made faster progress than I had anticipated and by 0900hrs,
with forty miles on the log, we were off the towering peninsula of the
Mull of Galloway, with a sluicing tide doing its best to wash us back to
Maryport. Battling through the water at 5 knots, the Farymann bravely
held *Amulet*'s nose into it, but we had plenty of time for bird watching
and studying the stonework of the lighthouse through binoculars. For
over an hour there were times when the whitewashed tower seemed to
be moving ahead faster than we were, but at least it was warm and
sunny and, apart from a few swirls which shunted *Amulet* sideways
occasionally, there was no sign of the Mull's notorious tide race. Several
schools of porpoise shot past us, taking advantage of the tide to head
south and cheer the hearts of the Isle of Man Tourist Board by
entertaining the holiday-makers in Port Erin, and a large three-masted
sail training ship appeared, surging along from the direction of Ireland,
its square sails hanging limp on the yards but with a plume of black
exhaust smoke acknowledging allegiance to the mechanical topsail that
has shattered forever the romantic image of 'a painted ship upon a
painted ocean'. When at last the tide began to ease its fierce grip on

Amulet's bow, the lighthouse gradually fell astern and we entered the North Channel, the twenty one mile wide seaway between Scotland and Northern Ireland. The Scottish side is noted for its wild scenery though, unfortunately for cruising yachtsfolk, it has rather more of it than it has havens of refuge. The only bolt hole is Portpatrick, fifteen miles north of the Mull, and though I wanted to make the best of the weather and keep going to reach the Clyde, Patricia dangled the carrot of a pub meal and a cool drink and, weary after a fourteen hour spell at sea, I swallowed it like a mackerel taking a fly.

The port takes its name from the famous Irish saint who, according to legend, crossed the North Channel in a single stride and left a deep footprint on a rock in the harbour. The Scots showed their displeasure at his arrival by cutting his head off but, undeterred, Patrick jumped into the sea and, with his head in his teeth, swam back to Ireland. Since his teeth were presumably still in his head, how he managed to do that the legend doesn't elaborate on, but that's the way historians tell it, so who am I to argue? During the construction of the harbour the Saint's footprint was removed, but for the benefit of seamen two leading marks were erected and I lined *Amulet* up on them and nosed gently into the outer harbour until a sheltered inner basin opened up to port, where Patricia shinned up a dubious-looking iron ladder and secured the warps. The log read seventy-four miles and we had averaged a touch over five knots.

Reputed to be the only non-tidal harbour on the English and Scottish coasts available to pleasure craft between North Wales and the Clyde, and a mere twenty one miles from Donaghadee on the Irish coast, Portpatrick is an incredibly popular and often congested haven; but, as was explained to me later by the eager chap who clambered aboard to extract harbour dues, the school holidays had not yet started and we had the berth to ourselves. In its heyday there was a regular ferry service from Portpatrick to Ireland and a railway that linked with Stranraer, a harbour at the foot of Loch Ryan on the eastern side of the Galloway Peninsula, and as the visitors flocked in, so the number of pubs increased. Washed clean of sweat and salt and spruced up in fresh clothes we went in search of one. Built round the harbour the village was a picturesque cluster of cottages and houses huddled close together for protection from the winter storms, but it had that unmistakable stamp of a one-time seafaring community that had long given up harvesting fish and concentrated on the more lucrative shoals of tourists. Nothing wrong with that, except that in their haste to get their hands on the tourists' cash, the proprietors of the pub we were in seemed to have forgotten that in return they were supposed to provide a service. Having given our orders, we were left twiddling our thumbs and ravenously crunching through packets of crisps for nearly an hour before the food arrived. Not impressed with the service or the food we didn't linger in the pub and, disappointed with our run ashore at Portpatrick, we strolled back to *Amulet* for a whisky and an early night.

With the pointer on the barometer still hard over to starboard when we turned in and the Clyde Coastguard weather bulletin on the VHF radio confirming no movement of the ridge of high pressure, the night was still and the surface of the harbour flat calm. I slept so well it wasn't until Patricia thrust a mug of tea under my nose that I raised a reluctant eyelid and realised where I was. "Time to get up," she announced cheerfully. "It's gone nine o'clock and the harbour master said that high water is at midday. I've got some fresh bread for breakfast!" She had been out to the village shop, come back and cranked the stove into life to make tea, and I hadn't heard a thing. The harbour master's information about high water saved me having to consult the tide table. Those who sail in the English Channel will be accustomed to the flood tide flowing east and the ebb flowing west while for us west coast types, with the exception of the North Channel, the flood normally heads north and ebb flows south. Having to leave Portpatrick at high water to catch an ebb that flows north is a strange experience and since, at springs, it can reach a rate of over 4 knots and there is no arguing with it, I had left a note on the chart table to remind me to check the tide times.

We had a leisurely breakfast in the cockpit and while Patricia stowed gear away ready to put to sea, I checked the engine oil and pressed the starter to warm the engine up. Nothing happened; the battery was dead flat! Cursing loudly, I pulled the engine cover away and methodically checked every cable, but there was no sign of corrosion or a loose connection. Unlike conventional engines, the alternator on the Farymann was not mounted separately and belt driven, it was an integral part of the flywheel and impossible to reach. "You won't ever have to touch it, they rarely give any trouble," assured Steve Barnes, the engineer at the

Farymann main agents in Surrey, when I said I was uneasy about the arrangement." "Well, the bloody thing's giving trouble now," I snarled at Patricia when I checked the battery with a voltmeter and found it reading zero. "What is?" said Patricia, startled at my sudden outburst. "Oh, never mind. Just pass me the starting handle," I replied irritably. If I were in a position of power I would make it illegal for any engine to be installed in a boat, small or large, that could not be started by hand or some other means that made it independent of a battery. A marine engine that relies solely on an electrical system to start it is a menace, yet this is the type fitted in the majority of modern pleasure craft, and the reason is that few manufacturers make a genuine marine engine any more. They are mainly marinised versions of industrial engines, and if the electrical system fails at sea when the engine is needed in a hurry, tough luck. Fortunately manufacturers like the German company Farymann still make small electric-start marine diesel engines that are also fitted with a decompressor and a starting handle as a back up, and it only took a few swings before *Amulet*'s engine burst into life. The charging light on the control panel, which should have gone off when the engine started, flickered for a moment but stayed on, a sure sign that the alternator wasn't charging. I checked all the contacts again and even tried a new earth wire, but to no avail, the light stayed on. It drove home the realisation of how vulnerable a boat is if the power supply fails. With the control panel in the cockpit protected from the weather I had not noticed the charging light was on, and during the night passage the navigation lights had drained the battery. It was now completely flat and not capable of powering the VHF, the GPS or anything else. In a foul mood, I left the portable generator pumping new life into the battery and went ashore and phoned Steve Barnes for advice, but his secretary said he was out on a job and to ring back the following day. It seemed crazy that there was only one engineer in the company who knew anything about Farymann engines and I said so rather forcibly, but the secretary was adept at smoothing ruffled feathers and assured me she would get Steve to contact me on my mobile as soon as he appeared. Walking back to the harbour in the warmth of another gorgeous morning, I realised I had let myself get all steamed up over nothing. I had a secondary means of starting the engine, a portable generator for charging the battery and, though they were useful, I could live without the VHF and the GPS. It was just after midday and, feeling a lot happier, I climbed on board *Amulet*, apologised to Patricia for being a pain in the stern, swung the engine into life and we departed Portpatrick bound for the Clyde.

With the throttle set at cruising speed and a three knot tide under us, we shot northwards at eight knots over the ground and the masts of Portpatrick radio station rapidly fell astern. Before the political goons swept away a long-standing service to mariners, Portpatrick Radio was part of the network of maritime coastal radio stations through which it was possible to make a VHF link call and who, through a whole range of high-powered maritime radio equipment, were the lifeline of mariners hundreds of miles away in the Atlantic. The politicians handed over the maritime safety duties to Coastguard stations, then proceeded to close them down as well. What the old maritime nation of Great Britain is desperately in need of is a few influential politicians who are keen on sailing and the sea.

It was incredibly hot and there wasn't a breath of wind as we splashed through a tide ripple off Kilantringan lighthouse and bounced in the wake of a passing tanker, but cirrus cloud spreading across the sky from the direction of Ireland heralded a change in the weather and an hour later I noted a momentous occasion in the log. A light wind sprang up from the north west and, for the first time since her launch, *Amulet* was under sail. We were not breaking any speed records, in fact what speed we were making was largely thanks to the tide, but it was a wonderful feeling to have the main and genoa drawing and the engine silent and we held the port tack all the way to Corsewall Point lighthouse, eleven miles north of Portpatrick and the place where, for me at any rate, the North Channel ends and the lower Clyde begins. It is also close to the entrance of Loch Ryan, a cheerless and unwelcoming place for yachts, largely taken over by the Ro-Ro ferries that ply between Stranraer and Northern Ireland. As we approached, a brace of those shapeless brutes came surging out at thirty knots, while another one was fast approaching from Ireland, and we were in the middle. We could only keep going and hope that as well as identifying a blip on the radar screen, someone on the bridge had spotted a tiny blue yacht with white sails rising and falling in the swell dead ahead of them. In the end they passed at a comfortable distance, but the wake from three gigantic tin boxes being shoved through the water at high speed kicked up a sea that flung *Amulet* about like an empty beer can.

Sailing north from Corsewall Point opens up a panorama that to describe as 'breathtaking' doesn't really do it justice. If the visibility is good, the coast of Northern Ireland can clearly be seen on the port side, sprawling out towards the gap that separates it from the great bulk of Scotland's Mull of Kintyre. To the right of Kintyre is the exquisitely beautiful Island of Arran, its skyline bristling with sharp rocky peaks, and to the right of that the entrance to the Firth of Clyde and the Ayrshire coast that sweeps south in a long curve and ends at Loch Ryan. It is the gateway to one of the finest sailing areas in the world, and those who discover it never want to leave.

Halfway between Corsewall Point and the Island of Arran is Ailsa Craig, a small but very steep island shaped like an upturned basin. Affectionately known far and wide as 'Paddy's Milestone', it is actually the summit of a granite mountain, and for many years it was quarried and the stone used for fine buildings in Ayrshire and beyond. It is one of the best landmarks in the Clyde and with a lively increase in the north westerly breeze drawing *Amulet* along, we lay over on the port tack and steered towards it. Helped by the new flood heading up the Clyde we made good progress but, just when we were about a mile abeam of Ailsa Craig lighthouse, the wind died away and left us wallowing in a lumpy sea. The engine fired into life with the first swing of the handle, but almost immediately another good breeze sprang up and I stopped the engine and sheeted in the main. *Amulet* creamed along on her ear for a couple of miles, then the wind died again, so abruptly we were nearly flipped backwards out of the cockpit. I felt someone was playing games with us, and when the same thing happened again half an hour later I sent Patricia forward to drop the sails. It was a good move. The sea went calm and the sun smiled out of a blue sky; and with the engine going well and the autopilot steering for Lamlash Bay on Arran, Patricia went below and emerged with tea and ham sandwiches. It was now 8pm and an absolutely lovely evening but, though the mountains of Arran seemed to tower over us, the chart showed we still had ten miles to go. I pumped the bilge and was horrified when it took fifty strokes; but when I went below with a torch to search for leaks, it was clear what had happened. When *Amulet* had been heeling over while sailing, it immersed planks above the waterline that hadn't yet 'taken up', and a large amount of water had seeped through. I was busy sponging water off my bunk when Patricia shouted that there was a strange ship ahead and, pulling myself into the cockpit, I saw it was a Royal Navy ship about two miles away and going round in circles as if it were out of control. Whether the skipper was chasing a submarine or had downed two many pink gins we never got close enough to find out. He suddenly opened up both engines and within minutes was a dot on the horizon.

As we got closer to Arran, the red orb of the sun set the sky ablaze with a spectacular finale of colour, and the tall pillar of the lighthouse on the tiny island of Pladda seemed to be floating on a sea of liquid gold. It was one of those sunsets that have photographers going berserk, and Patricia helped the president of Kodak put a down payment on his new Cadillac by shooting off yards of film, but as we approached the entrance to Lamlash Bay, between Arran and Holy Island, the sun was lost behind the mountains. The anchorage in front of the village was crowded with yachts of all sizes and I had to drop the hook in deeper water than I would normally have chosen, but it was a quiet night and the forecast was for continuing hot weather. It was nearly 10pm and it had taken us ten hours to cover thirty-four miles, but it didn't matter. As far as we were concerned sailing is all about the enjoyment of cruising at a leisurely and unhurried pace, and we had certainly done that.

About twenty miles long by seven wide, the Island of Arran has always been popular as a holiday resort and the knife-edge mountain ridges and sharp peaks are a mecca for hillwalkers. Only Lamlash on the south east side of the island and Loch Ranza on the north west provide sheltered anchorages for yachtsfolk, but it would be a sad day if the natural amenities of this lovely island were desecrated by the building of a marina and boats were herded into a hideous floating compound like sheep into a pen. Lamlash is a large natural deepwater bay which, in the days of the pushing and shoving of glacier activity was conveniently provided with an elongated mountain top that formed a high natural breakwater with an entrance to the bay at either end. The early Gaelic-speaking settlers called it 'Loch an Eilean,' the loch of the island, a much more romantic name than Lamlash, and the island was named 'Eilean Molaise', the island of Molaise, after an Irish Saint who is said to have preached there about 600AD. Someone with influence who couldn't get his tongue round the Gaelic name found it easier to call it Holy Island, and the name stuck. A refuge for centuries of sailing ships, the bay was a thriving naval base during wartime, but nowadays Lamlash and its lovely anchorage looks to the tourist and visiting yachts for its salvation.

I was keen to get in touch with Steve Barnes about the engine, but there was no signal on my mobile phone and after breakfast we rowed ashore to find a telephone box. Steve's secretary said he had been involved in an accident with a car while cycling to work and was recuperating at home, but let me have his number. He sounded shaken and explained that an idiotic motorist had knocked him off his bike, but he had, fortunately, escaped with only a few cuts and bruises. I apologised for disturbing him and explained the problem with the electrics but, apart from suggesting it could be that heat in the restricted engine compartment had caused the failure of a sealed control box mounted on the engine, he wasn't sure what was causing the trouble. I said I could remove the control box and send it back to him, if necessary, then I left him in peace to nurse his wounds.

I had often walked and camped on Arran and wanted to take Patricia on one of my favourite walks through the mountains, so while I was talking to Steve she went in search of a bus timetable. The local people on Arran have always had a reputation for their warm hospitality and friendliness but, as we discovered in Portpatrick, the downside of a boom in tourism is the undermining of old-fashioned values. When Patricia went into a shop to buy postcards, the shopkeeper was very offhand and unhelpful when she asked about a bus timetable. In another the shopkeeper was decidedly nasty, but in the post office the postmaster was a true highland gentleman, both pleasant and helpful, and Patricia, who had once worked as a midwife in the poorer parts of Glasgow, came away with her admiration for the Scots restored, and clutching a bus timetable. There wasn't a cloud in the sky or a breath of wind, and by noon it was so hot the interior of *Amulet* was like an oven; but I was determined to tackle the engine and, stripped to swimming trunks, I took away the engine cover and began systematically checking every inch of the wiring. Patricia plunged over the side for a swim but, when she came face to face with a large shoal of orange jellyfish, I'm not sure who got the biggest fright. She made a rapid exit from the water as if Jaws were in pursuit, and retreated to the foredeck with a book. Buried up to my shoulders in the engine compartment, the heat was intense and I was dripping so much sweat into the bilge I felt sure it would increase the pumping rate to a hundred; but when I prised open a fibreglass connector that joined the wires from the alternator to the wires from the control box and found the fault, it was worth every drop of sweat and the blood that dripped from a finger I cut on a sharp piece of one of the engine mountings. The metal inserts in the connector had not been securely joined, and the arcing of the high voltage from the alternator had gradually melted them away and cut off the charge to the battery. I removed the connector, joined the wires direct with crimp joints and started the engine. The charging light went out and the problem was solved. I let out a yell of triumph that scattered every gull in the bay and, dozing on the foredeck, Patricia nearly hit the top of the mast with fright.

The tranquillity of the afternoon was shattered by a bunch of morons on jet skis tearing in and out of the anchored boats and causing *Amulet* to roll violently, but as the great God in the clouds insists on being compassionate to imbeciles, my urgent prayer that they should collide with each other and sink in deep water went unheeded. When the motion eased, Patricia unearthed our boots and rucksacks from the forecabin ready for our mountain walk, and I spread an Ordnance Survey map out in the cockpit to show her the route. We would catch the 7.40am bus to Sannox, about eight miles north of Lamlash, walk up Glen Sannox and over a high pass close to the summit of Goat Fell 2840 feet, (874 metres) the islands highest mountain, then drop down into Glen Rosa and finish at Brodick, the main town and ferry terminal, to catch the bus back to Lamlash.

Amulet rolled heavily all night, but this time it was not the fault of the jet skis but a brisk easterly wind that sprang up late in the evening and sent a moderate swell rolling into the bay. Every time *Amulet* rose to the swell, the anchor chain went bar taut with a bang that shook every timber and I was forced out of my bunk to pay out more chain and rig a nylon rope snubber between the chain and the Samson post.

It cured the banging, but I slept fitfully and when the alarm clock burst into life at 6am my enthusiasm for catching an early bus to go clambering up mountains had worn rather thin. I tried snuggling deeper into my sleeping bag, but Patricia shook me and waved a mug of tea. "Shall I bring the dinghy alongside?" It sounded innocent enough, but I knew it was her way of saying "If you don't get up we'll miss the bus, and if we miss the bus we won't get a day on the hills like you promised, and if we don't get a day on the hills you needn't think I'm going to cook your dinner tonight." I got up. The swell was still rolling in from the east and, with walking boots protected in plastic bags, we piled into the dinghy and surfed towards the lea side of a stone jetty. Leaving the dinghy well above the high water mark, we trooped onto the bus with a handful of locals on a shopping spree and had a most enjoyable scenic run along the coast. At Brodick the bus filled to capacity with a Glasgow hiking club that had come over on the ferry but, mercifully, they all got off before we did and when we set off up Glen Sannox we had it to ourselves. By Scottish mainland standards the mountains of Arran are not high, but they rise straight out of the sea and as we tramped along a meandering path, the high, jagged peaks ahead and on both sides of the glen looked very formidable. We were out of the wind and it was scorching hot, but the dry weather of the past weeks had done us a favour and dried up the long expanses of boggy ground that in wet conditions would have made walking a nightmare. As we neared the head of the glen and the start of a long steep climb to the summit ridge, we came across a man and a woman staring intently at the sky through binoculars and they explained they had been watching a buzzard chasing off a golden eagle. It turned out they had a farm on the west side of the island and knew people I knew in the farming world, and for an hour we stood talking about farming and sheep, and about politicians who hadn't the brains of a sheep, until Patricia jogged my arm and reminded me we had a bus to catch on the other side of the mountain. "What a really interesting couple," Patricia enthused as we continued on our way. "Yes," I replied. "The salt of the earth those sort of people, and I bet government officials quake in their boots when that lady starts to ask questions at farmers' meetings. I wish I'd got their names." Patricia glanced at a piece of paper she had scribbled on. "Well, the man was called Duncan and I think the woman was Les. The conversation was fascinating, I'd love to meet them again."

The path became rougher and steeper as it left the level floor of the glen and reached the foot of a rocky gully which, at first glance, looked awesome, but inside provided a few hundred feet of exhilarating and airy scrambling that brought us out onto The Saddle, a dip between the summit of Goat Fell, 2840 feet, (874metres) and Cir Mhor, 2593feet, (798metres). The view down Glen Sannox and across the knife-edge ridges on either side of us was stunning and we took dozens of photographs, hoping that at least some of them would capture the atmosphere and give a true impression of the view. A walk of only a few yards across the saddle brought us to a path descending into Glen Rosa, much greener and very different in character to Glen Sannox but equally beautiful, and we gazed down on it from a heather-covered ledge and ate our sandwiches and drank tea. The walk down the glen, at times alongside a sparkling river, was a sheer delight and I was sorry when the path gave way to a track, which in turn joined a main road leading down to Brodick and the bus stop at the ferry terminal. The pier and terminal building were swarming with walkers and day trippers waiting for the ferry across to Ardrossan on the mainland, and ice cream vendors were doing a roaring trade. For a reason that the ferry operators, Caledonian MacBrayne, never got round to explaining to the waiting masses, the ferry was an hour late in arriving, but it eventually docked and, after a frenzied scurrying of vehicles and people, it departed again in a welter of foam stirred up by its hurrying propellers. Loaded with passengers, our bus pulled away from the terminal and we were on our way to Lamlash. The swell was still running into the bay when we got back aboard *Amulet* but, undeterred, Patricia dived overboard to cool off while I watched from the comfort of the cockpit and dissipated my bodily heat with a cold beer. We had walked ten miles through the mountains, and our visit to Arran had been truly memorable.

Through sheer laziness on my part, we endured another uncomfortable night being thrown about by the swell, and were slow to get out of our bunks the following morning. I've never met that 'prudent mariner' who is mentioned in every seafaring text book but, had he been the skipper of *Amulet*, I've no doubt he would have considered the well-being of his vessel and crew and moved across the bay to anchor in the lea of Holy Island; though, like me, he might have been put off by the thought of having to heave in thirty metres of chain by hand after a tiring day on the hills. *Amulet* did not have the luxury of an anchor winch and when, at 10.30am, we were ready to leave Lamlash and escape the relentless swell, Patricia had the unenviable and very wet job of hauling in the chain and anchor by hand, while I reduced the strain as much as I could by moving *Amulet* forward with the aid of the engine. It took half an hour of strenuous work before the anchor appeared and was lashed on the foredeck and Patricia flopped, exhausted, into the cockpit with her face the colour of a port-side lamp. There was a good breeze and I would have liked the sails up, but I sensed that any mention of it might provoke expressions unbecoming of a lady, so I kept quiet and motored out of the bay. Clear of Holy Island the easterly wind was a steady 10 knots and ideal for heading north and, never one to miss a good sail, Patricia read my thoughts and within minutes the main and genoa were up and *Amulet* was surging along with the pale green water of the Firth of Clyde washing her gunwale. We shot past Brodick and timed our speed at 5.4 knots through the water between the posts of two measured miles set up on the coast of Arran for the speed trials of ships like the famous Cunard liners 'Queen Mary' and 'Queen Elizabeth' during the halcyon days of shipbuilding on the Clyde. The wind died almost as soon as we passed the marks and left us wallowing in a lumpy sea so I started the engine and we motored along enjoying a sparse lunch of biscuits and cheese and bottled beer and keeping a wary eye on a sinister-looking nuclear submarine crossing ahead of us. Like the whole of the west coast of Scotland, the Clyde area is a sailor's paradise of sea lochs, islands and sounds and, leaving the blue mountains of Arran behind, we entered Loch Fyne, fabled for its breakfast kippers and, with the wind in helpful mood, a possible reach of over twenty miles from Ardlamont point at the entrance to Cairndow at its head, though most cruising yachtsfolk abandon the last few miles in favour of the attractions of the historic village of Inveraray and a peek at the Duke of Argyll's castle.

The easterly breeze sprang up again with a touch of south in it, but it didn't last and under a hot sun we drifted with the tide past the harbour town of Tarbert and stared longingly at an ice cream van parked on the quay. Now on the itinerary of the ever-expanding fleets of charter yachts, the harbour is often choked with a forest of aluminium masts where once the great fleets of drifters unloaded the 'silver herring' and made the Loch Fyne kipper world famous. As long ago as the 17th century the Loch Fyne herring industry employed 20,000 people, but by the 1930s there was hardly a herring left in the loch and, though the kipper legend lives on, a local restaurant owner once admitted to me that he bought his herrings from Norway. But there is no nationalism in a hungry belly and the thousands of 'yotters' who descend on Tarbert and pack the eating places and pubs have probably saved this fine little town from obscurity. It looked so inviting from the loch that Patricia insisted on putting in to explore the shops, but a cracking breeze sprang up and, distracted with my promise of a hot shower when we reached Ardrishaig, she took the helm and we pressed on. A little after 6.30pm we reached the entrance to the Crinan Canal, where *Amulet* was swiftly raised twenty feet above sea level by means of sluices, gates and two cheery lock keepers, and we motored into the basin and tied up alongside an elegant wooden sloop called *Morvern*. There was no sign of anyone on board, but a brass builders plaque in the cockpit revealed she was a true classic and, like myself, had been built in 1934, though by more famous parents than mine, the renowned yard of Robertsons of Sandbank, in Argyll. With *Amulet* snugged down and pumped out, a rather disturbing fifty strokes, we commandeered the immaculate shower facilities provided by British Waterways and, always ready to appreciate value for money, Patricia emerged, jubilant that she had soaked for eight minutes for £1.

The owner of *Morvern*, a very pleasant chap wearing a kilt, was aboard when we stepped gingerly across his beautifully laid deck, and in the course of conversation we were thrilled to discover he was Robin Bryer, who had not only skippered the legendary gaff cutter *Jolie Brise*, but had written a book about her. *Amulet* was crammed with sailing books, but unfortunately *Jolie Brise* was not one of them, and we missed an opportunity to own a copy signed by the author.

Full of colour photographs of sun-drenched scenes and with not a rain cloud or a Scottish midge in sight, the canal company's guide to the Crinan gives plenty of information about the nine mile journey, and tells the historically minded that the canal was constructed during 1793 to 1801. It was built in conjunction with the Forth and Clyde canal between Edinburgh and Glasgow to provide a sheltered passage for ships from the Firth of Forth, central Scotland, through Argyll by way of the Caledonian Canal at Fort William, to the Moray Firth at Inverness. Hoping to dangle an offer investors couldn't refuse, the prospectus assured them the canal would be a money spinner because 'It will not only enable the inhabitants to avoid entirely the very dangerous passage around the Mull of Kintyre but by affording a ready market for all the products of the Western Isles, it will invite the people to pursue a variety of kinds of industry to which they have hitherto been strangers. Above all it will enable them to supply themselves with salt and coals.' Alas the canal wasn't the licence to print money that the investors had hoped for, even with royal patronage. Queen Victoria described how she went through the canal 'in an most magnificently decorated barge drawn by three horses ridden by postillions dressed in scarlet', but the canal company no longer provides that level of service and unless you have plenty of crew or go through in the company of other boats, it is incredibly wearying, and if single-handed, almost impossible.

Having been through the Crinan many times before in a wide range of boats, I knew what we were in for and, when we motored into the first lock at 8.30am the following morning, I was far from happy. My state of mind was not improved by a sour-faced duo manning the only other boat to set off with us, and we had only negotiated two locks when I began to get needled by their bolshy 'We've done this before and we know better than you' attitude. As crew, Patricia was worth ten of either of them, but they obviously had a hang up about women in boats and gave her so much verbal harassment when she helped with the sluices and the lock gates I told them to continue on their own, and we tied up alongside a pontoon. Half an hour later a small armada of yachts, led by *Papa Westray* a large, heavily built motor launch, came steaming up the canal and when we dropped in behind, it helped to make up for the bad start to the day. The owner of the motor launch, a ship owner from Ayrshire, organised the lock opening and closing operations with such efficiency we seemed to race along the canal and we all had a most enjoyable time. We caught up with the two obnoxious gents in the yacht and they joined our flotilla, but they had the sense to keep their mouths shut and when we reached the end of the canal and tied up alongside a large yacht in Crinan basin, they went through the lock into the sea.

Whether it was the unrelenting heat of the day or the strain of passing through the canal that had unbalanced Patricia's normally sensible approach to parting with money I never found out; but she disappeared after we had tied up and came back with the news that she had booked a table for dinner at the Crinan Hotel, a renowned watering hole for well-heeled yachting types. When I looked startled and asked if she had mortgaged *Amulet*, she gave me a withering look that said plainly, "I'm paying and don't you dare ask how much it will cost," then aloud said, "It's a rather smart dining room, don't you think you ought to wear something presentable?" "But what's the point of eating there?" I protested. "We could go through the sea lock and I know lots of quiet anchorages where we could drop the hook and have an undisturbed meal." "Yes," she said fiercely, "and guess who would be expected to make it. It's a lovely evening, I'm having a break and we're dining at the Crinan, and that's the end of it!" I was forced to put on my best sailing trousers and shirt and sit in splendour in an elegant dining room while a delightful French waitress fed me first with oysters and then lobster and filled my glass with good wine. I kept thinking about Admiral Nelson's warning that harbours were the ruination of good seamen, but it wasn't just a meal, it was an experience and as the evening wore on and the superb courses came and went and the wine flowed, I was enjoying myself. "Sod Nelson," I slurred to the French waitress. "Pardon, m'sieur, my Engleesh is not very good," "Never mind; can we have another bottle of wine please?"

It is a sure sign I have been drinking quality red wine when I wake up in the morning after a night out and haven't got a splitting headache; and when a trawler tied up ahead of *Amulet* and the noise of the crew unloading the night's catch got me out of my bunk, I felt tremendous. There was no sign of Patricia and I was studying a chart spread out in the cockpit when one of the lock-keepers walked by. "Where are you making for?" he called. "Oban," I replied. "Och well, you'll not be needing a chart to get you to Oban," he said with a wry laugh, "just follow the line of beer cans; the Highland Week racing boats went through a few days ago." Patricia returned after searching unsuccessfully for a shower block and we prepared for sea, pumping the bilge dry with twenty five strokes, a vast improvement, and stowing loose gear. At 9.30am when the 'Gateway to the West', the creaking barricades of Crinan sea lock, swung open and the Farymann pushed us out into tidal water I set course for the Dorus Mor, a gap between Garbh Reisa island and Craignish Point on the mainland, and made a mistake that had me really worried that advancing years were beginning to make their mark on me. Leaving Patricia at the helm, I went below to check the engine, and coming back into the cockpit became totally disorientated and gave Patricia the wrong course to steer. I had sailed that way a great many times, yet it took me ten minutes to sort myself out and get back on the right course and safely away from a group of submerged rocks that would have delighted in getting their teeth into *Amulet*'s hull. In fifty years of sailing I had never done anything so stupid, and I felt thoroughly ashamed. One of the problems was that I refused to believe the GPS, yet it was the Furuno that eventually saved us from disaster. I told myself it was about time the Japanese wizard and I started to get on together.

The Dorus Mor has an unsavoury reputation but, as with every other place where there is a strong tidal stream, a lot depends on the weather; and on a flat calm, sunny day and taking the last of the flood, we hardly saw a ripple as we motored through and turned to starboard into Loch Shuna. This area is another paradise of islands and sea lochs and I was considerably annoyed when, some years ago, one of my favourite anchorages, a group of small islands close to the mainland, were engulfed in a marina complex the developers called Craobh Haven. But time heals all wounds and I have to admit it now sits comfortably into the landscape and provides a useful service for those who cannot spend a night on a boat unless plugged into all the home comforts. I quickly steered *Amulet* past the entrance and by the wooded Shuna Island to Cuan Sound before Patricia had a chance to talk wistfully of showers and hair washes. Cuan Sound is a very narrow channel between the islands of Luing and Seil and when the full power of a spring tide is on the move it squirts through in both directions at over 7 knots. Only boats with powerful engines have any chance of getting through from Loch Shuna against the ebb, and *Amulet* not being in that category we anchored in a sheltered bay at the north end of Luing to wait for the tide, and had lunch under a blazing sun. A few seals swam round the boat, but sniffed suspiciously at the pieces of bread Patricia threw over the side and sank beneath the surface leaving them untouched. The tide began to turn at about 7pm and brought an abrupt change of weather. The sun and blue sky were rapidly devoured by an ugly bank of grey cloud that sprinkled *Amulet* with light rain and had us rushing to fling the cockpit cushions below. I helped Patricia to heave the anchor and it broke the surface encased in thick tendrils of bladder weed that took ages to cut away, and when we nosed into the Sound the tide was a horizontal waterfall that zipped *Amulet* along at a cracking pace and spewed her out into the Firth of Lorne like a piece of drift wood. Imagining what the conditions would have been like had the fierce tide been met by a strong westerly wind was best left to the writers of horror stories, and we ploughed on for Oban across a leaden sea, trying to identify headlands through a murky drizzle. My new pal, the Furuno GPS, indicated that we were in the Sound of Insh on course for Kerrera Sound and the entrance to Oban Bay, and half an hour later when we suddenly motored out of the murk and into glorious sunshine and there before us was the Island of Kerrera and the Sound, I had to agree it was right. I wanted to anchor for the night in Little Horseshoe Bay, a lovely peaceful anchorage on the Kerrera side of the Sound, but we were low on diesel and I reluctantly continued on to the boatyard at Ardentrive, the northern tip of Kerrera that forms part of Oban Bay. It was late in the evening and the facilities were closed, but as I was pulling away a friendly chap enjoying an evening drink in his cockpit shouted that there was a mooring we could use if we wanted it. He said it was the owner's permanent mooring but he was away for the night and would not mind us using it. Wilting after a long day, it was just the gesture of camaraderie we needed and, calling our thanks, we picked up the mooring and sipped whisky while the evening meal was cooking.

Apologising for disturbing him at a late hour, I phoned Malcolm Robertson, the Furuno agent in Oban, to arrange for him connect up the GPS navigator to the new Simrad DSC unit to enable it to give our position in the event of us sending out a distress call. In Cumbria, marine radio technicians are as rare as visiting government ministers and the unit had not been fully installed. Malcolm said he was in bed suffering from a migraine attack, but he would be at Oban's north pier at noon on the following day.

The morning of the 26th of July was overcast but warm and we inflated the dinghy and went across to the boatyard to fill jerrycans with diesel. I winced when I noticed that a miniature marina of pontoons, all crammed with yachts, had been installed since my last visit and the whole place was swarming with people. No one seemed to want to tell me what was going on, but Patricia could easily talk her way into a masonic lodge and disarmed one of the committee into disclosing that it was a stopping-off place on the Clyde Cruising Club's annual binge, when club members and lots of other whisky-loving boat owners sail in a vast armada and visit the distilleries of Islay, Oban and Skye. I went pale when Patricia said they were expecting over two hundred boats that day and were preparing one of the sheds for a mammoth party, complete with piper. "Let's get the hell out of here," I implored. "Yes, as soon as we can!" she said eagerly. "I'll go and pay for the diesel." She came back a few minutes later looking downcast. "You're not going to believe this," she said, "but they've charged me £10 for using the mooring." "They've done what?" I said in amazement. "But they must already have had a year's mooring fee from the owner and we only stayed so we could buy diesel from the yard." "That's what I tried to explain," said Patricia, "but the man in the office wouldn't listen." "What a bloody rip off!" I exploded. "Times have certainly changed since it was a working boatyard; they went out of their way to be helpful when I brought my charter ketch in for occasional repairs: but since we've paid for the mooring we'll use it and stay here until we're ready to go across to the north pier."

From the mooring we had a magnificent panoramic view of Oban bay and the town, and a shaft of sunlight breaking through the clouds illuminated McCaig's tower that dominates the skyline. Started in 1897 by John McCaig, a local banker, to provide work for unemployed locals, it was never finished and is rather unfairly referred to in tourist guides as 'McCaigs Folly'. His only folly was that through spending all his money helping others who were experiencing desperate times, he soon found himself in the same plight. Oban is a lovely town and the heart from which flows the lifeblood of many of the islands and remote communities of the inner and outer Hebrides; but, in a lifetime of sailing the entire length of the west of Scotland and the isles, if there is a harbour that is less welcoming to yachts than Oban I have yet to find it. Many suggestions have been put forward for improving the harbour and providing facilities for the fleets of yachtsfolk who come in from the sea every year and pour money into the pubs and shops, but the town fathers are doing so well out of the many thousands of tourists who come by land they have neither the incentive nor the imagination to cater for sailors as well. When I chartered out of Oban there were a few incredibly popular and reasonably- priced pontoons for visiting yachts on the south side of the harbour, in the care of the very helpful and obliging lifeboat coxswain, but they were removed to make way for a new fish landing quay. Nowadays, trying to get ashore to explore the town or to take on stores is a considerable hassle unless the seaborne visitor is fortunate to find a vacant mooring, nigh impossible in the summer, or is prepared to go across to Kerrera Island and Ardantrive yacht centre and use their launch. Depending on the mood of the harbour master and at the mercy of the wash from passing vessels, it is sometimes possible to tie up alongside Oban's north pier, but when I phoned to ask permission to come alongside, it was obviously a day when small yachts were out of favour and he came up with every excuse in the book why it was not possible. It was only when I mentioned Malcolm Robertson's name that he relented, but he was waiting for us when we cast off from the mooring and motored across the bay to the pier and, ignoring the warps I flung up, he demanded to know how long we would be staying. With what sounded suspiciously like muttered swear words, Patricia climbed swiftly up a ladder and, grabbing the warps, secured *Amulet* to bollards while I searched for diplomatic words to indicate we would be staying as long as it took to get the radio fixed. Malcolm did not arrive until 4pm and he was still suffering from the migraine attack, but got out his tool kit and wiring diagrams, and within half an hour the job was done. Meantime Patricia had disappeared into the town to get groceries and, battered against the pier legs by the wash of launches picking up and landing passengers at nearby stone steps and having my ears bent every few minutes by the harbour master demanding to know when I was leaving, I was close to blowing a safety valve and had to work hard at stopping myself from letting go a broadside of language that would have lifted his hat off. Patricia cooled the potential explosion by arriving in a taxi loaded with stores and so many plastic buckets and miscellaneous bits and pieces of fishing tackle it looked as if she had done a ram raid on Woolworths. At 5pm and with enormous relief I revved the engine and pulled away from the pier, but not until the harbour master had relieved Patricia of £2-50 and sent us on our way with one of his best scowls. I had known Oban since my youth and the old Highland town evoked many happy memories, but it had changed and the people with it. I was glad to leave and, under a warm evening sun and with the Farymann burbling merrily, we chugged up Kerrera sound and dropped anchor in the tranquil setting of Horseshoe Bay. There was not a breath of wind; the only sound was the baa-ing of sheep grazing on the island and the only movement a herd of wild goats picking amongst the seaweed on the shore.

Old Pals Reunion - Spanish Gold - Skinny Dippers

In the course of a year many hundreds of yachts sail past the island of Kerrera heading for Oban Bay and, apart from reading what the sailing directions have to say about anchorages and the facilities at Ardantrive, probably never give it another thought. For anyone who enjoys a leg stretch in between bouts of sailing, Kerrera is a little gem. Only five miles long by two wide, it is perfect for a circumnavigation on foot and after an early breakfast the next morning, with rucksacks packed with flasks and sandwiches, we paid out an extra few fathoms of anchor chain, climbed into the dinghy and rowed the few yards to the shore. It was another lovely day with fleecy white clouds in a blue sky and warm enough to walk in a tee shirt and shorts. There are no roads on the island, just tracks and wild scenery, giving the impression that, despite the proximity of bustling Oban, the world has passed it by and it is the haunt of a few inhabitants, sheep and wild goats. It's all of this, but because tourist boards have an unfortunate habit of justifying their existence by focusing attention on quiet places, the island is now very much on the tourist trail and the handful that once crossed on the ferry to enjoy the magic of Kerrera has now increased to droves. Hence the reason for our early start, and we strode past Little Horse Shoe Bay and followed a stony track that climbed above the Sound. It wound southwards to a jagged coast indented with narrow bays strewn with all manner of flotsam that had us poking amongst it like a pair of Oyster Catchers. I've come across amazing finds in remote coves, including a container full of Russian charts on the Island of Lewis. It was at the height of the 'Cold War', and they were whisked away by two grim-faced gents from Special Branch who interrogated me as if I were a spy.

Perched on the edge of a high cliff, though clinging to it is perhaps a better description, is Gylen Castle, a 16th century stronghold of the MacDougalls of Lorne. Only about sixty feet long by thirty feet wide, it must be been way down the list of important Scottish castles, but there cannot be many that are more imposing. The MacDougalls must have felt very secure in their cliff top house and had a view of the islands of Mull, Scarba, Lunga and Jura that estate agents would go into a frenzy over; but, as so often happened in Scottish history, the castle was attacked and burnt and, in an attempt to prevent what has survived from falling into the sea, Scottish Heritage had erected scaffolding against the crumbling walls and, presumably with the help of volunteers with a good head for heights, were embarking on a restoration project.

Leaving the castle, we followed the coastline towards the west side of the island until boggy ground forced us back onto a track, climbing away from the sea to a fine viewpoint with an unrestricted view across to Mull. I was uneasy about a threatening bank of cloud approaching from the west, but away from it the sky was clear and we could see every detail on Lismore Island and beyond to Loch Linnhe and the breathtaking hills of the Morvern Peninsula. The panorama was lost when the track dropped steeply to Barnabuck Bay, but we were compensated for it by the sight of a magnificent wild billy goat with huge curved horns, perched on a rock, guarding his glen and his women like a true Highland patriarch. The track climbed out of the bay in a series of steep twists and we got the view back, but it denied us the final mile or so to the northern tip when it swung abruptly across the island and descended by the deserted island school to the ferry landing. A short walk along the shore and we were back at the dinghy and soon on board *Amulet*, gulping cold beer and hanging sweaty socks to dry in the sun. Circumnavigating Kerrera may not be the most demanding walk in Scotland, but it is certainly memorable.

Someone, I think the writer George Eliot, once said, 'Friendships begin with liking', and when, in the 1950s, I first met Robin Shaw, a scruffy Glasgow University student with a passion for mountains and boats, I liked him enormously and we have been friends ever since. With very little sailing experience he once applied for a job as an instructor at the Outward Bound Sea School at Aberdovey in North Wales and, to convince the unimpressed Outward Bound chiefs he could sail, he bought a very ancient boat on Loch Lomond, somehow got it down the normally un-navigable river Leven to Dumbarton on the Clyde, and sailed it single-handed down the North Channel and the Irish Sea to Aberdovey. He got the job!

I hadn't seen Robin for a long time when, in the course of a chance phone conversation with him, I discovered that he and his wife Celia kept their Nicholson 32 in Dunstaffnage Marina, a few miles north of

Oban, and that they were on board. Knowing that Patricia would understand, I abandoned all plans for heading out to the Hebrides and we heaved anchor the next morning and headed for Dunstaffnage. The cloud I had seen over Mull had moved in during the night and we motored through the Sound and out of Oban Bay's north entrance in thick fog and drizzle with the siren blasts of the Mull ferry uncomfortably close; but when we turned to follow the coast to Dunstaffnage, the fog miraculously cleared and we emerged into bright sunshine. Beautiful Dunstaffnage Bay was another quiet wildlife-filled anchorage of my youth that had succumbed to a marina development and, with one of those peculiar twists of irony that life sometimes throws at us, I had actually opened it. But it wasn't a ceremony accompanied by speeches and a brass band: I had spent a month sailing an open boat in the area and, battered by strong winds and heavy rain, had run for the shelter of Dunstaffnage. The shore was deserted except for two men in oilskin suits busy working on a jetty newly built of large boulders, and I asked if I could tie up against it. "Throw me your warps," one of them called with a big smile, "and welcome to Dunstaffnage marina, you're our first customer!" Within an hour, a reporter and a photographer from the *Oban Times* arrived and, having only come into the bay to get out of the storm and make a hot drink, my young crew and I found ourselves headlined in the local newspaper. Later, when I was chartering and had become completely disillusioned with Oban as a base and moved to a mooring in Dunstaffnage Bay, the owners of the marina were exceptionally helpful. But old habits die hard and, having been an incurable escapist all my life, I have never been able to throw off my dislike of being one of a herd and I have a 'hang up' about marinas that my friends find very difficult to understand.

Weaving carefully among the forest of masts, I brought *Amulet* alongside a pontoon close to Robin and Celia's boat *Souple Jade*, and after warm hugs all round we sat below and had a brew of tea, arranging to sail together to spend the night in Port Ramsay at the north end of Lismore Island en route for a day's hillwalking on Morvern. We left under sail ahead of *Souple Jade*; but the aristocratic Nicholson, with a genoa nearly as long as *Amulet*, was not going to be put to shame by a clinker-built upstart and soon caught up and swept effortlessly by as if we were at anchor. With a good breeze and a blue sky it was a perfect sailing day and we shot towards Lismore, turned right into the Lynn of Lorne, and goose-winged for six miles before hardening the sheets in the fast tide rip off the north tip of the island and surging into Loch Linnhe. All the way *Souple Jade* had been a speck in the distance, but when Robin stooged around waiting for us we caught up and sailed together towards the gigantic Glensanda granite quarry that has ripped an ugly scar across the lovely face of the Morvern peninsula. Many call the quarry an eyesore and a violation of the landscape, and so it is, but the whole of the west of Scotland is environmentally sensitive and though the wild places must be protected there has, unfortunately, to be times of compromise when the need for jobs to keep Highland communities alive takes priority over the view.

The wind dropped away before we reached the quarry and we stowed the sails and motored back to Lismore to anchor in Port Ramsay. If I had to choose only one of the many hundreds of anchorages I have enjoyed in the west of Scotland it would be Port Ramsay. A lagoon alive with seals and sea birds, the anchorage is utterly bewitching and the view across Loch Linnhe when the setting sun paints the sharp peaks and ridges of Morvern a rich ochre is quite beyond a description that would truly do it justice. Patricia put together a grand meal and, with Robin and Celia aboard *Amulet* and plenty of wine to loosen tongues, we had one of those evenings that linger in the memory of anyone who cruises under sail and enjoys the magic of a quiet anchorage and the company of good friends. When Robin and Celia returned to *Souple Jade* and I went on deck to hoist the paraffin anchor light, the velvet sky was filled with stars and it was absolutely flat calm. The only sound was the occasional splash of a rising fish and the squabbling of gulls on the tidal islets ringing the anchorage. It was heaven!

The hills were shrouded in mist and it was a flat calm morning when *Amulet* and *Souple Jade* nosed slowly out of Port Ramsay and headed under engine across Loch Linnhe on the four mile journey to the deep inlet of Loch a' Choire on Morvern. We anchored close to an old pier on the north side of the loch and inflated our dinghies, but as Robin and Celia hadn't got an outboard motor I took them in tow across the loch to the foot of a fairly tough slog up steep hills with tongue-twisting Gaelic names. We started with a strenuous hike up steep heather to a ridge that led us to the summit of Meall an Doire Dhuibh and the amazing sight of a herd of over twenty red deer stags. Spotting us, they bounded away up the ridge, their magnificent antlers silhouetted against the grey sky for a brief moment, then they were gone. Cameras were hurriedly uncovered in the hope that we would see the stags again but, more used to rifles being pointed at them than cameras, they kept well out of sight. An obliging breeze sprang up and cleared away the mist that had been swirling around the hill tops, then disappeared itself leaving behind a warm sun and a fantastic panoramic view of the sea and islands that stretched way down beyond Oban. In Loch a' Choire *Amulet* and *Souple Jade* sat side by side like two toy boats in a giant bathtub. The ridge curved round and with an easy scramble we reached a narrow rocky plateau and stopped to take in the view and eat a piece of chocolate. We were still not half way along our intended walk and, as Robin and Celia had arranged to be back at the marina by late afternoon, they set off back down the ridge. I wanted to continue the walk and Patricia was equally keen, so we pressed on, crossing the top of Glensanda Quarry and enjoying a brisk walk to the summit of Beinn Mheadhoin, 2402 feet, (739metres), a true rocky peak and the highest on the ridge. The view of the islands of Rhum, Eigg, Muck and Skye to the west and the whole panorama of mountains, islands and sea lochs on every point of the compass was spectacular. We saw a large herd of deer, including several stags, below us but they were too far away for taking photographs and we sat and watched them as they poured down the steep side of the hill and were swallowed up in a ravine. The ridge descended steeply to an expanse of peat bog, only to climb unrelentingly again to Meall na Greine, 1979 feet (609metres), before taking us down an even longer descent to the foot of a wearying climb up Sgurr Shalachain, 1748 feet, (538 metres), the last summit on the ridge.

An endearing feature of the little-known Scottish hills is that there are virtually no well tramped footpaths and you find your own way to the summits; likewise, there are often no obvious ways down and when we explored the sides of Sgurr Shalachain they appeared to be near-vertical heather and grass. Far below, the buildings of Kingairloch House and farm were laid out like models on a giant relief map and, carefully choosing a line that seemed feasible, I moved slowly down a heather gully with Patricia's boots slipping and sliding only inches from my head. It took a long time and a few frights before the angle eased and we could stand upright without hanging onto clumps of heather, and when we finally reached the floor of the glen we were so thirsty the sparkling clear water of the river was pure nectar. We were very tired and the walk along the shore of the loch to the dinghy seemed a lot longer than the mile it measured on the map, but back on board *Amulet* the bottles of cold beer had never tasted so good. We had walked about ten miles, climbed a lot of peaks and enjoyed wonderful views; it had been an absolutely superb day. Almost without any effort Patricia produced a meal, and afterwards we sat in the cockpit until the evening shadows crept up the ridges we had walked and a lovely day was turned into an enchanting night. The late weather forecast warned of an approaching low pressure system and strong winds, but we would be well sheltered by the time it arrived. It was only a few hours sail to Loch Aline, on Morvern, where my ex boatbuilder pal, John Hodgson, lived, and I was looking forward to seeing him again and showing him the completed *Amulet*.

The automatic bilge pump bursting into life shortly after midnight and again at dawn was a reminder that the persistent leak was not improving, and that visiting John was likely to be more than just a social call. When I pumped the bilge dry I could see a steady trickle seeping in from both sides of the keelson and, though they had been raked out and re-caulked twice, the culprit seemed to be the garboard seams. But there was nothing that could be done about it until *Amulet* was dried out, and we lingered in the sun trap of Loch a' Choire and caught up on small maintenance jobs until late in the morning. In the fond hope of enjoying regular hot showers, Patricia had invested in a large plastic bag with a tube which the label claimed was a solar shower and, suspending it from the boom she gave a pair of swans and some men working at a nearby fish farm a terrible fright by trying it out in the cockpit. She said it was invigorating, but when I stood under it and the freezing spray shrivelled my extremities, I got out quickly before I was reduced to a life of guarding the doors of a harem.

Reluctantly tearing ourselves away from the idyllic setting of the loch, we heaved anchor and motored out into Loch Linnhe, then turning south hugged the Morvern coast. There was not a breath of wind but, though it was hot, there was an oppressive feeling of an impending change in the weather, confirmed by a darkening of the western sky. The old fortification of Glensanda Castle, the seat of the MacLeans of Kingairloch, built on a high rock by the shore, seemed to be defiantly refusing to surrender to the quarrying operations. In stark contrast to this crumbling piece of Scotland's history, the huge modern freighter, the 'Yeoman Bridge', was being loaded at the quarry jetty and the ghosts of the crofters said to haunt the site of the ancient Glensanda township must have looked on in wonderment at the sight of the strange sea monster that, when it was hungry, came to their shore to be fed with rock out of the hill. It was about nine miles down the loch to the headland of Rubha an Ridire, at the southern tip of Morvern where Loch Linnhe meets the Sound of Mull and, with no hope of reaching Loch Aline at a convenient time to dry out alongside the village jetty, I set the engine at half throttle and we chugged slowly along, marvelling at the constantly-changing landscape and seascape that were unmistakably Scotland. At Rubha an Ridire the vast ebb of Loch Linnhe forces its way into the ebb of the Sound of Mull with some awe-inspiring tidal effects, especially with an opposing wind, but though it was springs and when we rounded the headland the ebb was tearing into us like a river, the sea gods were in a kindly mood and *Amulet* skipped through the tide rips with hardly a drop of water spilling onto the deck.

It was late afternoon and only four miles from Loch Aline, but I knew it was an extremely popular anchorage that would be teeming with activity, and I was keen to avoid it. As soon as we rounded the headland I steered for a group of small islets I was familiar with close to the Morvern shore, and dropped the hook behind Eilean Rubha an Ridire. An anchorage for connoisseurs of peace and quiet, and the haunt of playful seals who, when they think the occupants of anchored yachts are not looking, have a great time chasing each other in circles and diving off the rocks, it is an unbelievably beautiful place, and the view and the sunset over the hills of the Isle of Mull quite stupendous. I inflated the dinghy and rowed round to the west of the island to show Patricia a mast sticking out of the water that marked the last resting place of a coaster called the *Ballista* which, according to an old sea captain I knew who lived on Mull, lay across another coaster underneath it. Apparently the engine on the first coaster broke down and, loaded with coal, it drifted onto the rocks on Eilean Rubha an Ridire and was holed. The *Ballista* was sent to unload the cargo of coal, but it also hit a rock and was holed and both ships finally slid into the water and were abandoned. They now provide a home for lobsters and a playground for sub-aqua divers. Another home for lobsters, but out of bounds to divers, is the Royal Navy frigate *H.M.S. Dartmouth*, a wreck quite close to the coasters but unfortunately in about 30 feet of water and unable to be seen from the surface. According to records the *Dartmouth*, 80ft loa with a beam of 25ft and a draft of 12ft, was built in Portsmouth in 1655, and carried a crew of 135 and 32 guns. She was engaged in peacekeeping duties at a time when there was a lot of Jacobite sympathy in Scotland and on October 19, 1690, was torn from her moorings in a frenzied storm that lashed the Scottish coast and was smashed to pieces on the rocks. The Captain and all but six of his men were lost. It's a melancholy story, but it doesn't spoil the enjoyment of a jewel of an anchorage.

To ensure we would be up early and arrive at Loch Aline quay at high water, Patricia set her dreadful clanging alarm clock for 6am and it dutifully drove us out of our bunks at the appointed hour. The low pressure system had arrived during the night and battered the cabin top with heavy rain and, though it had eased to a drizzle when I went on deck to douse the anchor light, the visibility was down to about a mile and Mull was completely obscured. A breeze sprang up from the south east while we were hauling the anchor so we quickly hoisted sail and cleared the islands on a brisk reach. The squat white tower of Ardtornish Light soon hove in sight, and by 8am we were tied up to the north side of the stone-built quay at Loch Aline, nicely tucked away from the influence of a tidal flow that at springs reaches 3 knots. John appeared at 9am and had a poke around in the bilges, then departed saying he would be back at low water with some special mastic and a gas torch to dry out the seams. The scourge of arthritis had forced him to give up boatbuilding and repair work, and he had opened a picture-framing business in Loch Aline village and had to attend to it. The aroma of frying bacon from a tea bar on the quay lured Patricia ashore and she came back with an instant breakfast of large bacon rolls and mugs of tea, and we sat on the quayside and watched a large barge yacht, the *Audrey*, registered in Goole, come alongside the quay to take on water. The mooring warps had hardly touched the ground before her crew of young boys swarmed over the side and rushed gleefully up to the village shop to squander their pocket money.

Patricia had a blitz on the forecabin, and spread so much gear along the quay it attracted the attention of passengers waiting for the ferry to Mull and they asked me if we were holding a jumble sale; but it was a useful opportunity to unearth bags of clothes and miscellaneous gear I had forgotten about. All the floorboards and the engine casing were dumped on the quay and, armed with a big torch, I methodically checked every plank, every nail and every skin fitting; I also examined the stern gland on the propeller shaft but the only sign of seepage was on either side of the keelson. It had to be the garboards. We snaked the anchor chain along the side deck to give *Amulet* a cant against the wall when the keel settled on the bottom but it was 2pm before she completely dried out and John arrived with the gas torch and mastic. Dressed in his shop clothes he wasn't able to get under the hull and check the seams, but he made a few suggestions before leaving to go back to his shop. I pulled on my overalls and crawled over the wet shingle under *Amulet* and shone the torch along the garboards looking for tell-tale rivulets on the planking, indicating that if water was running out it was a place where it could also get back in, but there was nothing. I climbed on board and checked the keel bolt nuts, but they were absolutely tight. Completely mystified, I got Patricia to pull the quayside water hose on board and fill the bilge with water up to the level of the floorboards then I went back under the hull with the torch. A few drops were oozing through a plank seam above the garboard on the port side, and after a few minutes there were signs of seepage in the garboards. It didn't amount to much, but I felt I had to do something to justify drying out, so the water was pumped out of the bilges and, starting at the bow I raked out every caulkable seam, dried it off gently with the gas torch, hammered in new lengths of cotton and finished them off with John's superior mastic. For good measure I dried off as many plank seams as I could, and ran a bead of mastic along them. I felt sure *Amulet* would never leak again, but when the tide came in she did, albeit not as badly as before she was dried out, but badly enough, and it was very disappointing.

To add to the frustration, the damp, drizzly conditions were paradise for swarms of midges and we were driven frantic by the brutes as we rushed to stow the gear in the forecabin and fit the floorboards. On his way home, John came down to see how we had got on and said we would be able to get a drink in the local social club but, keen to escape from the midges, we left the quay and anchored in the loch. While we were eating our evening meal the wet, grey mist rolled away and we enjoyed coffee and a dram in the cockpit, bathed in warm sunshine. It was some compensation for a day full of disappointments, and from the anchorage we had an uninterrupted view of the loch and Ardtornish House. One of a rapidly shrinking number of large Scottish estates that has an owner who takes an active personal interest in it, Ardtornish has a quality of beauty, isolation and immense freedom of space that I have not yet seen equalled by any other, and it is by far my favourite. The ease of access to the sheltered loch and a good shop for stores has made it a popular stopping-off place for cruising yachtsfolk, but few venture very far beyond the shore, and are unaware of the wild deer, eagles, foxes and wild cat, and the abundance of wild flowers that make Ardtornish estate a very special place. When the poet Tennyson stayed at Ardtornish in 1853, he became so enchanted with it he cancelled a trip to the Isle of Skye and made the house visitors' book a collector's item by writing:-

'If he did not see Loch Coruisk
He ought to be forgiven;
For though he miss'd a day on Skye,
He spent a day in Heaven.

What descriptive words Tennyson would have penned to describe the racket which echoed across the loch and shattered the peace of our evening we'll never know, but I could have composed a powerful line or two myself when a machine at the sand mine close to the village suddenly burst into life and kept up an ear-splitting whine that was unbearable and drove us into the cabin. Like the rest of Ardtornish, the sand mine is unique and is one of the few places in Europe where high grade sand used in the manufacture of optical glass is found and ships arrive regularly to export it to many countries.

With a promise of a fresh wind, we were up early the next morning and by 7.30am had cleared Loch Aline and were beating up the Sound of Mull bound for Tobermory; but had only sailed about three miles when we were confronted with a fast- approaching armada of sails that completely filled the Sound. "What a wonderful sight!" exclaimed Patricia. "They've all got their spinnakers drawing." But I wasn't as thrilled. We had obviously run smack into one of the West Highland Week races and there was very little room for us to manoeuvre. There must have been well over two hundred boats, all running with the wind and on different tacks but, though we were beating to windward on the starboard tack and technically had right of way, it was clear we would create mayhem if we stood our ground, so Patricia quickly dropped the sails while I started the engine. Threading a way through the pack was a hairy experience, especially when one or two racing fanatics who were concentrating more on the set of their sails than on looking where they were going nearly rammed us, but we emerged unscathed and earned a hoot of thanks and a wave from a committee boat.

Tobermory, the 'capital' of the Isle of Mull, is the harbour of all harbours, the fleshpot of all fleshpots for the cruising and racing fraternity, and at the height of the summer I normally avoid it like the plague; but it is also a most attractive little harbour village and one place that yachtsfolk lock on to like a waypoint is the Mishnish Hotel. Run for many years by the incomparable accordionist and Scottish dance band leader Bobby MacLeod, and now by his family, it has always extended a warm welcome to the annual influx of the great unwashed that comes in from the sea, and provides hot showers and towels. I have a theory that the reason why women are so successful at non-stop long-distance yacht racing is because they are in such a hurry to get ashore and have a shower and wash their hair. On *Amulet* we could be dying of thirst or hunger or weakened with scurvy for want of fresh fruit, but as soon as we reached a harbour, Patricia's number one priority was a shower and hair wash, and when we had picked up a visitor's mooring and inflated the dinghy she headed for the Mishnish and insisted that I went as well. For £1, towel included, it was incredible value and I spent so long enjoying the caressing warmth that when I came out Patricia had gone to raid the grocery shelves of the local Co-op. I wandered along the seafront and popped into a bank, not to get money but to soak up a bit of nostalgia. In my youth when I was a lighthouse keeper at Ardnamurchan lighthouse, I opened an account at

the bank but was hopeless at handling money, and one day I received
an irate letter from Angus MacIntyre, the then bank manager, that read,
'When you opened your account you said it would be lively, heaven
knows it. But make it lively on the credit side or you'll have to close it.'
I got to know him later and he was a man with a tremendous sense of
humour, who wrote hilarious rhyming verse and some fine poetry.
Computerised banking and faceless managers are a poor substitute.

While searching through my pockets to pay for an Ordnance Survey
map of the Ardnamurchan Peninsula showing the hills I wanted to
climb, I came across a slip of paper with the telephone number of my
other boatbuilder friend, Sandy Macdonald and his wife Liz, who lived
on the shore of Loch Sunart on the opposite side of the Sound of Mull.
When I phoned to ask if it would be alright to call on them that
afternoon on our way down the loch, Liz was very welcoming and said
to pick up their mooring and they would watch out for us. I met
Patricia pushing a loaded supermarket trolley and she was delighted
with the news, but said she needed another hour as she had left some
clothes at a launderette. We unloaded the trolley into the dinghy and
had tea and sticky buns in a café while I read a booklet I had bought
about the famous Spanish galleon *Almirante de Florencia*, reputed to have
sunk in Tobermory bay laden with treasure. When Sir Francis Drake
finished his leisurely game of bowls at Plymouth in 1588, swapped his
trainers for seaboots and sailed the Golden Hind out into the English
Channel, defeating the invading Spanish Armada, the galleon *Almirante
de Florencia* fled up the west coast of Ireland and Scotland and sought
refuge in Tobermory bay, but was captured by Sir Lachlan MacLean of
Duart Castle and the Captain and crew were flung into his dungeons.
But MacLean did a deal with the Captain, promising to let him go and
to provide supplies for the voyage back to Spain in return for him
helping to attack his old rival, MacLean of Coll. It was the swashbuckling
stuff Errol Flynn movies were made of, and full of the intrigue and
treachery that Highland chiefs thrived on. Maybe the Captain suspected
he was being set up or that MacLean was scheming to get his hands on
the fabulous treasure rumoured to be hidden on board, but for
whatever reason the deal went sour, and in a fit of peak MacLean is
said to have sacked the ship and set fire to her where she lay at anchor
in the bay. When the flames reached the powder magazine she blew up

and sank less than a hundred yards off shore in eleven fathoms.

Another and more romantic version of the story of the *Almirante de Florencia* that has a 'Romeo and Juliet' touch, rare in Highland history, tells of the beautiful Spanish Princess, Clara Bheola, who was haunted by the vision of a man in her dreams. Driven to finding him, she sailed with the invading Armada aboard the *Florencia*, and when the ship arrived at Tobermory and she clapped eyes on Sir Lachlan MacLean she knew she had found the man of her dreams and turned on the charm. But Lady MacLean didn't take kindly to the Spanish beauty flashing her castanets at her man and, waiting until MacLean was on board, ostensibly to see the Captain, she sent someone with a message that he was urgently required at home. As soon as MacLean had left the ship, the messenger dropped a slow-burning fuse in the magazine and minutes later the ship was blown to bits and all on board killed, including the Princess. Days later her body was washed up on Morvern and she was buried in the churchyard at Loch Aline. But the story doesn't end there. Some time later the Princess appeared in a dream to MacLean, crying that she couldn't rest until her bones were buried in Spain, so Sir Lachlan sailed over to Loch Aline, had the remains put in a coffin, and personally escorted it to Spain. King Philip was overjoyed and sent MacLean home with a large treasure, but when it was discovered that her skull was missing, he accused MacLean of treachery and sent a ship to capture him and recover the treasure. Luckily for the line of the MacLeans of Duart, the Spaniards failed to catch him. There have been many attempts to salvage the wreck of the *Florencia*, notably a determined effort by the Duke of Argyll, helped by the Royal Navy, but the ship is buried under thirty feet of clay and until underwater exploration techniques are improved that is where she will stay.

The waitresses in the café were talking excitedly about one of the crew of the racing fleet they had taken a fancy to, and when I heard that all the boats would be returning to Tobermory that evening it was an incentive to leave and at 4.30pm we let go the mooring and, assisted by an obliging breeze from the west, reached across the Sound and past the menacing Stirk rocks, unmarked and awash at high water, and by Auliston Point on Morvern into spectacular Loch Sunart. There were several yachts heading in the same direction, though I was relieved when they made for the entrance of Loch Drumbuie, one of the most perfectly sheltered anchorages imaginable and it attracts cruising yachts like moths to a candle. Our destination was further down the Loch in a sheltered bay where, having secured *Amulet* to Sandy's mooring, we were whisked by Landrover to the house and the pleasure of Liz's venison casserole. After weeks on *Amulet*, it was sheer luxury to relax in the comfort of an armchair and spend an evening with interesting people, and we made rather a large dent in Sandy's whisky supply. The time went by all too quickly and, hoping for an early start to climb Ben Resipol, six miles down the loch, we very reluctantly returned to the boat. It was going dark and the sky was clear and the air still, but the late weather bulletin was depressing and forecast rain with a fresh to strong wind.

The mountains of western Scotland often confound the space age technology of the weather gurus and upset predictions, but for once the forecast was right and I woke next morning to the sound of rain pattering on the cabin top. When I looked out, cloud level was down to about 300feet. There was a light wind, and as the tide was flooding up the loch we decided to go with it in the faint hope that the met. man had got his calculations wrong and the cloud would clear away and give us a good day on Resipol. Had the glacial action that created this area been less active, the great peninsulas of Morvern and Ardnamurchan might have been joined together, but a final mighty heave separated them for all time with a seventeen mile long narrow sea loch the locals called Sunart. The glacial heave deposited three islands at the mouth of the loch, deeply indented Oronsay that neatly forms one side of the anchorage of Drumbuie, flat and insignificant Risga, and a high heather-covered beauty called Carna. The islands and the high hills on either side of the loch play havoc with wind direction and strength and though the wind was fitful when we set off, it was blowing a good fifteen knots when we rounded Carna and we variously ran and reached down the loch and anchored in the pretty bay of Garbh Eilean at the foot of Ben Resipol. The cloud had hardly moved and Ben Resipol was hidden in a great mound of dirty cotton wool that cascaded water over us. It wasn't a day for the hills nor for comfortable sailing, but perfect for what old Brab Davies used to refer to as 'festerin', sitting below with the cabin stove blasting out heat and drinking mugs of tea. We added 'a good book' to Brab's essentials and lay back on our bunks and read for a few hours. Liz had invited us to supper and when in the afternoon a rising wind moaning through the rigging reminded us that we had to get back down the loch, we left the shelter of the bay under full sail and immediately a gust of wind knocked *Amulet* over on her ear and water slopped into the cockpit. We tore across the loch like a demon but it was so difficult to steer we hove to and put two reefs in the main. Compressed by the hills, the wind was lashing into us with vicious squalls and attempting to beat to windward just smothered us in a welter of foaming water. There was no joy in it, and in the lea of a headland we downed sail and started the engine. Icy water still crashed over us when *Amulet* fell into the troughs, but at least we were upright and we plugged into it until we almost reached Carna, where to our relief the wind eased and we picked up Sandy's mooring, very wet and cold but very elated. Liz's offer of hot baths at the house was too much to resist, and with frozen limbs thawed out and warm and dry in fresh clothes, we sat down to another super meal and further increased the dent in Sandy's whisky supply. The weather forecast gave no hint of a return of the warm weather but promised light winds from the south. It was just what we needed to get round Ardnamurchan Point and, eager to make an early start, we left Sandy and Liz with our heartfelt thanks for their warm hospitality, and went back to *Amulet*. Tomorrow we would be on our way to the Hebrides.

The sadistic alarm clock roused us at 7am and with sails drawing well we eased out of the bay in very murky conditions of mist and drizzle. The coast of Ardnamurchan was barely visible and the Mull coast completely hidden but, keeping a sharp look-out for fishing boats, we made good progress past Kilchoan. At 9.30am I got a bearing on Ardmore light on Mull, but the wind increased and became very squally and an hour later it had veered to the west and increased to force 5 (20 knots). To take the sting out of the squalls we hove to and put two reefs in the main, but with wind against tide it kicked up a nasty sea and I knew that the nearer we sailed to Ardnamurchan Point the worse it would get. When I met Patricia's eyes under the dripping hood of her waterproofs we were thinking the same thing, "Let's turn back while we can!" I had got beyond the challenges of macho youth when I revelled in long thrashes to windward in rough seas, and shared Patricia's view that sailing had to be fun or there was no point to it. She clambered forward and dropped the main and under working jib, helped by the engine to push against the tide, we slowly made our way back down the Sound and, not wanting to impose on Sandy and Liz again, we steered for Loch Drumbuie. Leaving rough water and going through the narrow rocky entrance into an anchorage where there was hardly a breath of wind was like entering a lost world and, enormously thankful, we dropped anchor under a headland and devoured hot bacon sandwiches washed down with coffee and a large tot of rum. It was early afternoon, and though still raining slightly it was pleasant enough for a walk and, inflating the dinghy, we went ashore, joining an ancient right of way that starts at Loch Aline and in its day had been an important link between Morvern and Ardnamurchan. We followed it a mile or so to Dorlinn, a calling point for a ferry that was once rowed across Loch Sunart, and the entrance to a rock-strewn channel leading into the hidden grandeur of Loch Teacuis. The scenery was magnificent, straight from a Landseer painting, though the stags were missing. There were plenty of heaps of dung revealing that they were around, but they kept themselves well hidden. On the way back to *Amulet* we rowed the dinghy round Drumbuie to take photographs and have a closer look at a handsome wooden ketch, anchored close inshore.

Having been duped by what turned out to be a very inaccurate forecast, I didn't believe the man giving the late night weather bulletin. He was right about heavy rain, it battered on the cabin roof all night and kept me awake, but he had said it would turn to sunny weather and, when I stuck my head out of the hatch at breakfast time, it was obvious the prediction was just another of his little jokes. It was a dull Highland morning, flat calm, continuous drizzle and very poor visibility. I stayed in the warmth of my sleeping bag and studied my charts. One of the pleasures of poring over charts is that the sun is always shining, the sea kindly and the wind favourable, and at a glance you can travel long distances or pick a way through a maze of submerged rocks with ease. My little game of fantasy was interrupted by Patricia shouting from the deck, "Come and look, it's stopped raining and the mist is clearing away." The ship's clock said 11.45am, the met. man was right after all, and there was still enough of the flood to help us along the twelve miles to Ardnamurchan Point. Shafts of sunlight were already mopping up the wet mist when we scrambled to raise the anchor and, by the time we had pumped the bilge, eighteen strokes, cleared Drumbuie and were heading at a fast lick up the Sound, the sun had lifted to the hill tops and the horizon was clear to the Island of Coll, twenty miles away. Patricia went below and re-appeared a few minutes later with a plate of egg sandwiches, and it wasn't until I had hungrily swallowed one that I was aware it reeked of paraffin. Somehow, while filling the stove tank she had spilt paraffin on the galley worktop, and the sandwich bread had conveniently soaked it up. It provoked an immediate reaction in my gut and the discharge of paraffin-charged gas was so lethal I was afraid that each time I passed wind I might set off an explosion and blow a hole in the side of the boat. I tried drinking strong coffee and eating chocolate, and even sucked a lemon, but I could not get rid of the taste of paraffin. I only temporarily forgot about it when the wooden ketch that had been anchored in Drumbuie overtook us at full speed and went across our bow so close I had to go full astern to avoid a collision. The idiot at the wheel gave a limp wave of apology, though it might have been an acknowledgement of the words I called him, and the ketch made off to the west. At 3pm we were abeam of the tall granite tower of Ardnamurchan lighthouse. Tourist brochures will tell you that Ardnamurchan is Gaelic for the Point of the Great Ocean, the tower is 118 feet (36 metres) high, it stands on a 60 foot (18 metre) cliff and that it is the most westerly point on the UK mainland, reaching into the Atlantic twenty-three miles further than Land's End. Sadly, the light is now automatic, the keepers' houses are holiday homes, and the engine room a heritage centre; but I can never pass its grey granite tower without it bringing back memories of when I was a young keeper there. At that time there were only two of us manning it and the one in charge used to have fits of madness and stand right on the top of the tower, nearly two hundred feet above the sea hanging on to the weather vane and howling at the moon. He would let out blood-curdling screams that echoed up the inside of the tower, and regularly threatened me with a knife. Once he deliberately stamped on my fingers while I was clinging to a metal ladder with one hand while painting the dome with the other. There were no safety harnesses in those days and, had I not been a keen mountaineer and rock climber and used my slings and karabiners to clip myself on to something secure whilst working aloft on the tower, I would have plunged into the sea. Scared out of my wits by this maniac, I used to do my watch at night armed with a loaded deerstalking rifle. During the day he seemed normal, and no one would believe what he was like when darkness came, least of all the Commissioners of Northern Lights in Edinburgh. He had the same status as a ship's captain and was beyond the condemnation of subordinates.

A puff of wind tempted us into hoisting the main and genoa, but it died away as quickly as it came and though we drifted round the Point with the tide, it was clear that the only way we would reach an anchorage before nightfall would be with the help of the engine. One of the few joys of being a lighthouse keeper at Ardnamurchan was the incredible view of what are known jokingly as the 'cocktail islands', Rum, Eigg, and Muck, and seen across an expanse of rolling blue sea from the cockpit of *Amulet*, they looked magnificent. Muck, the nearest to Ardnamurchan and the smallest of the three, is fascinating to explore, and the MacEwen family, the resident owners, are very welcoming; But I wanted to climb the Sgurr, a vast prominence that dominates the skyline of the island of Eigg. There was a sizeable swell between the Point and the isle of Muck, and we climbed up and surfed down watery hills, passing the large ketch *Renaissance* on the way, and at 6.15pm dropped anchor close to the diving and survey boat *Ocean Bounty*, in the south east corner of Eigg, where the detached lump of Castle Island helps to form a small bay, horribly exposed to the south but tenable in settled weather. Sitting in the cockpit after dinner with a dram and observing a large black expanse of cloud advancing from the south, I began to doubt whether anchoring at Eigg had been a wise move, but there had been nothing alarming in Oban coastguard's evening weather bulletin. Even so, an uneasy swell crept into the bay in the evening and *Amulet* leapt about on her anchor chain like a fish on the end of a line, and the distant mournful sound of the foghorn at Ardnamurchan lighthouse moaning its warning was a sure indication that visibility had closed in and yet another weather front was approaching.

Staring miserably at it through the cabin window the next morning, it wasn't so much a change as just more of what had plagued us on and off for days, continuous rain and poor visibility. The *Ocean Bounty* was barely visible a few yards away, let alone the Sgurr of Eigg. Hill walking was definitely out, and so was another day at anchor. The swell made life on board very uncomfortable and, tired of juggling with airborne pieces of breakfast toast and hanging on to mugs of coffee, we heaved anchor, and with the aid of the trusty GPS felt our way round Castle Island and were greeted by a useful breeze that sprang up from the south. It was raining steadily but we were in good spirits, and with main and working jib spread out we ran up the side of Eigg, keeping about half a mile offshore. Moving through the water at four knots and with a two knot tide under us, it didn't take long to sail the five miles to the northern tip of the island, where our arrival coincided with a rapid improvement in the visibility when the grey mist curtain rolled aside and revealed the breathtaking panorama of the sharp peaks of the island of Rum and the even more stupendous mountain backdrop of the Cuillins of the Isle of Skye. I set a course for Loch Scresort, an inlet on the east side of Rum and about six miles from Eigg, but the wind died and left us wallowing and it was the Farymann that pushed *Amulet* across the top of the Sound of Rum, occasionally scattering flocks of Manx shearwater that had gathered in great rafts on the sea. We motored into Loch Scresort and anchored well seaward of a stone quay that dried at low water, and well away from construction work that was going on to build a jetty to accommodate roll-on/roll-off ferries. Scresort would never win an award for the most sheltered anchorage in the west and keelboat sailors have to be careful - the loch dries out a long way - but it was a vast improvement on Eigg and had a view of the great mansion of Kinloch Castle that sent Patricia into raptures.

A 19th century visitor called Rum 'the wildest and most repulsive of all islands', and wild it is; but as for being repulsive, the man must have seen it from the deck of a ferry on a wild, wet day when torrents of water were pouring down the hillsides and the summits were swathed in black cloud. It's a lovely island, at least that's what John Bullough, a Lancashire industrialist thought when he bought it in 1886; and his son George, when he inherited it, built himself a castle from red sandstone imported from the island of Arran, and created gardens with soil brought in from Ayrshire. George loved his island but wanted it for himself, and banned all curious visitors from landing. Intrigued by the 'forbidden island', I paddled over in a canoe from Glen Brittle in Skye when I was in my teens, landed next to the old stone quay, and found myself staring into the barrel of a rifle held by a stalker who threatened to blow my head off, "If you put as much as the nail of your toe on Sir

George's land." Happily, Highland hospitality got the better of him and he took me to his cottage and gave me tea and scones. Rum was bought by the Nature Conservancy Council in the 1950s, and later taken over by Scottish National Heritage (SNH), and though the island is now in the grip of intractable bureaucracy it is at least, subject to a few restrictions like no dogs or bikes, open to visitors. Threatening the island with neither dogs nor bikes, we inflated the dinghy and went ashore to boost the local shop's takings with the purchase of a handful of postcards and a few groceries. The lady running the shop was surprisingly terse and unhelpful and, as we wandered round the grounds of the castle, SNH staff walked by without a word and I found it most unsettling. When Sir George's widow sold the island it included the castle, fully furnished with all her husband's curiosities collected from all over the world; and, like so many owners of grand houses, the Scottish National Heritage leased it for use as a hotel. Patricia tried to book an evening meal for us but was told that it was not possible, as the castle had been taken over for a conference of international geologists. The delegates arrived on a MacBrayne ferry from Mallaig as we rowed back to *Amulet*, and we watched the captain deftly manoeuvre his ship while group after group of intense-looking scientists and their baggage were unceremoniously lowered into the island motor boat and ferried ashore. On the completion of the new Ro-Ro jetty, future high-powered delegates will arrive on Rum with no more loss of dignity than it would take for them to walk down the ship's gangplank, but it will be the end of a romantic part of island life that has gone on for centuries. The Manx shearwater we had startled on our way to Rum were truly fascinating seabirds who flew inland every night and nested in huge underground burrows near the summit of Hallival, a 2333 feet, (718 metre) peak close to the loch. Keen to take photographs of them, we planned to climb it the following day and, getting out the ordnance survey map of the island and leaving our boots and rucksacks at the ready, we turned in early to catch up on lost sleep.

It was terribly disappointing when I looked out at 7am on a wet morning and saw that all the hills were shrouded in thick cloud that reached down almost to the edge of the loch; but though we had to ditch the plan to climb Hallival, we were determined to have a walk and set off in drizzly rain for Kilmory, a deserted settlement in a bay about

five miles from Scresort on the north side of Rum. The glens teemed
with red deer and, with stags so tame they walked up to us, there were
plenty of photo opportunities. Set in a sheltered bay with interesting
cliffs, a lovely beach and a great view of Skye, Kilmory had once been a
thriving community, but there was an air of sadness about it not helped
by a headstone in the tiny graveyard that revealed the appalling
suffering of the Matheson family who, within three days in 1873, lost
five of their children to diphtheria. Such an awful tragedy, surrounded
by so much beauty. It was an eerie place, and leaving it to the ghosts we
returned along the track to Scresort in thick drizzle and warm, humid
conditions, and among the trees by Kinloch Castle walked right into
the fearsome embraces of a native Scot, hated by Tourist Boards and
renowned and feared throughout the world.

"The midge in Scotland," thundered Sir Alexander McGregor, "may
not be a carrier of infection, but its biting properties make it a serious
source of irritation both to the Scottish people themselves and to the
many tourists who visit our beauty spots." Sir Alex was the chairman of
a scientific advisory committee set up way back in 1944 by the
Department of Health for Scotland to see what could be done to
combat the midge menace and to produce a midge repellent. The
setting up of the committee was the first shot in a battle against the
Scottish midge that has raged for almost sixty years, and though
scientists have since put men on the moon, explored the depths of the
deepest ocean and invented a little box that can work out the position
of a yacht to within a metre, they are no nearer to finding a means of
controlling the midge. John Hirst, after visiting Skye in 1919, advised:

> "Climbers who would go to Skye
> where midge may bite and sun may broil
> ere you set forth, be sure to buy
> a well-corked bottle labelled "Oil, of Citronella."

The scientists ignored this advice and, urged on by the Scottish
Tourist Board, concocted their own potion which they claimed was
effective and tested it on forestry workers, anglers, road workers and
schoolchildren throughout the Highlands. But it was only temporary
respite from the hordes and the nasty, aggressive Calicoides Impunctatas

and the other fourteen species of biting midge developed a taste for it, gobbled it up as if it were an aphrodisiac, and went forth and multiplied. Individually the midge is minute, but in swarms of thousands it is a monster that has caused schools to close, farm work to be halted, animals to collapse with exhaustion, forestry workers to be driven from woods and military establishments to be abandoned. The great universities of Scotland have devoted their might to finding a way of interrupting the breeding cycle and so rid the country of the pestilence - it is said that some have even studied the Bible for guidance - but verily, he that taketh on the task of midge castrator will surely needeth exceptionally good eyesight.

We arrived back on *Amulet* smarting from midge bites and gasping with thirst, and the first bottle of lager retrieved from the cool depths of the bilge hardly touched the sides of my throat and it required another before parched thirst buds were relieved. Antihistamine cream soothed the burning sensation of the bites, but Rum had left its mark on us in a variety of ways and we were both keen to move on. The weather pattern seemed to have got into the habit of clearing up in the afternoon and when, at 4pm, the rain stopped, the mist cleared away and left behind clear skies and a fair wind, we hoisted sail, left Loch Scresort behind, and had a most enjoyable sail across twelve miles of gentle swell to Loch na Cuilce, an almost hidden pool at the head of Loch Scavaig. All the way from Rum the awe-inspiring backdrop of the truly savage rocky skyline of the Cuillins grew larger and larger as we sailed towards Skye and, when we lowered the sails beneath near-vertical crags reaching a thousand feet above us and motored cautiously through the tight rock-strewn entrance of the pool, it felt as if we were entering the lair of a mountain king. Anchored in the middle of the pool, we sat in the cockpit with mugs of coffee and marvelled at the mountains and a tremendous waterfall crashing down the cliffs into the loch. Loch na Cuilce has been described as the most spectacular anchorage in Europe, and it is not an exaggeration. It is an anchorage that has to be experienced to be fully appreciated, though it is certainly not a place to arrive at and discover you have run out of tea. It is extremely remote and in the days before yachts had engines, 'yotters' could find themselves embayed for weeks and run seriously short of food if the wind blew from the south with any strength.

Unfortunately, many of what were once little-known and remote anchorages in the west of Scotland are now on the 'must visit' list of the hordes of charter boats, and just when we were hoping we would have a peaceful night, the first one announced its arrival by hitting one of the submerged rocks at the entrance with an almighty crash that echoed round the crags. It was followed by no less than nine other boats that managed to avoid the rock but got themselves into a frantic tangle trying to decide where to anchor. They dropped their anchors without thinking about swinging room, collided with each other, then with a whine of electric winches up would come the anchors and they dashed to another part of the pool and did the same all over again. We felt as if we were squatting in the middle of a fairground ring while dodgem cars crashed into each other all around us. Finally two boats managed to get their anchors on the bottom and the rest gave up trying and rafted alongside. It seemed to be a school party of teenagers, and a very liberated one at that. When the dinghies were inflated, several hardy lads and girls rowed across to the waterfall, stripped to their skins, and splashed around in the torrents. It was all-revealing, but very likely a shrewd move by the teachers. They could sip their gin and tonics on board confident that the freezing water splashing around the boys' masculine bits would inhibit their interest in the girls' feminine bits, the school's reputation would be unblemished, and it would feature high in the government's league table of achievers with an exceptionally high pass rate in GCE Anatomy!

The high mountain range of Skye, which all but surrounded our anchorage, was the Cuillins, which learned men say is from the Norse 'Kjollen', meaning keel-shaped ridges; though the name was interpreted with rather less reverence by a wag who famously wrote in a hotel visitors' book, 'The mountains of the Isle of Skye are cool-in spring and seldom dry'. His cry of despair could easily have applied to the month of July as well for, during the night, the temperature dipped to teeth-chattering level and torrential rain beat a tattoo on the cabin roof as if the Norse gods were practising for a drum festival. It was an intimidating scene when I slid back the hatch at 8am. Water was cascading down the crags in thunderous torrents and, buffeted by downdrafts of wind from the hidden mountain tops, streamers of greyish-black cloud were twisting and swirling around the bowl of the tiny loch like tormented souls suspended above a witch's cauldron. *Amulet* was snatching at her anchor chain as if aware of the chilling warning in the Pilot Book, and in a hurry to be off. The most spectacular anchorage in Europe it may have been, but Loch Na Cuilce had an evil reputation for sudden and violent squalls that drove clouds of foam before them with a roar like thunder and with such a force it could knock a boat over and drag its anchor. I looked across at the two rafts of five boats swinging innocently to their single anchors and hoped that the mountain king would spare them his fury.

Many of the world's greatest landscape painters and poets used to come by boat to this remote corner of Skye, but their pilgrimage took them beyond our anchorage and up a short steep climb to the hidden magnificence of Loch Coruisk. One and a half miles long and enclosed in a horseshoe of incredibly steep mountains, it is one of the most stunning and dramatic settings of any fresh water loch in Scotland and ironically, apart from a strenuous trek along a coastal path or through the mountains, it can only be reached from the sea. I had walked round Coruisk many times, marvelling at its beauty, and wanted to take Patricia, but it was raining heavily when we rowed ashore from *Amulet* and climbed the path to a viewpoint that appears on countless calendars and picture postcards of Skye. Having reached the same viewpoint, the writer and poet Sir Walter Scott wrote scathingly that Coruisk had 'No tree, nor shrub, nor plant, nor flower, nor aught of vegetative power,' but maybe, like ours, his view was blotted out by a vast curtain of rain sweeping across the loch. I had enthused about Coruisk to Patricia and it was terribly disappointing that she could not see it in all its beauty, but she was game to walk round its shore and we squelched through bogs and waded across streams hoping for a miracle that would bring the sun. But we were out of luck. The bogs got deeper and the streams wider, our boots filled with water and the driving rain hammered into our so-called 'waterproof' anoraks and over-trousers with such force we were soon soaked to the skin. We had hardly covered a mile, but there was no pleasure in walking in such appalling conditions and we returned to *Amulet*, flung our wet clothes into the forecabin and thawed out in our sleeping bags, helped by hot coffee and a giant tot of rum.

The school convoy had departed and we had the anchorage to

ourselves, but the evening brought two more charter boats with another display of panic-stricken shouting and several dummy runs before they succeeded in attaching the anchors to the bottom. A few minutes later a very smart motor yacht came in and, with a rattle of chain and a touch astern on the engines, gave a very practised display of how it should be done. The Coastguard weather bulletin put out a strong wind warning for an area to the south of us, but the 'Caledonia' forecast was for light winds in the morning, when we planned to set off for Loch Nevis, and increasing to force 5 from the west in the afternoon, when, hopefully, we would be safely at anchor. We turned in with the intention of making an early start.

It was flat calm and raining gently when I got out of my bunk at 6.30am, but the cloud had lifted and was spread across the mountain peaks. It took only twenty strokes to pump the bilge out, which was cheering. Though I had never been able to trace the source of the leak, at least it was not getting worse, and pumping out night and morning had become routine. We cleared the anchorage at 8.30am and, watched by a few curious seals and a row of impassive cormorants on the tiny islet of En Reamhar, we hoisted sail and in a very light wind cruised past Soay, a flat shrub-covered island assured of a place in history for being the home of the breed of sheep of the same name and the base of a one-time shark fishing enterprise run by the island's then owner, the author Gavin Maxwell, and his charismatic partner, Joe (Tex) Geddes. It also had one of the few harbours in the west of Scotland with a tidal bar at the entrance.

Away from the protection of Soay, and on course for the Point of Sleat, ten miles away, we found a good westerly breeze that bowled us along at 5 knots in a lumpy sea for an hour until, pushed by a nasty-looking bank of black cloud, it increased to force 5 and heaped the seas up with it. We were on a reach and absolutely tearing along on the starboard tack, and though *Amulet* was now over canvassed and difficult to steer, I hung on, enjoying the excitement of a fast keelboat surging through the water at maximum speed. A mile or so past the Point of Sleat we needed to change course to go up the Sound of Sleat but, each time I attempted to go about a big sea hit *Amulet*'s bow and stopped her dead, and backing the jib was no help. The only solution was to jibe, and gritting my teeth I waited for a 'smooth', then calling to

Patricia to haul in the mainsheet, I heaved the helm up. A sea lifted *Amulet*'s stern and swung her round, and instantly the wind snatched the mainsail and flung the boom across the boat like a missile, tearing the main sheet through Patricia's hands as it went. It hit the shrouds with a tremendous crash and for a moment I thought the mast would go, but the stout galvanised rigging withstood the impact and on the port tack we raced up the Sound until the massive bulk of the Sleat Peninsula gave us a lea and the wind eased to a light breeze. We were off the entrance to the busy harbour of Mallaig when a MacBrayne ferry came charging out and made straight for us. Having served for a short time on the bridge of a coasting freighter, I could well understand that, during the summer months when there are more yachts bobbing up and down on the sea than there are gulls, it must at times be very frustrating for the captain of a ferry with a course and a time schedule to maintain and I always gave them a wide berth; but though he could easily have gone round our stern, he came straight for us and I had to make a hurried jibe to get out of his way. I had an urge to call the captain on the VHF and ask him what the hell he was playing at, but I knew he wouldn't answer. He would be well aware of the Highland saying:-

> The earth belongs unto the Lord
> And all that it contains
> Except the Scottish Western Isles
> And they belong to McBraynes.

Off the wide entrance to Loch Nevis, the wind died completely and I started the engine and motored into the loch, past the welcoming outstretched arms of a huge white statue of an angel standing on a headland, and anchored off Glaschcoille House on the north west side of Inverie Bay at 2pm. It was a suntrap and with our saturated hill walking clothes and boots spread out on the deck to dry, we relaxed in the cockpit. It was good to be back on Knoydart estate; I had known it for years and it held many happy memories.

The Anchor Drags - A Dinghy With Legs - Rolling To Canna

Knoydart is a strikingly beautiful mountainous peninsula jutting out from the Scottish mainland into the Sound of Sleat and bounded by the dramatic fiords of Loch Nevis, (the loch of Heaven) on its southern shore and Loch Hourn, (the loch of Hell) to the north. It is often described as 'the last great wilderness' but how an area that teems with deer and is the home of eagles, wildcats and all manner of wildlife and is carpeted with vegetation, qualifies as a wilderness I have never been able to figure out. Wild and sparsely habited country it certainly is, and that it is only accessible along rough tracks or from the sea has helped to keep it that way through many centuries. I first discovered it in the 1950s when I went to live not far away and canoed across Loch Hourn to climb the Knoydart hills and was so captivated I returned regularly for many years under sail, on foot and even on horseback. Like most Highland estates, its complex and turbulent history is well sprinkled with blood and treachery and in more modern times a strong whiff of intrigue. The laird's 'big house' and the estate workers cottages formed the tiny hamlet of Inverie on Loch Nevis and in the hands of successive owners, who all left their own particular mark, the estate had been run with varying degrees of success. It was an owner with deeply religious convictions who had the statue of the angel with outstretched arms placed on the headland at the entrance to the Loch, though when I was researching for a book about Knoydart and asked a local about it he was obviously not of the same persuasion. "Och, it's an angel with its arms outstretched," he exclaimed scornfully. "But I don't know whether it's blessing the Loch or telling us about the fish that got away."

In 1948 a handful of crofters seized land from the then proprietor, Lord Brocket, but were forced to give it up when the court ruled that the estate would only survive as a single unit. Ironically, and much to the horror and despair of many of the old workers, the estate changed hands in the 1990s and was sold piecemeal to many different buyers. It was a sad end for the old Knoydart estate but a new beginning for cruising yachtsfolk. The village pub was bought by an enterprising couple who laid a string of visitors' moorings off Inverie pier, offered meals and showers, and put Knoydart very much on the cruising map. It was with a meal and a shower in mind that Patricia wanted to walk the mile or so round the bay to Inverie and we inflated the dinghy and went ashore. I wasn't very happy about leaving *Amulet* anchored at Glaschoille as the bottom was thick kelp and notoriously bad holding ground but the conditions were settled and we set off and enjoyed the pleasant walk to the pub. The worst thing about returning to a place you have known and loved after a long absence is that the changes are often unbearable. Old estate shepherds I had known had gone to the graveyard and their cottages had taken on the dreary unlived in appearance of a holiday home, the little church had been converted to a house, the 'big house' looked tatty and neglected and the only face I recognised was a man who used to look after the laird's motor cruiser. "Och, its all change here since the Major sold up," he said sadly when I asked him what life was like under the new management. "The incomers are putting new life into the old place, right enough, but I liked it the way it was." The visitors' moorings were full of boats and when we stuck our heads round the door of the pub and saw it was crowded we went along the road to a nearby café where a friendly girl served us with tea and fresh scones with jam. Through the window I could see that a fresh westerly breeze had sprung up and the boats were straining at their moorings. "It's a shame to waste that wind," I said to Patricia. "Instead of spending the night at Glaschoille let's sail down the Loch to Tarbet, it a lovely little anchorage and we can walk over the hills to Loch Morar." Patricia was all for it and we went back round the bay at a fast walk. As we neared Glaschoille I could see that *Amulet* had dragged her anchor but when I got a transit on two trees I realised to my horror she had not only dragged anchor but was drifting out into the Loch. Yelling at Patricia to hurry we ran for all we were worth to the dinghy and dragged it down the shore to the water. I rowed like fury but had only gone a short distance when both rowlocks snapped with the strain and we each took an oar and using it as a paddle drove the dinghy in pursuit of the fast retreating blue hull. The effort was exhausting but we dare not slow the pace and ignoring aching arms and cramped muscles we forced ourselves to keep going. Each weary splash of the paddles brought us nearer and nearer to *Amulet* until with a final heave I managed to grab the gunwale and clung on gasping for breath. Twenty fathoms of chain and a heavy anchor were hanging vertically from the stem and, already worn out from the effort of paddling, it took us a long time to haul it aboard and chop an absolute wad of thick rubbery kelp off the anchor. We narrowly avoided a disaster and I was angry with myself for allowing it to happen. I knew it was poor holding ground and even though I had let out plenty of chain I should have put out a kedge before leaving the boat unattended, but it is always easy to be wise after the event. It had been a nasty shock and it wasn't over. When I started the engine the ignition light stayed on, a sign that the charging problem had flared up again. I was too weary to fiddle with it and in any case Patricia had hoisted the sails and with a lively force 4 on the quarter we creamed across Inverie Bay and in less than an hour we had covered the five miles down Loch Nevis to the tiny horseshoe-shaped inlet of Tarbet and anchored close inshore. Flanked by steep hillsides the anchorage was completely protected, and though the surface of the Loch was covered with white caps, inside the bay there was hardly a breath of wind and after a meal we sat in the cockpit soaking up the evening sun. It had been an eventful day and when the sun dipped behind the hills I needed no persuading to get into my bunk.

The sun rose the next morning in a cloudless blue sky and spread a shimmer of gold over the bay and the surrounding hills and it was dazzlingly beautiful. When Patricia had finished hanging wet anoraks, boots and clothing in the rigging to dry, *Amulet* looked rather like one of the family-owned Chinese junks I had seen plying up and down the Yangtse river, always with long lines of multi-coloured shirts and underwear fluttering from the mast and when the lovely old ferry, the *Western Isles*, came into the bay some of the crowd on deck must have thought so as well and photographed us from every angle. The *Western Isles* discharged a few passengers in the time-honoured manner of taking them ashore in a small dinghy, and in the days when Tarbet boasted the most isolated post office in the UK they would have delivered a mail sack as well, but times had changed.

Turning my attention to finding out why the ignition light would not go out when the engine was running, I discovered that the wires from the alternator had completely sheared off due to engine vibration and, hidden behind the starter motor, the two ends protruding through the flywheel housing were incredibly difficult to reach. With the aid of the portable generator and an electric soldering iron, and with sweat pouring off me with the effort, I felt like a bomb disposal expert as I very carefully lowered the hot soldering iron down to the broken wires and with more luck than skill managed to apply solder and attach a length of wire to each of the two ends. What a relief when I started the engine and the ignition light went out; the alternator was charging again. To celebrate we took a picnic lunch in a rucksack, paddled ashore in the dinghy and followed a stony track that climbed high above Tarbet before it descended to Loch Morar, which at over 1,000 feet claimed the honour of being the deepest loch in Scotland. During the 1939/45 war when a large part of the west of Scotland was used as a training ground for commandos, miniature submarine crews and special forces, Morar had the unique distinction of being the training base of espionage groups and it was from there that incredibly brave people like Odette and Peter Churchill were sent behind enemy lines. An epoch now just a distant memory and the people involved all but forgotten.

To get a view of both Loch Morar and Loch Nevis, we climbed a hill above the track and from the summit gazed in rapture at the endless panorama of mountain ranges. Far below in Tarbet bay the sun glinted on *Amulet*'s varnished mast and two yachts with white sails lay motionless on Loch Nevis. It was a perfect day for 'festerin' and the west of Scotland was looking at its best. There was nowhere else on earth to equal it.

Warmed by the sun and thoroughly happy, we made our way back down the track and reached Tarbet just as a few of the new breed of young 'locals' were moving a small flock of sheep. One of them managed to grunt a response to our greetings but there was a distinct feeling that we were not welcome, and it was so uncharacteristic of the native highlanders I had known who lived in the remote communities I felt as if I were in a foreign country. After such a pleasant, warm day, the Coastguard weather bulletin was disappointingly gloomy and gave a strong wind warning for our area. At Tarbet we would be sheltered from it so decided to stay another night, and while I repaired the broken rowlocks on the dinghy Patricia commandeered the galley and prepared a gastronomic anonymity she claimed were salmon fish cakes. During the evening I was surprised to hear Robin Shaw calling me on the VHF and though he was very faint I was able to make contact and, when I learnt he was on a mooring at Armadale on Skye, we arranged to meet up the following day.

During the night the wind moaned over the hills above Tarbet but *Amulet* hardly moved, and though the morning dawned rather dull and overcast it was fine and warm and a gentle breeze wafted us out into the loch at 8.30am. But as soon as we cleared the shelter of the headlands the breeze rapidly increased to force 5 and we had an exhilarating sail up the loch with *Amulet* showing a large expanse of keel and Patricia and me with feet firmly braced against the cockpit coaming watching green water rushing past our toe caps. We lost the wind in the lea of the hills at the entrance to the loch until the ebb carried us out into open water off Mallaig and we found it again. It had dropped to a light breeze and it started to rain, but we sailed on and at 10am arrived at Armadale and picked up a visitor's mooring ahead of *Souple Jade*. The saloon of Robin and Celia's boat seemed like a ballroom after the confines of *Amulet* and we lingered over coffee and conversation until Patricia reminded me that we needed to go ashore and stock up on groceries.

At the ferry terminal, surrounded by camera-clicking Japanese tourists and an American couple visibly overcome with emotion, a kilted piper was greeting the incoming passengers with a melancholy rendering of the Skye Boat Song. A song that stirs patriotic fervour amongst Highlanders and on the repertoire of singers of Scottish songs the world over, it is often used as atmospheric background music in Highland Tourist Board information offices, though oddly enough the song was written by an Englishman, Sir Harold Boulton, in 1884.

"Speed bonny boat, like a bird on the wing,
   Onward," the sailors cry.
"Carry the lad that's born to be King
   Over the sea to Skye."

It is a very plaintive song, but some accuse it of being over sentimental and associated with the popular romantic myth about a young and beautiful girl, Flora MacDonald, who was in love with Bonnie Prince Charlie and with only minutes to spare before the English soldiers captured him, she braved storm and tempest in a tiny boat and, single-handed, sailed her exhausted Prince over to Skye when he was on the run after the disastrous Jacobite Rebellion of 1745. Hollywood film directors might like to see it that way, but they would be as far from the truth as Skye is from California. The brave 24 year old Flora MacDonald certainly met the fleeing Prince near her home on South Uist in the Outer Hebrides, and to get him away before the English soldiers closed in she agreed to cross to Skye on the pretence of returning to her mother who was living at Armadale and take the Prince with her disguised as her maid. The open boat carrying the party sailed from Rossinish on Benbecula, but when they were close to the coast of Skye they were caught out in bad weather and also fired on by troops on the shore. They struggled on and finally landed in Kilbride Bay on Loch Snizort, where the Prince was hidden on the beach before walking with a trusted guide to Portree. Flora made the journey on horseback and they met up again at an inn in Portree, where they parted, and the Prince was taken by boat to the island of Raasay. Some say he gave her a lock of his hair, others argue it was the garters from the maid's clothing he wore as a disguise; but, as ever, historians squabble over the details. Flora was later captured and it is generally believed she spent a night or two in Dunstaffnage Castle, (close to the marina,) before being taken to London and later released. She returned to Skye, married and had seven children, gave Johnson and Boswell dinner, bed and breakfast on their tour of the Hebrides and, when she died in 1790 at the age of sixty eight, she was buried at Kilmuir not far from where she landed with the Prince. For fear of endangering her friends and family, it was only reluctantly that Flora MacDonald risked her life to save the Prince and, were it not that her stepfather used his influence to save her from the sadistic naval captain who captured her, the story might have had a very different end. But the popular legend lives on.

A well-filled shop at Ardvasar village, a mile or so from Armadale, provided all the groceries Patricia wanted and we went back to *Amulet* to have lunch and write postcards. It was still raining heavily, but I was keen to leave and sail the ten miles or so up the Sound of Sleat to Isleornsay, where there was a good anchorage sheltered from the wind blowing into Armadale, and away from the uncomfortable wash of MacBrayne's ferry that came and went at regular intervals. Warm and cosy by their cabin stove, Robin and Celia were understandably reluctant to stray from it, and we had set off when, through the binoculars, I saw them hoisting sail and following us. To our delight the rain cleared away, and in warm sunshine with a good breeze astern and the main and genoa goose-winging, we rolled our way up the Sound at 5 knots. Abeam of Ornsay lighthouse a huge Norwegian freighter of the LYS Line came up rapidly from astern and I headed for the Knoydart shore to give it a wide berth. We were perhaps fortunate to have kept out of its way; some time later under auto-pilot and with no one keeping watch, it sailed down the Sound of Mull and piled into rocks on Morvern. Robin had caught up and gone ahead of us into Isleornsay bay and was anchored when we entered, and with plenty of room to manoeuvre and a steady wind we tacked up to *Souple Jade*, rounded up smartly, and dropped the hook. It was very satisfying to come up to anchor under sail; my old sailing trawlerman friend Brab Davies would have grunted his approval.

I was quite happy to retain my acquired bodily 'warmth', but Patricia's uncontrollable urge to have a shower and wash her hair when in sniffing distance of civilisation meant I had to inflate the dinghy and run ashore so that she could book the facilities of the Isleornsay Hotel. When the Shaws also declared their intention to pamper their bodies with soap and hot water, I was shamed into making it a foursome - though the eager anticipation of a new experience melted when the ladies made it very clear that 'making it a foursome' only meant sharing the cost! The owners of the hotel were very hospitable and gave us the use of a room with a shower, but when we were all clean, glowing and very hungry and hurried to the bar to order a meal it was crowded, and we waited in agony for an hour before it arrived. It was dark, the sky starry and the bay very peaceful when we rowed back to the boats and, after coffee and a large dram on *Souple Jade*, we turned in well satisfied with an exciting day.

Robin and Celia departed for Mull early the next morning and, with plenty of time to wait for a favourable tide to take us up the Sound of Sleat and through the fast flowing narrow channel of Kyle Rhea into Loch Alsh, Patricia busied herself with various jobs while I did some chart work then took photographs of the island of Ornsay that gave shelter to the bay and, oddly, the name 'Isleornsay' to the community on the mainland. It was a bright and cheerful little place when I took my photographs, but in the 1840s it must have been associated with great sadness when, at the height of the Highland Clearance, brutal lairds and landlords evicted hundreds of crofting families from their homes. Many from Knoydart and the surrounding area were transported to Canada on ships sent to Isleornsay to fill their holds with human cargo. Who knows what mental and physical torment those wretched people endured when young and old, male and female, they were herded with their few pathetic belongings into boats at Isleornsay quay and rowed out to ships waiting at anchor in the bay. John MacKay, an old shepherd on Knoydart, told me that his grandmother remembered how, as a young girl, she stood with her parents on a cliff top on Knoydart and watched the ships sailing out of Isleornsay and down the Sound of Sleat making for the Atlantic, their decks crowded with people. Her father lit a bonfire as a last farewell to family and friends they would never see again. He was allowed to stay because he was a skilled shepherd and was needed to care for the huge flocks of sheep that had been brought in to replace the crofters. There is no need to look beyond the shores of the UK for examples of man's inhumanity to man. Atrocities committed in the Highlands by the conquering army after the rebellion of 1745, and the obscenity of the Highland Clearance in the 19th century, would have been enough to have kept a human rights tribunal going for a long time.

Aware that *Amulet* was probably anchored in the very place where the ships loaded the immigrants rather depressed me, and I suggested to Patricia that instead of waiting at Isleornsay for the tide to change we should go across the Sound and explore a little of Loch Hourn. Always keen to visit new places, she was full of enthusiasm and we heaved anchor and set off on a 'sight-seeing' trip. Seen on a wet day when evil black clouds fill the sky and the mountains turn dark and threatening, the loch of Hell is no misnomer; but seen on a bright, sunny day when the sky and the water are blue and the mountains a patchwork of browns and greens, Loch Hourn is astonishingly beautiful. It was a superb day and *Amulet*'s bow cut a silver vee through the still surface of the loch as we motored slowly past the remote community of Arnisdale, from where I had first canoed over to Knoydart to climb the mighty Ladhar Bheinn, 3448 feet (1061metres). The air was warm and it was so deserted, with not a movement on either the loch or the land, it was difficult to believe that in the 18th century the lower half of Loch Hourn was a major herring fishing base, with a great fleet of boats and 'a multitude of little occasional hovels and tents on the shore for the accommodation of the crews... an unexpected sight at a distance of thirteen miles from the sea, amidst the wildest scene in nature.' The shoals were so vast it was reported that when a boat was rowed on the loch the oars made the herring fly out of the water like flying fish. But one day the silver herring left for good, and with it the boats and the people. The bonanza was finished forever. Nowadays, magical Loch Hourn draws stressed urbanites to its remote holiday homes and adventurous cruising yachts to its hidden anchorages.

We were so mesmerised by the wonderful scenery we forgot the time and, with the engine at full throttle, sped out of the loch and past Sandaig Islands in the Sound of Sleat, the setting for Gavin Maxwell's 'Ring of Bright Water', and on to the narrow entrance to the Kyle Rhea channel. It was here in the days before ferries that drovers from Skye swam their cattle across to the mainland on their way to the markets in the south, but the swim would have had to be timed very carefully. Ebbing or flowing, the tide is squeezed through an opening barely a quarter of a mile wide with a force that sometimes exceeds 8 knots. When we left Loch Hourn I was worried that we might have left it too late but, in the company of three intrepid canoeists, *Amulet* was whizzed through into Loch Alsh on the tail of the flood and, resisting the pull of the bright lights of the bustling town of Kyle of Lochalsh on the mainland, we picked up a visitor's mooring in front of a row of houses at Kyleakin on Skye. A good meal and a nip of malt whisky induced sleep, and not even the ear-blasting racket from a group of lads with a transistor radio working on a car by the houses disturbed it.

Prior to the unprecedented boom in the popularity of sailing, a yacht wanting to tie up at Kyle of Lochalsh had to take its chance among the fleet of fishing boats, but the council have generously provided a visitor's pontoon, and to be on it when the shops opened we motored across early the next morning. The weather had completely changed again and it was very dull, very overcast and very wet. In fact with poor visibility as well it was decidedly miserable; but the shopkeepers and the people of Kyle of Lochalsh made up for it by being friendly and helpful, and the harbourmaster was one of the most obliging officials I had met in a long time. With boats tied up at his fuelling berth taking in diesel by the ton, I felt hesitant about producing two cans and asking for ten gallons, but with a ready smile he left the shelter of his office and turned out in the pouring rain to fill them. The cruise ship *Hebridean Princess* came in while Patricia was away shopping and, having travelled on it many times when it was the MacBrayne ferry *Columba*, I was curious to see what changes the new owners had made. The passengers were disembarking for a coach tour, and when an elderly lady mistook me for one of the crew and asked what time the ship would be leaving again it was an opportunity to have a chat. She was obviously on her own and rather lonely, and told me her husband had been a banker and when he was alive they both hoped that they would retire to the Highlands, but it wasn't to be and she said the next best thing was to take a cruise on the *Hebridean Princess*, where she would be well looked after. I was telling her about *Amulet* and about our walking and sailing tour when she was called away to join the coach, and I returned to the pontoon. Later, when Patricia had finished shopping and we had filled the drinking-water tanks and were pulling away, we passed close to the *Hebridean Princess*, and there was my friend sitting at a table in the dining saloon having lunch. When she saw me, she came to the window and waved excitedly and I waved back. It would be nice to think that the chance encounter with the man with the little yacht at Kyle of Lochalsh was one of the highlights of her cruise.

The rain was pouring down in torrents and the visibility dreadful and, preferring to enjoy the full majesty of the islands rather than plough on through a grey wall of rain and see nothing, we picked up the mooring at Kyleakin again to wait for the weather to improve. The influence of the Viking raiders crops up frequently in the Highlands and Kyleakin gets its name from Hakon, a 13th century Norse king who built himself a castle not far from where we were moored, though weathering and age had reduced it to a heap of historic rubble. Another enterprising Norwegian, a princess this time and married to a chief of the Clan MacDonald, had a flair for making money that must have kept her bank manager very happy. She had a chain strung between the castle and the mainland and no boat was allowed to pass over it without paying dues. It is amazing that cash-hungry politicians haven't latched on to this money spinner down the centuries; though the latter day princes of power, believing themselves to be clever and forward-thinking, granted private enterprise an even more effective means of prising money out of visitors and residents. In 1995 a toll bridge was completed that linked Skye to the mainland near Kyle of Lochalsh and, apart from the enormous controversy it caused, in one fell swoop it brought 400 years of continuous ferry service between Kyle of Lochalsh and Kyleakin to an end, destroyed the romance of Skye as an island and with it the livelihoods of all who crewed and maintained the ferries, deprived the shops of Lochalsh of a considerable income and consigned Kyleakin to virtual oblivion. As a piece of modern architecture it would be churlish to say the bridge was not well designed, though it fits as naturally into the landscape of the highlands and islands as a giraffe in a crofter's hay field. But this alien concrete invasion appears to have stirred the anger of the ghosts of the ancient chieftains and it could be they are attempting to protect their beloved isle. According to scientists, the Island of Skye is moving away from the mainland a few millimetres each year and the bridge is slowly being stretched.

Much as I disliked the bridge, I was pleased to see it when, a little after 2pm, the cloud lifted and it towered over us, lit by the sun, only a few hundred yards from our mooring. The rain gradually cleared away and, having been rolled about violently by the wash of a seemingly endless procession of fishing boats coming in to land their catch, and naval vessels heading to and from the submarine testing range off the Isle of Raasay, it was a great relief to leave Kyleakin, pay reluctant homage to the bridge builders by passing underneath it, and break out into the open waters of the Inner Sound bound for Portree on the east side of Skye. Caolas, Caol and Kyle are names that appear frequently on charts of western Scotland and are Gaelic, meaning 'narrow straight'. The inshore passage I favoured followed the coast of Skye and took us through Caolas Pabay, between Skye and Pabay island, which is deep water and Caolas Scalpay, between Skye and Scalpay island, which has a rocky causeway that dried out. It was neaps and I had worked out that although the tide would only just be starting to flood when we reached it, we would have enough water to get through the narrows and over the causeway which, according to the pilot book and the chart, was marked with a beacon and buoys. The channel got narrower and narrower and the bulks of Scalpay to starboard and Skye to port loomed ever larger, but there was no sign of the promised beacon marking the causeway and the echo sounder showed the depth beginning to drop. We both scanned ahead with binoculars but there was absolutely no sign of any markers, and with Patricia calling out the depth and me steering for what I hoped was the deepest part of the channel, we crept forward hardly daring to breathe. "Two metres," said Patricia anxiously. "One and a half. One. Half a metre. Zero." I went cold, expecting that any moment *Amulet* would hit the bottom and a rock would tear into her side, but nothing happened. Patricia's face was white with fear. "It's still on zero," she said, almost in a whisper. I had slowed the engine right down and *Amulet* barely had steerage way, but ahead I could see the channel was widening. "It's moving again," shouted Patricia. "Half a metre, one metre. It's holding on one metre. No it's not, it's moving again. Two metres. Three metres, five metres. We're through!" She almost screamed the last two words and I felt inclined to do the same, but instead I put the engine in neutral and looked back on the channel with the binoculars. There was no marker beacon and no buoys. *Amulet*'s keel must have scratched the backs of a few barnacles snoozing on the bottom as we went over the causeway, and we had been very lucky. But there was no point in blaming the chart or the pilot book. Keeping my large stock of charts corrected and up to date was an ongoing job I had never been able to devote the time to, and the information in pilot books is often out of date before it leaves the printers.

Safe in deep water, we were motoring past the entrance to Loch Ainort and I was preparing to hoist sail when the sky turned dark and a fierce wind-squall came storming off the distinctive cone-shaped hill of Glamaig, 2509 feet, (772 metres), churning the loch into a maelstrom and sweeping over *Amulet* like a tornado. The nearest I can get to

finding a word that justly describes the fiendish power of the blasts of
wind that are often forced down off the mountains into the sounds and
anchorages of the west of Scotland is 'horrific' and, concerned the sails
would be blown to shreds if we tried to beat up the loch, I left the ties
on and we continued under engine. The squalls got worse and off
Suishnish Point, the southern tip of Raasay Island, the wind was so
strong we were heeling under bare pole, and a small car ferry crossing
ahead of us on the short passage from Skye to Raasay frequently
disappeared in a confusion of foaming sea. With salt spray stinging my
eyes it was difficult to make out the green and red buoys marking a
narrow channel where the islands of Skye and Raasay almost touched
and it was a warming sight when, dead ahead, I spotted a bright green
conical buoy rearing out of the surf. The passage through the narrows
was like going from one world to another. It was unbelievable. At one
end the wind had been howling and the sea rough and at the other,
where we emerged into the Sound of Raasay, there was hardly a breeze
and the sea was calm. With the engine at full speed *Amulet* raced up the
Sound, but even with the tide under us it seemed to take forever to
cover the five miles to Portree and it was 7.30pm when, wet and weary
and ready for a hot meal, we entered the harbour and picked up a
visitor's mooring.

The author of a motorist's gazetteer for tourists who said of
Portree, 'It is by courtesy called a town but is actually hardly larger than
a village,' was being rather dismissive of the island's 'capital' and he
would perhaps have appreciated it more had he arrived by boat rather
than by car. Thanks to a visit by King James V in 1540 the name of the
town was changed from the rather uninspiring 'Kiltraglean' to 'Port-
righ', the King's Port; though if the monarch had built an imposing
castle dominating the entrance to the harbour it would have done more
for its image. Guide books are full of accounts of the town's
association with Bonnie Prince Charlie and Flora MacDonald, but there
is not much else of historical interest and for some reason they never
mention 'The Blackening', a quaint old Portree marriage custom that is
still practised and which, when we went ashore the next day, was
causing great excitement. The young couple to be married were being
driven round the town in the back of a pickup truck, the modern
equivalent of a horse-drawn cart, and local people, including

shopkeepers, were pelting them with porridge, fish, eggs, treacle and all manner of ghastly rubbish. It was a bit of harmless fun that would certainly have provided a few shots not normally seen in an album of wedding photographs, though in bygone days it may well have been a ritual punishment ordered by the church elders who suspected the couple might already have consummated the relationship. On the other hand, since a considerable time must have gone by before the couple managed to get completely rid of the clinging noxious mass and smell sweet enough to be interested in a close encounter, it could have been the local council's way of delaying an increase in the town's population.

Carrying a rucksack full of clothes, Patricia went in search of a launderette while I wandered round the town centre that had not changed very much since the days when I used to come ashore from a fishing boat, and there was a group of old fishermen sitting on benches smoking their pipes. An intense-looking young chap went by carrying a placard that read, 'The Blood of Christ will save all sinners', and they stared at it solemnly until a big rugged type, wearing a fisherman's cap and with a face that advertised every brand of alcohol that had ever been invented, applied a fresh match to his pipe, puffed out a cloud of smoke and said, "Och, well now, Sandy, if the Lord was to be giving his blood to save the sins of yourself, I'm thinking the good man would soon be needing one of them trans-fooshans." "Aye, right enough," replied Sandy, "and if Dracula was needing a dram of whisky it's the veins of yourself he would be making for." The old men rolled about laughing, but the man with the placard looked pained and, bowing his head, obviously said a few words on their behalf.

Well organised, Patricia had gone shopping for groceries while the clothes were being laundered and all I had to do was help her carry everything back to the dinghy and row back to *Amulet*. It was a gorgeous day, and although one of my favourite Scottish fiddlers was performing at a Ceilidh in the town that very evening, I was keen to visit the Island of Rona, above Raasay. A weather chart on the quay had shown a vigorous depression close to Scotland and I felt we should be on our way before it arrived. At 4.30pm a light breeze sprang up and slipping the mooring we sailed out of the harbour and turned north up the Sound of Raasay. It was about twelve miles to Rona and with the wind behind us, a warm sun and fabulous scenery, we ran gently up the

Sound enjoying the views of Raasay to starboard and Skye to port. Abeam of the Storr, a 2327 feet, (716 metres,) peak on Skye, I was searching with the binoculars for the 'Old Man of Storr,' a great rocky pinnacle, when Patricia shouted, "Look at that!" I thought she had spotted the pinnacle, but when I followed the direction of her outstretched arm she was pointing to an incredibly threatening bank of black cloud, advancing rapidly from the south and enveloping the sun and the blue sky. Through the binoculars I could see that below it the surface of the Sound was churned up like a tide rip. "It's a nasty squall," I said, "let's get the sails down now before it hits us." I rounded up and we just had time to tie the sails before it was on us like a pack of screaming demons, tearing at the rigging with astounding ferocity and laying *Amulet* on her side. Fortunately, we were near Eilean Fladday, a small island close to the side of Raasay, but what I thought would be a brief, violent squall was in fact the sudden arrival of a gale and, turning for Fladday, we had a beam sea and even under engine it was a boisterous two miles before, with huge sighs of relief, we crept round the foaming rocks at the north end of the island and dropped anchor in a narrow pool. High above the mast the wind roared like a passing train and heavy rain drummed on the cabin roof, but tucked safely under the lea of the island we enjoyed our evening meal undisturbed.

It rained and blew all night though, after dawn, the wind eased to a light breeze, and by breakfast time an apologetic sun was peering through the clouds and doing its best to warm the anchorage. Stornoway Coastguard's weather bulletin promised that high pressure and good weather were on their way, so we decided to wait and go for a walk on Raasay. Eilean Fladday has two anchorages, Caol Fladday, our anchorage, and Fladday Harbour, separated at low water by a rocky causeway from which a path, hewn out of the side of Raasay by generations of Fladday crofters, climbed airily from the sea and round Beinn na Iolaire, the hill of the eagle, to a well-defined track that led to the northern tip of Raasay or south to eventually take on the status of a motor road leading to the main community of Inverarish and the ferry to Skye. A long thin island, Raasay is about 22 kilometres long by 6 kilometres wide at its base, gradually tapering to a point. It is an island renowned for its rugged beauty and the final five miles or so, starting almost opposite Fladda Island, are wild, hilly, rough and boggy. The original purpose of the track we followed north was for the crofters of old to drive their cattle to the summer pastures where, in the shielings - tiny dry stone houses thatched with heather - the women and girls spent the summer looking after the animals, and made butter and spun wool while the men stayed behind and worked the crofts. At least that is the version in the tourist literature. Stories handed down by ancient crofters I have known tell of hot-blooded lads walking many miles to the shielings to do their courting and the custom being what it was, the older women kept their eyes down and concentrated on their wool spinning. With other pleasures in mind it's doubtful that the amorous lads would have paused to appreciate the view across the Inner Sound to the Torridon Hills as they hurried along the track, but we did and it was quite breathtaking. As frequent VHF radio broadcasts to cruising yachts by the range control on Rona make it very clear, the Inner Sound, between Raasay and the mainland, is a submarine testing area and we could see a couple of the black monsters cruising along on the surface far below us. Having in the past had my sailing plans interrupted by the activities of submarines in the Inner Sound, it can be very irritating; but I have come to accept that, in this crazy world, were it not for the vigilance of the submarines we might not have the freedom to sail at all.

A sharp shower of rain had us rushing for our waterproofs, and when it steadily increased to a continuous downfall we were delighted to stumble on a shieling that had been renovated by the Mountain Bothies Association, a little known organisation that deserves wider recognition for its work in providing free shelters, with sparse sleeping accommodation, in the wild areas of Scotland. We ate our lunch while the rain rattled on the corrugated iron roof of the bothy and, having duly signed the visitors' book, walked the short distance to Caol Rona, the narrow straight between Raasay and Rona, hoping we might see otters, but nothing stirred except for a few seals and a small cargo ship steaming between the islands. Retracing our steps along the same route was wearying, but at least the rain stopped and we could see across the Sound as far south as the Skye bridge and Kyleakin. Back at the harbour I groaned when I found the tide out and had to carry the dinghy over my head across the causeway through a wide expanse of boulders draped with seaweed. I slipped and slid, cursed and swore, banged my shins and filled my boots with smelly slime but, instead of helping, Patricia just fell about in a fit of uncontrollable laughter. "You would be more useful if you would help me instead of standing there laughing like a damned hyena," I shouted irritably. "What's so funny anyway?" "I'm sorry," she said, still having difficulty controlling the giggles, "but it looks as if the dinghy had been transformed into a giant turtle and is walking over the rocks. Oh, if only I had brought my camera." She burst into another fit of laughter and I angrily dropped the dinghy into the water and made her row us back to the boat, but once on board and in dry clothes I soon recovered. The hill of the eagle lived up to its name when we sat in the cockpit with a dram after our evening meal and we were treated to an unforgettable sight. Completely unaware of us, a golden eagle flew across from Raasay and perched on a gnarled tree on Fladday only yards away from *Amulet*. We kept perfectly still and it took off and soared around and above us before landing on a rock near the tree, resting for a few minutes then launching into the air again and soaring out of view on the opposite side of the island. It was the perfect end to a most enjoyable day.

It rained all night but at 7am patches of blue sky began to appear, and an hour later, when we raised the anchor and departed Fladday to sail round the top of Skye, it was a nice bright morning. There was a light wind, but it was so variable it was exasperating and, after jibing uncontrollably for the fifth time, I dropped the sails and we motored with the autopilot at the helm. With a fair tide and a lumpy following sea we made good progress and Staffin Island, close to the Skye shore, was soon astern; but then the steering became very erratic and I discovered that a screw on the bracket holding the autopilot had fallen off and found its way overboard. Patricia steered while I found a replacement screw, and with the autopilot in control again Eilean Flodigarry was left to port and we steered for the lighthouse on Trodday, an island off the top of Skye, and ran full tilt into a sudden heavy shower of rain that forced us to hide under the shelter of the cockpit canopy until it had eased. A strong tidal stream whizzed *Amulet* through the channel between Trodday and The Aird, the northern tip of Skye, and a light easterly breeze was healthy enough to fill the main and genoa and help the tide rush us past the headland of Rubha

Hunish, where I confirmed on the chart we had rounded the top of the vast Island of Skye. The island is sixty miles long but has so many indentations and bits sticking out all over the place it would defy anyone but the most determined surveyor to decide how wide it is. The north side of Skye, which faces the Minch and looks across to the Outer Hebrides, is deeply indented by the massive expanse of Loch Snizort, which is separated from Loch Dunvegan by the huge headland of Waternish Point, which in turn is separated from Loch Pooltiel, a mere dewdrop in comparison to its neighbours, by Dunvegan Head. It is spectacular landscape and seascape on a massive scale and the invading Vikings must have felt very much at home in the fiords of Skye. It was ten miles across the wide mouth of Loch Snizort to the great headland of Waternish Point but, washed by the rain the air was crystal clear, the visibility exceptional and distances deceiving. I could clearly see the lighthouse on the Island of Scalpay, off the coast of Harris fifteen miles away, without needing the binoculars, and every whitewashed cottage along the Hebridean coast shone like a beacon in the sunlight. Three huge freighters, hulls well down in the water and flying the Norwegian, Panamanian and Dutch flags, passed us heading in convoy up the Minch to Cape Wrath and the world beyond; and though someone on the wing bridge of the Norwegian ship studied *Amulet* closely through binoculars, he missed a good view of her underside when, later, the wake of the ships tossed her about like a piece of flotsam.

At 1pm the heavens darkened and another monsoon shower sent us scurrying under the canopy, and the decks had hardly dried when half an hour later, passing close to the gaunt cliffs of Waternish Point, we splashed through a tide rip and dipped the bow under a couple of times. With Waternish Point behind, I set a course which would take us into Loch Dunvegan, but by the time we reached Isay Island inside the mouth of the loch, the wind had died, the tide had turned and it was like motoring through thick porridge. The journey down the loch seemed endless and, to add to the ordeal, rain squalls raged into us so violently I could hardly open my eyes to check my position. Mercifully, there was a respite from the onslaught as the head of the loch narrowed, and near Dunvegan Castle we picked up a visitor's mooring in a sheltered pool close to an old stone quay. It was almost 4pm and we had covered forty-seven miles.

There are still places in the west of Scotland where visitors' moorings are free and normally we always repaid the hospitality by having a meal in the local pub, buying groceries in the shop or visiting local attractions, but I'm ashamed to say we didn't put a foot ashore at Dunvegan. I had been many times before and meant to inflate the dinghy and show Patricia around, but the rain cleared away and a hot sun was hanging in a blue sky, so we hung our wet walking clothes in the rigging and sat reading in the cockpit in shorts and tee shirts. There wasn't a ripple on the water and on the mooring it was utterly peaceful, whereas on the shore two motor coaches had arrived and noisy photo-snapping tourists were swarming about like ants. We were both allergic to crowds and stayed put. Afternoon became evening, and the sunset was so wonderful we savoured every minute of it until the shadows of darkness crept down from the hills and covered the loch in black velvet.

We woke to a staggeringly beautiful, flat calm morning and, as we lingered over breakfast it had gone 9am before the mooring was cast off and we motored slowly out of the narrow pool and turned to port in front of Dunvegan Castle and lined *Amulet* up to head between small islands into the open water of Loch Dunvegan. I felt badly about leaving without at least saying 'thanks for the use of the mooring' by taking Patricia to visit Dunvegan Castle, the ancestral home of the Clan MacLeod and claimed to be the oldest inhabited house in Scotland. Having cycled the length of Skye with a girl friend to visit the castle in the 1950s, when we were the only visitors on a horribly wet day, the then Clan Chief, Dame Flora MacLeod, gave us a personal tour and, while we dripped water onto her kitchen floor gave us tea and told us that the MacLeods were descended from a Norse King who ruled the Isle of Man and was given the Isle of Skye as compensation when Norway gave up its claim to the Isle of Man and the Outer Hebrides in the 13th century. The castle was a fascinating place and a shrine for MacLeods from all over the world, but in the course of time it had become a high-pressure, money-spinning tourist attraction, which was not what we had sailed to the Highlands to see.

The surface of the loch was so calm it had the look of an unbroken vastness of blue glass that opened at the touch of *Amulet*'s bow and closed again behind her stern and, far ahead over the Little Minch, the mountainous Hebridean island of Harris floated in a purple haze. Across this fairy sea we motored for an hour before we left the loch behind and rounded the imposing vertical wall of Dunvegan Head, rising to almost 1,000 feet, (300 metres,) out of the sea. "Isn't that an interesting coincidence," exclaimed Patricia who had been studying the log. "Just as we were abeam of Dunvegan Head the log recorded we have travelled five hundred miles since we left Maryport. We ought to celebrate!" And we did, though not with anything stronger than hot coffee and digestive biscuits, but the wind gods also marked the occasion and gave us a wonderful present of a steady breeze that came up suddenly from astern. With the boom let out to the fullest extent of the mainsheet and the genoa held out with the spinnaker pole, it was like being in a trade wind as we surged and rolled past the whitewashed tower of Neist Point lighthouse and down the west coast of Skye at five knots. "Where are we going to put in for the night?" asked Patricia, hanging on to the tiller and gritting her teeth every time the boom lifted and threatened an involuntary jibe. "I'm not sure yet," I replied. "This is rare sailing, let's see where the wind takes us." We were just five miles abeam of the wide entrance to Loch Bracadale which had lots of fine anchorages but, though I was tempted, not least by the prospect of renewing an old acquaintance, it was such a marvellous day with a perfect wind I could not bear to give it up. Twenty miles down wind of us was the island of Canna; that would do very nicely.

Amulet was rolling steadily, and to give Patricia a break I took the helm and wedged myself on the starboard side of the cockpit so that I would have a good view of the Skye coast. I couldn't suppress a little laugh to myself when I looked over to Loch Bracadale and remembered a friend of mine who lived there telling me about the days of his youth and two brothers who were crofter/fishermen. They owned a boat called *Nelly*, and during a storm it broke loose and was driven across Loch Bracadale onto rocks on the far side. Telephones were few and far between in those days and the younger brother was sent on the long journey by road round the loch with instructions to send a telegram home from the nearest post office when he had examined the boat. Archie duly sent the telegram but, more used to expressing himself in Gaelic, he shocked the postmistress with a telegram that read, "Looked at Nelly's bottom, found no hole."

"What on earth are you laughing at?" quizzed Patricia, emerging from the cabin with a plate of sandwiches and a mug of tea. "Oh, I was just looking at Loch Bracadale and remembering a tale a friend told me; it's not for ladies."

"H'm," she sniffed. "If it's one of those tales you tell when you've had a whisky too many, I'd rather not hear it." She took the helm and, steadying myself against the constant rolling, I clipped a safety harness onto a guard wire, carried my sandwiches and tea to the foredeck and leant back against the mast. Sheltered from the wind it was surprisingly warm and while I chewed my sandwiches I scanned the sea in the hope of spotting a whale or basking shark. At one time they were plentiful around Skye and the Inner Hebrides but, though a shoal of porpoises kept a respectable distance ahead for a while before disappearing, there was not a whale or shark to be seen and I worried that they had fallen victim to the ever growing hazard of sea pollution. We were on a converging course with a fishing boat I had been keeping an eye on, and when I returned to the cockpit to take a closer look through the binoculars I could see he was trawling and we would have to give him a wide berth round his stern. It was a bit hairy having to jibe in the swell, but it went off without mishap and, with a courtesy not always characteristic of fishermen, the skipper came out of his wheelhouse and gave us a wave of acknowledgement. At 4pm we were about seven miles north of Canna and had superb views of Rum, Soay, the spiky peaks of the Cuillins and a flotilla of Royal Navy ships steaming towards the Hebrides complete with a helicopter buzzing around their masts. I was hoping to sail right into Canna harbour, but the wind was fluky and it was the Farymann that carried us in to anchor amongst a mass of yachts of all shapes and sizes. We had had a run of thirty-five miles, goosewinging all the way in the most perfect sailing conditions imaginable. As Para Handy, the west of Scotland's most famous seaman and skipper of the mythical cargo vessel the *Vital Spark* would have said, "It was chust sublime."

How many islands there are off Scotland's west coast is not easy to determine. Many folk have tried counting them and some have written books about them, but life isn't long enough to spend time arguing about when is an island an islet and an islet a rock. One sure fact is that the west has a lot of them and, while they all have their individual charm, the one that has always been rather special to me is Canna. I first landed on the island while I was 'at the fishing'; and when my skipper sent me to buy milk and eggs from the farm I discovered there was something quite unique about it, not least that the Laird, Mr John Campbell, was something of a folk hero with the fishermen and he and the writer Compton Mackenzie had founded a society to protect the fishing industry in the west of Scotland. Almost throughout history Canna was a very popular haven for fishing boats and crews used to paint the name of their boat on a rock face by the jetty, but in modern times successive governments have used the fishing industry as a pawn in the political game and systematically destroyed the UK fishing fleets by allowing foreign boats to plunder our waters. A few fishing boats still call at Canna, but the harbour is now very much on the 'must visit' list of cruising yachts, and a regular stopping-off place for 'tall ships' and the growing fleet of ex-fishing vessels converted to take scuba divers out to the Hebrides and St Kilda. Before he died, friend of the fishermen, Gaelic scholar and historian Dr John Lorne Campbell gave Canna to the National Trust for Scotland, which unfortunately means that the island is run by 'experts' based in Edinburgh, much as Trust land in the English Lake District is run by 'experts' in London. On the positive side, it should mean that in the ownership of the National Trust for Scotland, the natural beauty of the island and its peaceful harbour will never be desecrated by speculators.

I knew the harbour well but had never explored the land beyond it and, fresh after a good night's rest, we gave *Amulet* extra anchor chain to allow for the rise of a spring tide and rowed ashore in the dinghy with boots and rucksacks to walk round the island. A friendly local working on his boat showed us a track that would take us in the direction of Compass Hill, at 474 feet, (146 metres,) one of the high points on the island, and laughingly said we were lucky to be escaping from the crowds. When we looked puzzled he explained that three fishing boats were due to arrive from Mallaig carrying two hundred people on an annual RNLI outing. It was an incentive to get moving and, after taking a quick look round an attractive little chapel, we followed the track to a high viewpoint above the harbour that overlooked An Coroghon, a knife-edged stack rising above the beach, on which was perched a primitive tower. According to legend, one of the Chiefs of Canna imprisoned his young wife in the tower when he found he was sharing her favours with one of the MacLeods of Dunvegan. It was a grim place to be marooned, and the story would have had a romantic ending worthy of a highland hero had MacLeod rescued her and carried her over to Skye in his Galley, but no one came to her aid and she died in the tower. The Clan Chiefs seemed to have been rather fond of having their way with their neighbours' wives. Malcolm, the third Chief of the MacLeods, is reputed to have killed a bull that attacked him while he was returning from a clandestine visit to the wife of Fraser of Glenelg on the mainland, and it could well have been the reincarnation of a revengeful husband out to get him. Way back in the dark days of history, it was a Chief's privilege to spend the wedding night with the bride of any of his tenants who got married; a barbaric custom that must have caused great distress and filled the communities with lots of lookalike children.

Leaving the ghost of the unfortunate lady to her misery, we climbed through grass and heather to the summit of Compass Hill, cursed by early mariners for being full of deposits of iron which seriously affected the compass of any ship in the vicinity of the island. The air was clear and there was a remarkable view of the Cuillins of Skye, the island of Soay and the hills of Rum and, as we walked along the northern edge of the island, we were amazed at the grandeur of the high cliffs which plunged vertically into the sea. The sky was alive with seabirds, and the lush grass ablaze with wild flowers. Canna was looking its finest and it was easy to see why it had been a favourite with the Vikings, and when in later years it was cultivated and stocked with cattle, it provided rich pickings for pirates. The map showed that Canna was six miles long by two miles wide, but gave little indication that the western half of the island was a mixture of rolling hills and boggy hollows, flanking one of the island's highest hills, Sliabh Meadhonach, 484 feet, (149 metres,) and they seemed to extend interminably into the distance. With leg muscles aching and throats parched by the hot sun we reached Garrisdale Point, the westerly tip of the island, and followed the cliffs round to sink thankfully against an Ordnance Survey trig point and sip orange juice. We had a wonderful bird's eye view of the small island of Heisker with its tall lighthouse warning shipping away from the treacherous reefs and islands surrounding it. When I was a keeper at

Ardnamurchan lighthouse and in daily radio contact with the keepers on Heisker, they told me that the island was alive with seals and that the people from Canna had said that in the 19th century the islanders went out once a year to kill them for their blubber. When it was melted down they fed it to cattle, rubbed it on their chests when they had a bad cold, and even drank it!

Walking back along the south side of the island we had marvellous views of Rum and the island of Sanday, that formed part of the harbour and was joined to Canna by a footbridge built to enable children to get to the island school. Following the rim of the broad horseshoe of Tarbert Bay, we joined a wide track that had been bulldozed nearly three miles from the harbour to access farm buildings and we trudged along it until, just as we were passing a wooden shack that was the island's post office, the sun went behind a black cloud and heavy rain drove us inside. It was as if the postmistress drummed up business by waiting for visitors to appear then pressing a button to release a deluge. We took the hint and bought postcards and stamps and used the public telephone to phone home and report all was well. When we reached the harbour it was late afternoon and many of the yachts that had been anchored near *Amulet* had gone. The skippers would have written in their logs, 'departed Canna', but very few would have seen the real Canna or enjoyed their visit to the island as much as we did.

The Virgin's Infidelity - On Fire - Lassoed By A Lifeboat

To be told that there is a water shortage in the west of Scotland is a bit like listening to the assurance of politicians that never again will they put up income tax. It takes a lot of believing; yet when we motored *Amulet* over to the jetty the following morning to fill our water tank, the skipper of a fishing boat, who had also come in for water, said that many of the islands were suffering a water shortage and he had heard that on the island of Coll, our next destination, the situation had become so serious supplies had been shipped out in a tanker from Oban. The skipper was from Harris and when I said that, with all the rain that came in from the Atlantic, there should always be plenty of water in the Hebrides, he laughed and with a twinkle in his eyes said, "Aye, right enough, but water is not a thing we would be bothering our heads with. If an island runs out of whisky it's a tragedy, but if it runs out of water it's only an emergency."

In a straight line the distance from Canna to the Cairns of Coll, a group of rocks at the eastern end of the Isle of Coll, is about twenty-three miles of open sea and when the sun is shining, the visibility superb, and there is a steady force 3 wind it is a most enjoyable sail. When we left Canna at 10am we had such a day and the only niggle was that the wind was on the nose but, though we had to beat to windward and it meant adding a few extra miles to the distance, there was a bonus; on the first tack we sailed parallel with the rugged coast of Rum as far as Harris Bay, where the Bullough family who owned Rum were buried in a pretentious mausoleum built in the style of a Greek temple.

It was in this area, in my charter ketch with my partner Jean during August 1986, that we had an alarming experience when two killer whales decided to accompany us, one on either side of the boat. The ketch was forty feet long and the enormous whales seemed to be almost the same size; and I dared not alter the engine speed or turn the boat to port or starboard in case it scared them and they flattened the boat with one flick of their massive tails. They stayed alongside for over a mile, then quietly sank below the waves and were gone. A marine biologist said later that they probably thought the boat was a female whale. I was highly relieved that August wasn't the mating season!

Off Harris Bay the wind died and the sails hung like rags, so we furled them and continued under engine with the autopilot at the helm while we relaxed in the sun. There was not a cloud in the sky and it was sweIteringly hot; but when we were about five miles from the Cairns of Coll we witnessed the most amazing phenomenon. A single massive column of black cloud sailed in from the west like a celestial water tanker, hovered directly over Coll and discharged its cargo of life-giving water in a sparkling thunderstorm. It was uncanny. The skipper of the fishing boat had said that the Coll islanders had been praying for rain. Mighty is the power of Scottish Free Presbyterian prayer!

We raced MacBrayne's Outer Isles ferry to the Cairns of Coll and actually got there first, but it had the last word and bounced us contemptuously up and down in its wake. It was seven miles from the Cairns to Loch Eatharna, Coll's fine harbour, and the village of Arinagour - though with a stiff tide against us it seemed longer - but just after 4pm we picked up one of a row of visitors' moorings, inflated the dinghy and rowed ashore for a leg stretch and a glass of something long and cool in the hotel. It was a fatal move. We had hardly got through the bar door before Patricia was enquiring about showers, and for the second time in as many weeks I found myself signed up for a hot soaping and shampooing. The bucket of seawater and a lathering with saltwater soap in the cockpit was fast becoming redundant. Worse, because of the water shortage the hotel guests had priority, and we were requested to come back at 10am the following day. Half a day's sailing lost for the sake of a hot shower. I complained bitterly but Patricia wouldn't budge.

Seen from a boat the island of Coll is a flat, uninviting, bleak, lunar landscape of bare rock, and the impression does not improve much when seen from a mooring in the harbour, but it is misleading. I had been to Coll many times and thoroughly enjoyed exploring the island on foot and by bike and, though it has always been considered the poor cousin of the adjacent prosperous island of Tiree, there are those, including me, who prefer Coll. When I once remarked on the difference between the two islands an old 'Collach' (local inhabitant,) said dryly, "When the good Lord was handing out the horn of plenty he dropped it, and it missed Coll and spilt all over Tiree."

Refreshed after our cool drinks we climbed above the hotel to a church on a hill and looked down on the narrow loch that was the harbour. The moored boats were shimmering in a heat haze and the row of picturesque whitewashed cottages along the 'main street' would have sent a watercolour artist into raptures. But most of the cottages were holiday homes, and for an island community to survive it has to have young people, and to keep them there it needs a strong economy. Coll was short of both. I had hoped we might hire bikes from the hotel and cycle to Gunna Sound, overlooking Tiree, but I was rather concerned that the leak had reared its ugly head again on the way over from Canna, so we went back to *Amulet*. When I lifted the floorboards there were no ominous gurgling sounds, but water was seeping along the keelson and appeared to be coming in where the plank ends were fastened to the stem. It was more of an irritation than a danger, and the daily pump strokes and the automatic bilge pump would be a good indication if the leak increased.

Climbing back into the cockpit to write my log in the warmth of the sun, I was stopped in my tracks by the sight of a steel ketch that had picked up a mooring while I had been checking the bilge. Except for colour it was identical to my charter ketch, and by even more of a coincidence it was on the mooring that I had been tied to for a couple of days in a fierce westerly gale, battened down with one of Prime Minister Maggie Thatcher's top advisers and his family. "You should have said how marvellous she was, you might have got a knighthood," said Patricia sarcastically when I told her. She had been an occupational health nurse during the Thatcher era and was no fan of the 'iron lady'. "He never even mentioned her," I said, "and not long afterwards we were chartered by one of her cabinet ministers, who didn't mention her either. Politicians are like anyone else on holiday, they want a complete break and the last thing they want to talk about is work." "That's probably why they chose your boat," she chided. "MI5 probably checked up on you and told them you had no interest in anything but boats and mountains." Just like the 'iron lady', she had to have the last word!

The Coastguard 'Caledonia' forecast on the VHF promised continuing fine weather with calm seas and little or no wind and it was difficult to decide what to do the following day. I left the decision to Patricia saying, "Since you insist on wasting time in the shower we can hire bikes and explore the island, but if we get away in plenty of time we can go across to the uninhabited Treshnish Islands, then have a look at Fingal's Cave on Staffa, and maybe even get ashore at Iona to visit the Abbey." "Oh, let's go to Staffa," she said joyously, "I love listening to Mendelssohn's Hebrides Overture and I've always wanted to visit Fingal's Cave." "O.K," I said. "Staffa it is then, and we'll look at the Treshnish isles on the way, but we leave before midday otherwise it's a bike ride round Coll."

It was another sparklingly beautiful morning and the surface of the harbour was like glass when we went ashore in the dinghy and left two five-gallon cans at the island shop to be filled with diesel while were we showering at the hotel. Though we were obviously intruding on their morning routine, the friendly hotel owners were most helpful and, conscious of the water shortage, we didn't linger under the shower. We were out within half an hour and had time for a leisurely pot of coffee in the hotel garden before collecting the diesel and a bag of groceries from the shop. Just after noon, with a tropical sun making it unbearable to walk on deck in bare feet, we slipped the mooring and headed out to sea. It was a perfect day for a bike ride round Coll, but that's one of the problems when sailing in the west of Scotland. There are so many wonderful places to visit you are spoilt for choice.

Looked down upon from high ground on the Isle of Mull when the sun is setting on a calm sea, the mystical Treshnish Islands float like purple jewels set in gold, but from a boat they are green and brown and just as lovely. Lunga, the largest and rising to 325 feet, (100 metres,) was once inhabited but, like the other islands of the group, is now home to a huge colony of seabirds of all shapes and sizes. We motored down the east side of the group to the 'Dutchmans Cap', a distinctive conical island at the southern end of the group, then turned for Staffa, five miles away. One popular account of the composer Felix Mendelssohn's visit to Staffa in 1829 tells of him being too seasick to take any interest in the scenery, but I find it hard to believe that he could have been inspired to write his marvellously descriptive Hebrides Overture without having gazed in wonderment at the spectacular basalt columns of Staffa and the enormous gaping chasm that is Fingal's

Cave. The cave was given its name in honour of a 3rd century Irishman, Finn MacCool - in Gaelic, Fionn na Ghal - who helped the Scots to defend the Hebrides against the Vikings. Apart from the fleets of motor boats which were unloading hordes of trippers onto the landing place and knocking on the head any hope we had of anchoring and getting ashore, we could not have arrived at a better time. The sea was flat calm and the afternoon sun was lighting up the columns and shining into the cave. We went berserk with our cameras, shooting off roll after roll of film and trying to get angles that did not have the top of the island bristling with people like penguins on an iceberg.

Conditions like that were so rare I could not bear to leave but, when more and more yachts began to arrive and a truculent individual on the flying bridge of a gin palace nearly backed his chrome-plated charge into us, I felt I needed more breathing space. Many of the yachts were obviously making for the popular and often hopelessly overcrowded anchorages in the Sound of Iona, and it was our cue to head in the opposite direction. I knew of a remote anchorage on the island of Ulva, close to the shore of Mull, and at 5pm we nosed carefully through the maze of rocks that make the approach to this anchorage so interesting and dropped the hook in a narrow pool between two headlands. The only other boat in sight, anchored in an adjacent bay, was the well-known charter yacht *Corryvreckan*, owned by Douglas Lindsay and his wife, of Oban, a couple who probably sailed more miles in a year than the average yacht owner does in a lifetime. The heat had made us lethargic and there wasn't a flicker of enthusiasm from Patricia when I suggested inflating the dinghy and going ashore to look round the sad ruins of the village of Cragaig where, during the Highland Clearance, the Laird's thugs evicted the people without warning and set fire to their houses. Instead we ate steak and salad sitting in the cockpit, opened a bottle of wine bought from the shop on Coll, and watched the sun sink in the west until the sea, the land and the sky merged into one and it was time to hoist the anchor light up the forestay.

It was low water when we were ready to leave the following morning, and the mass of exposed rocks in every direction made it a tricky place to get out of under sail with a fluky wind spiralling round the anchorage, so to save any embarrassment I kept the engine ticking over until we were safely into deep water. Clear of the rocks and with

the main and genoa drawing nicely in a light wind, I set course for the
Sound of Iona and its famous island about eight miles to the south.

"You know Iona well, don't you?" said Patricia, as we approached
the entrance to the Sound and slowed down to avoid a fleet of yachts
heading out. "Well, I'm no expert," I replied, "but if I had a tenner for
every time I have sailed to Mull and visited Iona and the abbey when I
was chartering I would be able to afford a larger boat than I've got
now. Our guests were fascinated with Iona and I gave them the tourist
spiel so often I reckon the Tourist Board should have given me a
guide's badge! Pilgrims come from all over the world to see where Saint
Columba founded his abbey, and you can bet your life the island will be
swarming with tourists on a lovely day like this. I wonder if that bunch
walking on the beach over there know that that's the place where the
Vikings massacred the abbot of Iona and fifteen monks. There's the
abbey on the right. I'll go close inshore and you'll be able to
photograph it." "You're beginning to sound like a guide already,"
Patricia sniggered, "and since I don't know anything about Iona you
may as well put on your guide's hat and tell me." I launched into the
story of St Columba but was distracted by a large gaff-rigged ketch,
with every stitch of canvas on board hanging from the spars and no
one keeping a proper look out, bearing down on us yawing wildly from
side to side, and I had to give a long blast with our foghorn to focus the
attention of the helmsman. It slid by within a few yards of us, flying the
tricolour of France, it's crew of waving youngsters cheerily oblivious of
the anti-European obscenities being hurled at them by the elderly ros-
boeuf on the petit bleu bateau they nearly collided with. "That was a
near one," breathed Patricia, waving to the youngsters as the French
boat slipped by.

"O.K. so St Columba was an Irish prince who was banished from
Ireland for stirring up a battle, and sailed from Ireland with twelve of
his mates in five sixty three, landed on the Garvellach Islands near
Oban, then sailed on to Iona and founded a Christian monastery. What
then. He sounds a man of many interests." I knew it would be like
waving a red rag at a bull, but I couldn't resist saying, "Well, one things
for certain, he wouldn't have been interested in you; he was a woman
hater and wouldn't allow women or cattle on the island, in fact he said,
'Where there's a cow there's a woman, and where there's a woman

there's mischief.' He kept well away from temptation; that's probably why he was a saint." She suddenly lost interest in peering at the abbey through binoculars and banged them down on the cockpit seat. "Huh," she snorted, "he might have been Scotland's first Christian, but if that was his opinion of women he was obviously the country's first chauvinist as well. I'm certainly not going ashore to visit any abbey that he built. Anyway you haven't given me the full tourist spiel yet. What happened to him?" "Oh," I said, "he spread Christianity throughout Scotland then returned to Iona and died when he was in his seventies, but the Vikings kept attacking the island, destroying the Abbey and killing the monks, and Columba's remains were dug up and removed for safe keeping so many times that no one is sure where they are now. Over the centuries the abbey was knocked down and rebuilt, but then it was left derelict for years until the Duke of Argyll gave the ruins to the Church of Scotland, who made an attempt at rebuilding. But it was when the Reverend George MacLeod founded the Iona Community in the 1930s that restoration really got going. A man I was in the lighthouse service with was in the Iona Community and they were an odd bunch, but they did marvellous work restoring the abbey and were all volunteers who gave up their holidays and spare time. It wasn't time wasted either, because Iona will never be destroyed. An old prophesy says that when the world ends, 'Columba's happy isle will rear her towers above the flood.' That'll be his reward for a lifetime of keeping out of the clutches of women." I ducked under the tiller to avoid the blow she threw at my head and reminded her that striking a ship's captain was punishable by being stripped naked and flogged before the mast.

I slowed *Amulet* down to keep clear of the Iona ferry bustling across the Sound with a load of pilgrims and said, "By the way, just to round off, I'd better mention that forty-eight Scottish Kings, including MacBeth, are buried on Iona along with a few Norwegian and French kings; and I forgot the period in the sixteenth century when, just to show how un-christianlike Christians can sometimes be to each other, the Abbey and a lot of the priceless treasures in it were destroyed by the followers of a new brand of Scottish religion who didn't agree with the brand practised on Iona. So much for the bit from the Bible that says, 'Love thy neighbour'. It's a funny old world." As the Abbey came abeam to starboard we didn't need binoculars to see that the building and the road all the way to the ferry landing were teeming with visitors, and I was not sorry when Patricia said she was quite happy to give Iona a miss. "O.K.," I said, "that suits me; we'll go along the south coast of Mull and see where the end of the day finds us. We pass the island of Erraid that features in Robert Louis Stevenson's book "Kidnapped"; in fact he wrote the book on the island and in all the years I've sailed round here I've never landed on it, so if its suits you we'll anchor just off Erraid and go ashore in the dinghy." "That's a great idea," she enthused, "Sounds better than struggling through a mass of tourists on Iona."

The writer Robert Louis Stevenson's association with Erraid drew tourists to the island by the hundreds but, to an ex lighthouse keeper like myself, what was even more interesting about the island was the Stevenson family's fame as the builders of famous lighthouses around Scotland and the Isle of Man, with perhaps the most famous of them all, the Skerryvore, perched on a rock about twenty-five miles west of Erraid. The story of the building of the Skerryvore lighthouse is an account of unbelievable skill and endurance, the like of which might never be repeated. The hundreds of granite blocks for the tower, hewn from a quarry on Mull overlooking the Sound of Iona, were individually curved and tapered, and it all was done by hand with a hammer and chisel. When completed the 138 feet, (46metre,) tower was less than an inch out of vertical and was designed to 'give' to the wind. Having on many an occasion stood with my back against the wall at the top of the Butt of Lewis lighthouse in the Hebrides at the height of a winter storm and felt the tower swaying, my visit to Erraid was to pay my humble respects to the champions of lighthouse builders.

The island, joined to Mull by a strip of sand at low water, is protected on the seaward side by a maze of rocks and islands which form the Tinker's Hole, another anchorage high on the 'must visit' list of charter yachts and, although it was by now almost noon, I was bitterly disappointed to see a forest of metal masts sticking up above the rocks and absolutely no room to anchor. I knew of other places nearby, but they were open to the south and with a slight swell coming in from that direction I was worried about leaving *Amulet* unattended at anchor, and reluctantly cancelled landing on Erraid and kept on round the coast. Just off this corner of Mull are the dreaded Torran Rocks which, like other sea monsters that lie hidden below the surface, can sometimes rise up and give the crews of passing boats an awful fright. The preferred channel through the rocks runs parallel to the coast of Mull for about two miles, and even in this the submerged rocks marked by breaking seas are unpleasantly close and it is no place to be caught out in poor visibility. There were stretches where a strong tide running across the swell bounced *Amulet* about like a cork, but the faithful Farymann pushed her steadily forward and eventually the last rock in the channel and the evil foaming seas breaking over it were behind us and we were in clear water.

Patricia gave an audible sigh of relief and I had a feeling that the perspiration on her forehead wasn't all due to the heat of the sun. "Thank goodness that's over!" she exclaimed. "The Torrans are enough to give anyone a nightmare." She shielded her eyes with a hand and then pointed south to a purple haze in the distance. "What's that island over there?" "It's Colonsay," I said, "then to the left is Islay, then Jura." Her face lit up, "Oh, I've read about Colonsay in W.H. Murray's book 'The Hebrides', and it sounds idyllic; can we go there?" "It's fine with me," I said. "It's about fifteen miles to the harbour of Scalasaig but, though the island may sound idyllic, it's a bloody awful place to tie up for the night. Someone has fastened a few boards against the pier legs to enable yachts to go alongside but there's not much room, and if the wind or a swell get up you have to get out quickly and there's nowhere to go except the old harbour, which is invariably crowded with fishing boats, and it dries out. I've cycled round Colonsay and its lovely but, unless the weather is exceptionally settled, it's my least favourite place to sail to; but we'll give it a try." I worked out a course on the chart, fixed the autopilot on the tiller and stretched out in the sun while *Amulet* nosed gently into the swell. "Apparently the rocks on the islands of Colonsay, Oronsay and Islay are geologically different to all the other islands." Patricia took her visits to islands seriously and had unearthed a book from the ship's library and was reading about Colonsay. "Fascinating stuff," I said casually, my eyes half-closed, trying not to let her see it was in fun, "but if we hit one it'll still sink us, and right now where the rocks are under *Amulet*'s keel is the limit of my interest in geology." She gave an impatient snort and went forward to continue reading the book on the foredeck.

As we approached Scalasaig, halfway down the east side of Colonsay, a large black-hulled yacht, the *Sirius*, motored ahead of us towards the pier and, when we got closer, we found it had gone aground close in to the shore. I shouted to two girls rowing around frantically in the ship's dinghy to bring a warp across to us but, though *Amulet*'s engine raced and the water foamed, *Sirius* would not budge. The tide was falling rapidly and she was stuck fast. A rather strange-looking wooden yacht, *Huff of Arklow* motored in and tied up astern of us at the pier, and it transpired that both boats were owned by the skipper of *Sirius*, Andrew Thornhill of Bristol, with business interests as diverse as Exeter Maritime Museum and a snuff factory in the Cumbrian town of Kendal. He invited us aboard the Uffa Fox designed *Huff of Arklow* for a beer, introduced us to the skipper, Dominic, and showed us over the most unusual and beautifully fitted-out boat. Taking our leave, Patricia went to the village shop while I went in search of the harbour master to ask if I could take *Amulet* into the old harbour to dry out against the wall to try to locate the leak. I met a retired farmer who said the harbour master was driving the island bus and would be along presently, so I passed a very enjoyable hour talking about farming and the future of crofting on the islands. The harbour master arrived while we were talking and, in the way that comes so easily to people born and bred in remote communities, he was most helpful and obliging and said that I could lie *Amulet* against the harbour wall in a berth normally occupied by a fishing boat. "And stay as long as you want and get your wee boat fit for the sea. High water is at ten o' clock tonight." Unfortunately for Patricia she had experienced another side of life on Colonsay and came back looking most upset. Not having been able to buy a bottle of wine at the shop, she had been directed by the kindly postmistress to the hotel but, far from being helpful and courteous when she asked about buying a bottle of wine and the possibility of having a shower, the person she spoke to was so objectionable she walked out. "What a change from friendly Coll," she said. "I thought we might have had a meal at the hotel tonight, but now I can't get away from here quick enough." When we returned to *Amulet* a small motor cruiser was tied alongside crewed by two Germans, a

father and son, who had trailed the boat from Cuxhaven to Oban and
were exploring Scotland at twenty knots. They were a most pleasant
pair and it had gone dark when we finished hearing about their tour; it
was time to motor *Amulet* into the harbour and tie up in a snug corner
against the wall. Probably feeling rather vulnerable against the huge
pier, the Germans followed us in. The Coastguard reading the evening
weather bulletin talked cheerfully of a continuing spell of fine weather,
but the synopsis on the navtex shipping forecast showed the approach
of a vigorous depression from the Atlantic.

There was no wind during the night but a gentle swell rolling into
the harbour kept *Amulet* on the move, and the fenders rasping and
scraping against the wall gave us a disturbed night until the tide receded
and peace returned. Dawn came early and, keen to get on with the job
of caulking the seams, I assembled my tools and waited for low water
but, utterly weary, I fell asleep and low water came and went. The noise
of an engine woke me and I couldn't believe it when I saw it was nearly
8am; I leapt to my feet in time to see the stern of the German boat
disappearing out of the harbour. When I looked over the side, water
was already well above *Amulet*'s keel and working on the hull was out of
the question. Furious with myself I stamped up and down in the
cockpit swearing angrily, but I had no one to blame but myself. "Do
make less noise," said a sleepy voice from the port bunk, "and put the
kettle on."

Our visit to Colonsay had not been the happiest, and by way of
some compensation to help us on our way a fresh breeze sprang up as
we cleared the harbour at a touch after 11am. With Patricia steering for
the entrance to the Sound of Islay, eighteen miles distant, and the main
and genoa straining at the sheets, we soared across a blue sea spattered
with silver.

We had been sailing along nicely for an hour when MacBrayne's
ferry ploughed by and took our wind back to Colonsay, leaving us
becalmed and floundering in its wake. With sails stowed and the
Farymann fired up, we continued and at 1.30pm we were abeam of the
white tower of Rubha a Mhail lighthouse at the entrance to the Sound.
From thereon it was like being in a power boat instead of a small yacht.
Caught in the grip of a 5 knot tidal stream and with the Farymann
spinning round at close on full revs, we shot down the Sound between

Islay and Jura at *Amulet*'s all-time record speed of ten knots. There was hardly time to glimpse the whisky distilleries and the little harbour of Port Askaig on the Islay shore, and the mighty hills of Jura, before we were decanted into the Sound of Jura and swirled around in a powerful eddy.

Rummaging through my stock of charts, I discovered that a chart of the Sound of Jura I had loaned to a friend had not been returned, and it was with the aid of an Ordnance Survey map and information gleaned from Dominic, the skipper of *Huff of Arklow*, that we navigated through a thick heat-haze along the coast of Jura and the narrow rock-strewn entrance to Craighouse Bay to pick up a visitor's mooring. A spectacular run of twenty-seven miles. The crews of several moored yachts were climbing noisily into their dinghies, obviously hell-bent on keeping the till ringing in the island's hotel, but after a disturbed night in Colonsay Patricia and I were both very tired, and turned in early. Two men cutting firewood on the shore did their best to keep us awake with a whining chain saw, but failed miserably.

Much refreshed after a sound sleep, we woke to a fine morning and a big decision. Should we go ashore and climb one of the Paps of Jura, or should we take advantage of the fair breeze and run fourteen miles across the Sound to visit the Island Gigha? Yearning to be on the mountains again, I was all for climbing one of the Paps; but a friend of Patricia's had wrecked his boat on Gigha and though, with the aid of his son it was rebuilt again, she wanted to see the place where the boat had gone aground. (see *Rescue and Recovery – Iskra's Ordeal in the Hebrides* by Frank Mulville. Pub. Seafarer Books) In the end the fair wind won but, though we had left the mooring under full sail in anticipation of a lively run to Gigha, it abandoned us after less than an hour. Astern the hills, sharp and inviting against a clear blue sky, seemed to mock me and I longed to return to Craighouse; I started the engine but it was too late, Patricia was already reading up about Gigha. "Did you know the island was once owned by the Horlicks family who made the famous bedtime drink?" she challenged. I said I did, and that the islanders had thought very highly of them. "Well, did you know that there is a stained glass window in the church dedicated to Kenneth MacLeod, the man who wrote that lovely song, 'The Road to the Isles'?" "Yes, I did," I said. "I'll sing it for you if you like." "No thanks," she said hurriedly.

"This tourist booklet also mentions a Russian factory ship that went aground on Gigha in 1991; do you know about that?" "As a matter of fact I do," I said, "I saw the ship not long after it went ashore and it was very tragic. The crew's personal possessions and clothing were scattered over the rocks. Apparently somewhere in the Atlantic off Islay it was struck by a huge wave that stove in the wheelhouse. One of the crew was killed and the captain lost both legs. The crew were taken off and the captain was in hospital in Glasgow for weeks. Word got round that the Russian trawler company had abandoned him, and the islanders on Gigha had a whip round and gave him quite a lot of money so that he could get home." Patricia looked shocked. "What a dreadful catastrophe, and how wonderful that the islanders helped the captain to get home. I like Gigha already!"

Taking avoiding action to keep clear of two fishing boats busy trawling, I found I was on a collision course with a MacBrayne ferry, thundering towards us on its way back from Islay to the mainland, but though he had right of way, the officer on watch clicked his autopilot to port and, with plenty of sea room, the ship swept round our stern. A strong tide was running against us when we entered the narrow Sound of Gigha between the island and the long, rambling Kintyre peninsula, but we were not in a hurry and the slow pace gave us more time to appreciate the full beauty of Gigha's eastern shoreline before we threaded our way through a maze of moored yachts in Ardminish Bay and picked up a visitor's mooring. Sitting in the cockpit in the blazing sun, sipping cold beer and looking across the blue water of the bay to the white sand of the beaches, it had all the atmosphere of a tropical island. It was difficult to imagine that it was in the same bay that Patricia's friend Frank Mulville and his wife Wendy were plucked to safety by a helicopter in a raging gale, and their yacht *Iskra* driven onto the rocks and badly damaged. Scottish weather can be very changeable, as a day later we were to experience ourselves.

We inflated the dinghy and went ashore to look at the place where *Iskra* had gone onto the rocks and was driven into a small cove. That the yacht had finished up where it did without being reduced to a heap of firewood was unbelievable, and that Mulville had managed to recover it was nothing short of a miracle. "It was entirely due to Frank's son Adrian that the boat was saved," said Patricia as we walked round the bay making for the island shop. "He was a Thames Barge skipper and experienced with boats and came all the way from Essex to rebuild *Iskra* with Ariane, a Dutch girl who was a boatbuilder and worked for the same company as David Showell, the shipwright who stayed with us and rebuilt *Amulet*'s cockpit. Frank has since died, but as far as I know *Iskra* is still being sailed." She disappeared while I was in the shop arranging to fill the diesel containers, and came back half an hour later all smiles. I should have known! She had been to the hotel to arrange for us to have showers. "The shower block by the jetty is owned by the hotel, and we can use that," she announced. "I've also booked a meal for tonight, I hope you have a clean shirt." *Amulet* was moored close to *Insouciance*, an enormous ketch from Northern Ireland, and the owner and his wife and their two guests arrived at the jetty in a dinghy on their way to the hotel at the same time as Patricia and me. Owners and crews of large yachts can often be very snooty towards lesser minions on small boats that could easily have been slung from davits on their floating stately homes, but George Ralston and his family were very laid back and friendly and when, in the course of the conversation on the way to the hotel, I mentioned my missing chart, he said he had a spare I could have. To me, sailing is all about keeping well away from the flesh pots of civilisation and appreciating the solitude of remote places, but I had to admit I thoroughly enjoyed the fine meal in the country house atmosphere of the Gigha hotel, and returned to *Amulet* full of peace and goodwill and rather more than my usual intake of whisky.

A cloudless sky and a dew on deck the following morning heralded another hot, windless day and we went ashore early to buy groceries in the shop and fill the diesel containers. I was sad to hear from a local man that an endearing part of life on Gigha was about to come to an end with the impending retirement of Seumas McSporran and his wife, who had run the island shop for many years. Not only was Seumas the proprietor of the island shop and post office he was also the postman, the coastguard, the fireman, the policeman and the registrar of births and deaths. There is no allowance for replacing unconventional characters in today's computerised world and, given the opportunity, the bureaucrats will have us all as regulated as peas in a pod and the unique way of life of the Scottish islands will fade into history.

We returned to *Amulet* just as George Ralston came over in his dinghy with the promised chart, and talked enthusiastically about the remote Ardmore Islands at the southern end of Islay. I had been to many places on Islay, but the Ardmore Islands were not one of them and, as the weather front that had been heading for Scotland was now hovering close, it was an opportunity to visit them while the weather was favourable. Cancelling our plans to cycle round Gigha, we slipped the mooring, motored south down the Sound, rounded Cara Island at the tip of Gigha and set course for Islay, hidden in a heat haze fifteen miles to the west. Two hours of motoring in flat calm conditions brought us abeam of a lighthouse on the northern extremity of the Ardmore Islands and I steered for Ardmore Point on Islay which marked the beginning of a canal-like channel leading into a large pool almost encircled by islands. Our hope that we would have the islands to ourselves was dashed when four yachts, coming from the direction of the Sound of Islay, nipped into the channel ahead of us; but when they occupied a smaller anchorage close to the Islay shore I turned *Amulet* into the large pool and dropped anchor. It was a birdwatchers' paradise. All around us there were hundreds of sea birds wheeling and diving and the rocks were covered in seals. It was a perfect evening for going ashore and exploring the islands but, rather than inflate the dinghy and risk frightening the wildlife away, we sat in the cockpit and had a grandstand view through binoculars. It was a brilliant sunset and around *Amulet* the surface of the water was like a mirror. When darkness came I lit the anchor light and we turned in, hoping for another fine day so that we could take the dinghy and explore all the islands and inlets. About 1am the rumbling of the anchor chain woke me and, startled to hear wind moaning through the rigging, I climbed into the cockpit. The wind was blowing a good force 5 (20 knots) from the east and I shone a powerful torch at the rocks round the pool to check that we hadn't dragged anchor. *Amulet* hadn't moved, but I let another couple of fathoms of chain out and retreated, shivering, to my bunk. The wind steadily increased from a moan to a howl and, when a sudden vicious gust laid *Amulet* over and nearly flung me off my bunk, I went outside again and shone the torch round. It was a frightening sight! The pool was a cauldron of boiling water and the wind so fierce I had to cling on to the guard wire to prevent myself being blown over the side. Every few seconds there was a tremendous bang as the anchor chain came taut and, fearing that the chain might part and *Amulet* would be driven onto the rocks, I went below and got dressed and told Patricia to do the same and to get the lifejackets ready. The roar of the wind was so loud we had to raise our voices to be heard, and *Amulet* was being thrown about so violently I was sure it was only a matter of time before the strain on the anchor or the chain would be too much and we would have to jump for our lives when the boat hit the rocks. I was so concerned about our situation I made ready to press the distress button on the new fangled DSC unit before we jumped, at least it would give our exact position. In the midst of the commotion Patricia bravely lit the stove and made a pot of tea, and it did wonders for morale. From time to time I stuck my head out of the hatch and shone the torch on the rocks to see if we had dragged, but all was well and for almost three hours the storm raged over us. From 4am the gusts became less frequent and the roar dropped to a moan and eventually fell away to a strong breeze that rattled the halliards. *Amulet*'s violent motion eased to a gentle roll and, completely exhausted, we fell asleep on our bunks fully dressed.

Rain falling on the cabin top woke me about 9am and I looked out on a view that had been completely transformed from the previous evening. The tranquil, sunlit scene with a blue sky and sea, the dark browns and greens of the islands, the air full of birds and the rocks packed with basking seals, had been wiped away and replaced with a dark threatening sky and a grey malevolent sea that angrily flung waves against the rocks in an explosion of foaming surf. The islands were a menacing black, and there was not a bird or any other living thing to be seen. It was raining steadily and a wet mist hung in the air, reducing visibility to less than a mile. Over breakfast we agreed we had missed the opportunity to see the islands at their best and it was not worth staying. Eighteen miles further north up the Sound of Jura were the MacCormaig Islands, close to the entrance of Loch Sween. The larger of the small group, Eilean Mor, was famous for its medieval chapel dedicated to St. Cormac, though there was a time when the locals on the mainland used it for less sacred purposes and installed an illicit whisky still in it. But of particular interest to me was that the pirate John Paul Jones was reputed to have had a base there, and the tiny,

sheltered harbour would have been an ideal hideaway. A native of
Kirkcudbright on the Scottish side of the Solway Firth, John Paul Jones
had nailed his flag to the American cause in the War of Independence
and hit the headlines by raiding the port of Whitehaven on the
Cumbrian coast, spiking the guns and setting fire to ships. I had done
some research on the notorious mercenary and the chance to visit one
of his hideouts was too good to miss. The CQR anchor had been
ploughed deep into the bottom of the pool by the tremendous pull on
the chain during the gale, and it took the combined strength of Patricia
and me to break it out and heave it up on deck. Even hauling on the
tripping line had no effect, and I made a mental note that fitting an
anchor winch was top priority. Having blasted us all night, the wind fell
away completely and, when we motored from the Ardmore Islands in
light rain about mid-morning it was flat calm. *Amulet* had hardly
travelled a couple of miles before the islands and the massive bulk of
Islay were swallowed up by low cloud and mist and, steering a compass
course, we saw nothing for an hour until a large freighter appeared out
of the gloom astern and swished by with two radar scanners spinning
round and its engine vibrating across the water. It seemed dangerously
close, but it was probably over a mile away. At 1pm the GPS and a
quick bearing on Skervuile light tower, marking an isolated rock in the
middle of the Sound, confirmed that the MacCormaigs were only three
miles ahead, and half an hour later we didn't need the GPS or the hand
bearing compass. The mist lifted as though someone had taken the lid
off a box and there in front of us, and bathed in sunlight, was the island
of Eilean Mor. Enraged by the sight of the harbour filled with modern
yachts, John Paul Jones might well have vented his fury by setting fire
to a few and making the crews walk the plank; but prevented by the
laws prohibiting piracy, I had no such gleeful option and could only
fume. I counted seven masts in an anchorage that could comfortably
take two or three, and with no hope of anchoring safely amongst such
congestion we turned away from the MacCormaigs and made for
Patricia's choice of an alternative haven for the night, Tayvallich, seven
miles up picturesque Loch Sween. Tayvallich is reckoned to have one
of the most attractive settings and be the best sheltered of any harbour
in the west of Scotland and, while that is a matter of opinion, there was

no denying its popularity as we threaded our way through an armada of yachts sailing from it, and were one of a convoy heading towards it.

"That's interesting. Did you know that Castle Sween, that ruin over to starboard, was attacked and taken by Robert the Bruce? That's the king who was saved from being captured when he hid in a cave and a spider wove its web across the entrance." I groaned inwardly. Patricia was reading a tourist brochure again. "No, I didn't," I said, "but I hope he got planning permission for all those caravans he's parked round it; they hardly fit into the landscape." "Trust you to say something silly," she said wearily. "Aren't you interested in learning about the history of the places we visit? "Of course I am," I said, "but it would be easier to appreciate it if local authorities were also interested enough in their heritage not to destroy the dignity of an historic castle by allowing modern development to overpower it." We were passing an extensive holiday complex spread along the shore by the castle and Patricia studied it through binoculars. "Yes, I see what you mean. I'll make some tea!"

Nestling in a sheltered, wooded hollow, almost enclosed behind a natural rocky breakwater, the harbour of Tayvallich was undeniably beautiful and it was so well protected it gave the impression of being unassailable by winds from any direction. A few modern houses had been introduced into the landscape, but mostly the village still retained its old-fashioned charm and it had everything we could have wished for with one exception, there was no room to anchor. Nor was there a vacant mooring; the harbour was crammed full of boats, including George Ralston's *Insoucience*. We anchored outside the harbour in the lee of a wooded headland and went ashore in the dinghy for a leg stretch, but the steep headland was so overgrown with long grass and birch trees it was like a jungle and, targeted by a persistent swarm of midges, we beat a hasty retreat back to *Amulet*. The red painted ketch *Renaissance*, that had passed us off the Island of Muck weeks before, came into the bay looking very workmanlike under full sail but pushed along by its engine; and, having inspected numerous locations decided on a spot close to *Amulet* and dropped anchor. "The skipper's got an all girl crew," said Patricia, studying the ketch through binoculars, "there must be at least ten of them." "What a way to die," I joked, "some skippers get all the best jobs." "You've got an all girl crew," she said, "what more do you want?" "Well, a girl who hadn't got the same birth date as Methuselah would be a help!" I managed to dive down into the cabin before the plastic cup she threw at me hit the hatchway.

What a contrast to the night in the Ardmore Islands. *Amulet* never made as much as a ripple on the water and there wasn't a breath of wind. We slept so soundly it was nearly 9.30am before we rolled out of our sleeping bags and sat in the morning sun savouring a mug of tea. It was an absolutely magical day and the water was so clear we could see shoals of fish swimming around the stern. An inquisitive seal surfaced close to the cockpit and we could have patted his head, but we kept perfectly still while he sniffed the air and stared at us with wide, dark eyes. He sank quickly beneath the surface when a roe deer barked somewhere in the trees on the headland, and we reached for our binoculars in time to see a fine roebuck bound along the shore and disappear into a clump of gorse. It was a Sunday and, used to the strict customs of the Hebrides, I was surprised when a passing fisherman we spoke to said that the village shop was open from 10am until 1pm. The water containers needed topping up and Patricia wanted milk and a few groceries, so with the outboard motor whirring away on the dinghy we did a few circuits round the harbour to look at the boats, then landed on the village jetty. I met George Ralston on his way back from the shop with an armful of newspapers and he told me that during the gale the wind had reached over 40 knots on his wind indicator and he had been forced to raise anchor during the night and go across the Sound of Gigha and find shelter in the lea of the Kintyre peninsula. He said he had a conscience about sending us over to the Ardmore Islands, but I assured him he had done us a favour. The easterly gale had certainly given us a pasting behind the islands, but it might well have been worse had we been in the exposed anchorage on Gigha.

Lovely Tayvallich was a place that was difficult to leave, but I was still keen to land on the MacCormaig Islands and as soon as we returned from the grocery run we pulled in the anchor and set off down Loch Sween. Though it was a Sunday and a lovely day, there were remarkably few boats around except for two gin palaces that overtook us and, as were nearing the MacCormaigs I felt cheered that, at last, we would be able to anchor in the harbour and stay the night. I could hardly contain my anger when, as we reached Eilean Mor, we found the gin palaces anchored and fastened stern to stern, completely blocking the entrance like a harbour defence boom. Clouds of black smoke were pouring out of them and they appeared to be on fire, so I was even more furious when I raced *Amulet* in to help only to discover that, far from being on fire, the smoke was billowing from two enormous barbecues clamped to their stern rails. The gruesome torture the portly chefs and their raucous friends would surely have been subjected to by the pirate John Paul Jones would have been child's play compared to what I could have conjured up for them, and, denied a landing on Eilean Mor yet again, I angrily swung *Amulet* round and steered up the Sound of Jura.

"Where are we heading for?" asked Patricia. We had been going for some time without a word being spoken. It was a lovely warm day, rafts of guillemots were drifting lazily on the surface of the sea, a lone gannet was making his spectacular dive in search of fish, and the charter yacht *Corryvreckan* drifted by like a ghost ship, sails limp and not a soul to be seen. The only sound to trespass on the peace was *Amulet*'s engine chugging along quietly and the occasional chattering oystercatchers flying low across the Sound. It was too nice a day to let it be spoilt by flying into a temper because I was prevented from landing on an island; there would be another time. "I'm not sure yet," I said, answering Patricia's question, "I'm giving it some thought. Sorry about the outburst back there." "Oh, think nothing of it," she laughed, "I've learnt a few words I've never heard before, and it was very inconsiderate of those people in the motor yachts to take over the harbour like that." I went below for the chart of the north end of the Sound of Jura and spread it out in the cockpit. "I fancy a walk on Jura, and since the tides are not right to risk going through the Gulf of Corryvreckan and past the whirlpool, we could do the next best thing and walk round the top of Jura and look at it." It had instant appeal. "That's a brilliant idea, I've read about the Corryvreckan whirlpool and it sounds terrifying. I'd much rather look at it from the land than from a boat." "The passage through the Gulf has to be treated with a lot of respect, but if conditions and tides are right it is possible to sail through. Anyway, if you look at the chart there's a place we can anchor and go ashore." I pointed to Kinuachdrachd Harbour in the north east corner of Jura, a little below the Gulf of Corryvreckan. "It looks a bit of a tongue twister but its pronounced 'Kinokty', and the name 'Harbour' gives the wrong impression. In fact, it's only a bay, but we can anchor there and it's only a couple of miles over the hill to the other side of Jura." "Let's do it," said Patricia keenly. "It'll be very exciting. We'll have lunch shortly then I'll get our boots out. Will tuna sandwiches and fresh coffee be alright?"

The autopilot took over he helm while we had lunch and I set it on a course that would take us close to Jura so we could enjoy the island's rugged coastline as we went along. "Did you know that George Orwell wrote his book, nineteen eighty four, on Jura?" I asked Patricia as we chugged by the lovely wooded bay of Ardlussa. "Goodness me, no, I didn't; how interesting! Where did he live?" "Well, oddly enough, in a cottage only a mile or so from the bay where we will be anchoring; depending on how much time we have we might go and see it on the way back from the Corryvreckan." "I'd love that, I've read the book and it would be thrilling to see where it was written." "Did you know that George Orwell was his pen name? His real name was Eric Blair," I said. She laughed out loud and said, "You accuse me of reading from tourist guides; now you're doing the same thing yourself." "No, I'm not," I protested. "I once stayed for a day or two with a friend of mine, Mike Akers, who was the doctor on Jura, and I got to know a bit about George Orwell and went to visit Barnhill, the farmhouse where he lived. Orwell was a friend of Lord Astor who owned a part of Jura and who probably told him that his neighbours, the Nelson family of Ardlussa, had a vacant farmhouse. He suffered from tuberculosis, so maybe he came for the clear air. According to an old man I spoke to who knew him, he arrived sometime in 1946 on his own, but his sister and his small son came to live with him shortly afterwards. He was a sick man and had to go into a sanatorium for a while, but came back to Jura to finish the book. Apparently he knew he was dying and worked almost non-stop. The old chap said it was called *Nineteen Eighty Four* because the book was finished in nineteen forty eight; he couldn't decide on a title, so he just reversed the last two numbers, but whether that's true I've no idea. In the end he was so ill he had to leave Jura, and died in hospital in Glasgow." "What a heart-rending story," said Patricia emotionally. "I always had the feeling that *Nineteen Eighty Four* was written by an unhappy person, and it seems I was right. I do hope we will have time to visit the house."

It was hot and humid, and a heat haze prevented us from having a clear view of Barnhill, set amidst green fields above the Sound, but there was no mistaking Kinuachdrachd Bay and Patricia let go the anchor close inshore. Once the dinghy was inflated I ran out the kedge anchor over the stern to provide extra security, and with boots, rucksacks and cameras we rowed ashore and joined a stony track that went as far as a little farm, then narrowed to a path that the Ordnance Survey map showed traversing round the northern tip of Jura. Above the farm was a vast panoramic view, opening out across to Crinan and swinging round in a wide left hand arc through Loch Craignish, the islands of Shuna and Luing, the Sound of Luing that was the sailors' highway to Oban and Mull, and the mountainous island of Scarba. Between Scarba and where we were standing poured the infamous Gulf of Corryvreckan, considered by the Admirality Pilot to be un-navigable, but regularly used by fishing vessels and when, and only when, conditions were ideal, by the crews of adventurous yachts. The tide was flooding, and though there was not a breath of wind the surface of the Gulf was white with breakers, and a large fishing boat going through was pitching and rolling as if in heavy seas. Following the path high above the Gulf we came to the west side of Jura and looked down on the maelstrom about which so much had been written, and which had featured prominently in a gripping 1940s movie I remembered seeing as a lad, called *I Know Where I'm Going*. Those who have studied its many moods say that to really get a fright and see the Corryvreckan at its most horrific, the place to be is looking down on it from the island of Scarba when a spring flood is running into full-blown westerly gale; but from where we were standing the foaming water, whirling round as if someone had pulled the plug to empty a bath tub, was impressive enough, and the spring flood was running without any opposition. "Thank God we're not out there in *Amulet*," said Patricia fervently. "What on earth causes the water to behave like that?" "Some friends of mine who are divers say that there is a pinnacle of rock sticking up about two hundred feet from the sea bed, with the top about sixty feet below the surface. The tide runs about eight knots and when it rushes past the pinnacle, particularly on the flood, it causes a swirling motion to build up and the worse the weather the more agitated the swirling." "I don't think I want to look at it any more," said Patricia, with a shiver. "Let's go." "Well, while we're here you'd better know that it's called the Corryvreckan after a Viking Prince who lost his life in the whirlpool because he trusted a woman." "Here we go again," she laughed, "you're just trying to wind me up." "Judge for yourself!" I said with a grin, "Corryvrekan means the Cauldron of Breakan who, according to legend, was a Viking Prince who fell in love with the daughter of the ruler of Jura and wanted to marry her, but the old boy had a crafty way of getting rid of unwanted suitors; he consented to the marriage on condition that Breakan showed how brave he was by anchoring his boat for three days and three nights in the whirlpool. The Prince accepted the challenge, sailed back to Norway and had three anchor ropes made, one of hemp, one of wool, and one made from the long tresses of virgins. Breakan had a notion that the purity and innocence of the virgins would give the rope extra strength. Anyway, he came back to Jura and anchored in the whirlpool and on the first day the hemp rope snapped, then on the second day the woollen rope snapped. On the third day the rope made from the hair of the virgins held, but just when he thought the Chief's daughter would be his, the rope of hair parted and the boat was sucked down into the whirlpool. It seems that one of the virgins who had contributed her hair wasn't, if you see what I mean, and because she wasn't it weakened the rope. The moral of the story for all yachtsmen is, never trust a girl who says she is a virgin and don't rely on a rope to hold your main anchor." There was a long intake of breath like the sighing of the wind, "What utter rot!" she said, with slow deliberation. "Only a man could invent a story like that. If you think I'm going to believe that load of sexist nonsense, you can think again." "Well, suit yourself," I said, "but poor Breakan was drowned and his faithful dog dragged his body ashore and it's buried in a cave in a bay just round this headland. Come on, I'll take you there."

Breakan's cave was in a bay just below the Gulf on the west side of Jura, and as we approached we came on a herd of wild goats grazing in a hollow. Leaving Patricia with the rucksacks I crawled through the heather with my camera and managed to fire off a few good shots before a fine curved-horned billy goat got wind of me and in a flash led his harem in a mad stampede down the hill, along the beach and around the far headland. The cave, hollowed out at the foot of a cliff, was massive and could easily have concealed a small army, and probably did in the days when the favourite pastime of the clans was massacring each other. A 17th century traveller reported that there was a tomb and an altar in the cave, which may well have been the resting place of the unfortunate Breakan, but there was no sign of it when we looked. Patricia was not terribly impressed and thought it creepy, so we followed a glen marked on the map that took us back to Kinuachdrachd. On the east side of the island, the Sound of Jura was flat calm and *Amulet* had hardly moved from where we had left her. "Do you still want to look at George Orwell's house?" I asked Patricia. "It's about a mile and a half from here." "Oh, yes please, I might never get another chance and we are so close it would be a shame not to take advantage of it." It was only a short distance on the map, but I had forgotten it was a long slog up a steep, rough track and in the heat of the sun it was hard work. The reward was a fine view of the house with the sun on it, but there was smoke coming out of a chimney and, not wishing to disturb the occupants' solitude, we crept as near as we dared and took photographs. "The atmosphere is almost overwhelming, it has a feeling of great sadness," said Patricia, almost in a whisper. "When I get home I'll read *Nineteen Eighty Four* again and I'll be able to imagine George Orwell in the house writing it." The visit seemed to have affected both of us and, deep in our own thoughts, we hardly spoke on the way back to *Amulet*.

"With a strong tide pouring up and down the Sound, this isn't the best of anchorages," I said, as we sat in the cockpit satisfying a raging thirst with cold beer. "If you are agreeable, I suggest we go over to Loch Craignish near Crinan; I know a lovely sheltered spot behind an island." Patricia was all for it and, heaving in both anchors, we motored over the Sound to Craignish Point where the ebb whizzed us through the Dorus Mor. We had crossed the track of our start from Crinan many weeks before but, with a six knot tide under *Amulet*'s keel, we were not given an opportunity to stop and celebrate and, turning into Loch Craignish, I steered through the tricky rock-threatening gap between the islands of Eilean Dubh and Eilean Mhic Chrion and dropped the hook in The Lagoon, a delightful traditional anchorage slowly being overwhelmed by the onslaught of invading moorings.

Though late in the evening it was warm and, having worked through a
refreshing salad for our evening meal and hung the anchor light in the
rigging, we sat in the cockpit in the dark with a glass of whisky listening
to the calls of the birds, the plops and splashes in the water and the
mysterious rustlings on the shore that are all part of the magic of an
anchorage in the Highlands.

Almost every day, the news bulletins on BBC Radio Scotland had
been reporting water shortages on the islands and in remote
communities, caused by one of the driest summers in the country for
many years; and to confirm that it had no intention of going away, the
sun climbed quickly into a clear blue sky the next morning and by 10am
it was too hot to walk on deck in bare feet. Patricia had bought a pile of
Sunday papers in Tayvallich and we spent an idle morning catching up
on world news and swapping the trendy supplements until, about 1pm,
Patricia went below to light the stove and prepare lunch. I had been
putting a new shackle on the anchor chain and had returned to the
cockpit to get my tool kit when there was an almighty 'whoosh' from
the cabin and a scream from Patricia. I looked down and saw a wall of
fire with Patricia in the middle of it. I leapt down the steps and,
grabbing a bunk cushion, furiously beat out the flames on Patricia's
clothes and on the bunks. A tin of methylated spirit, used to light the
paraffin stove, was spewing its burning contents over the cabin floor
and, grabbing another cushion, I flung it on the tin and stood on it
while I beat out the burning meths before it poured into the bilge. The
panic was over and the fire out in a matter of minutes, but Patricia was
deeply shocked, and when she removed her smouldering jeans her right
foot and ankle had been severely burnt. I wanted to get her to a doctor
but being a nurse, and stubborn with it, she insisted on treating it
herself and I hauled the first aid box out of the forecabin. Prepared as
she always was for every emergency from boils to childbirth, Patricia
had filled little *Amulet* with more medical equipment than was carried
on the QE2 and I had often complained about it; but now the space
taken up by special burn dressings and pain killers had been well
justified. She kept apologising for forgetting my warnings about the
dangers of pouring methylated spirits on to a hot burner, but we can all
suffer lapses of concentration. She had been lighting the cooker, but it
had gone out and, without thinking, she had poured fresh meths. onto

it and applied a match. The vaporising meths. exploded and ignited the meths. in the tin she was holding and, when she impulsively jumped back, the burning liquid had poured over her jeans and onto the bunks. She was clearly in considerable pain but, having dressed the horrible burn on her foot, she refused to rest and courageously lit the stove and made lunch.

Miraculously, apart from singed cushions and a charred carpet, the interior of *Amulet* was unscathed, but the accident had seriously affected Patricia's mobility and we stayed in The Lagoon for three days while she recovered from the ordeal and dressed the wound. She flatly refused to get a taxi to the nearest railhead and go home, and insisted she should help me sail *Amulet* back to Cumbria. By far the easiest way back to Maryport was to go round the Mull of Kintyre, have an overnight stop in Northern Island and then round the Mull of Galloway into the Solway Firth, and on a bright, windless morning, with Patricia clipped to a lifeline and hobbling about the deck like the one-legged pirate Long John Silver, she stowed the chain while I hauled in the anchor and we sailed back down the Sound of Jura to spend the night at Craighouse.

A study of the tide table showed we would have to leave Craighouse at 6.30am to take the ebb round the Mull of Kintyre, and at 4am the jangling alarm clock drove us out of our bunks. Determined it would be 'business as usual', Patricia cranked the paraffin stove into life and made tea. I staggered into the cockpit to sniff the weather and found it was still dark, but flat calm, and with the Clyde Coastguard weather bulletin promising a southerly wind, force two to three, with a smooth to slight sea and good visibility, it was an ideal day for rounding the notorious Mull of Kintyre and making for Larne in Northern Ireland. As the first rays of the dawn began to streak the sky above the distant island of Gigha, I shoved the engine into gear and headed *Amulet* out into the Sound while Patricia lashed the CQR onto the foredeck. Clear of Craighouse, *Amulet* rolled and wallowed in a slight swell and, as we passed the Ardmore islands, the hills of Islay were tinged pink by the rising sun. As the sun climbed higher it was a great morale booster to feel the warmth on our backs but, far ahead, the sprawling bulk of the Mull of Kintyre and the coast of Northern Ireland were half-hidden under a morose mantle of dark cloud. Around 10am, having made a full-throttle dash to port to avoid a coastal tanker intent on running us down, a freshening gusty wind indicated that the prediction of force two to three in the Coastguard weather bulletin was somewhat astray. By 11am, when we were well into the North Channel, about seven miles off the Mull of Kintyre lighthouse, with a twenty knot wind stemming a strong tide and *Amulet*'s foredeck constantly buried under tons of angry water, there was no doubt about it. An hour later, the wind had risen to such an extent the sea was streaked with spume, and huge breaking seas were regularly engulfing the entire boat. We were in a crisis situation; and with Patricia steering and me warning her to ride over it whenever a particularly nasty sea bore down on us, I altered course and we punched our way towards Sanda Island, a few miles east of the Mull, hoping to find shelter.

The motion of the boat was so violent everything below had been flung in a heap and it was impossible to study the chart or read a pilot, and, not being familiar with Sanda Island but aware that there was a nasty tide race between the island and the mainland, I called the Coastguard on the VHF and explained that we were in very heavy seas but under power and not in any immediate danger, and asked the operator if he would phone the Campbeltown lifeboat coxswain and ask if it would be safe to shelter behind Sanda Island. Twice I stressed that we did not need assistance and could hardly believe it when, after a long pause, the Coastguard radioed back with the news that the lifeboat had been launched and would be with us in an hour. I radioed back that we were under power and did not require the lifeboat, and in an hour's time we could be safely tucked in behind the island. Used to yacht skippers who bombard Coastguard stations with TRs (traffic reports) when only sailing very short distances, it is hardly surprising it conveys the impression to Coastguard radio operators that the majority of yachtsmen are totally incapable of judging a situation for themselves, and he just repeated that the lifeboat had been launched and was on its way. Watching an RNLI lifeboat ploughing towards you at full speed is a fine sight, even if you didn't ask for it, but by the time it arrived we were out of the worst of the seas and only a mile from Sanda Island. The faithful Farymann had never missed a beat, and on the radio I flatly refused the coxswain's offer of a tow and said we were not in any difficulty but would be happy to follow him through the Sound of

Sanda to Campbeltown. Half an hour later he came on the radio again to say that the tide was turning and without a tow we wouldn't be able to motor against it. I said I would come alongside and take his warp, but he insisted on launching an inflatable that surfed through the swell and deposited two crew on *Amulet* with a towline. They were a very competent and cheerful pair but looked anxious when, with a thundering roar of twin engines, the lifeboat took off as if it were in a power boat race, dragging *Amulet* behind it. Being towed at speed by the enormous lifeboat was terrifying and, though I desperately tried to steer a straight course, *Amulet* yawed about so violently she was in danger of being rolled over and pulled under the water. I grabbed the radio microphone and bellowed, "Cox, for Christ's sake slow down; you'll have us under." The speed dropped, but it was still too fast and by the time we reached Davaar Island at the mouth of Campbeltown Loch my arms felt as though they had been pulled out of their sockets. "OK Cox, thanks for your help, you can cast us adrift now," I called over the radio as *Amulet* was dragged like an exhausted shark into the calm waters of the loch, but there was no reply and we were pulled all the way to the yacht pontoon in Campbeltown Harbour. "Go and make your peace with the Coxswain," said Patricia, thrusting a twenty pound note into my hand for the RNLI fund. "If we've learnt anything, it's that we have the best lifeboat service in the world and you never know when we might really need them." I was annoyed that the Coastguard had launched the lifeboat, but to be fair they reacted in the way they thought was in our best interests, and the only message the lifeboat Cox had been given was that there was a yacht in difficulty off the Mull of Kintyre. Happily it all turned out well. The wind that had given us a pasting was the start of a vicious southerly gale that blew for nearly a week and enabled us to discover the delights of Campbeltown; and best of all, for some totally unaccountable reason, the tow by the lifeboat had completely cured *Amulet*'s leak!

Gale in the Kyles - Upmarket Urinals - Journey's End

After nearly a week of inactivity in Campbeltown due to gale force winds and heavy rain, I was suffering from what Patricia diagnosed as 'acute harbour rot'. To pass the time we had been to the cinema, bought bits and pieces at a real ship's chandlers that catered for the fishing fleet, and enjoyed the welcoming hospitality of the Ardsheil Hotel which had even laundered our clothes for us, but I wanted to be away before *Amulet*'s mooring warps became permanently welded to the pontoon. A strong wind warning on the Coastguard weather bulletin, an ominous sky and the flag over the RNLI building in danger of being flogged to shreds by the wind was no encouragement to leave and face a long thrash down the North Channel to the Solway Firth; but, blowing from the west, the wind was ideal for sailing up Kilbrannan Sound between the Kintyre peninsula and the isle of Arran. Patricia's foot was still very painful and restricted her movement, but she was happy to take the helm and, with two reefs in the main and the working jib in place of the genoa, we said goodbye to Campbeltown and set off down the loch. A posse of boats escorting an incoming submarine held us up for ten minutes while the sinister looking craft was manoeuvred towards an Admiralty jetty, but once on our way again, Davaar Island was soon astern. There was a hefty swell running in Kilbrannan Sound and the wind had been gusty in the loch, but it fell away to force 4 in the lea of the land and we had a fine sail all the way up the Sound. Just in time to get the 6pm shipping forecast, we picked up a visitor's mooring in Loch Ranza, a superb anchorage almost enclosed by high hills, in the north west corner of Arran. A slight swell was running into the loch, but it was by no means uncomfortable and we had a huge dinner and a comparable dram to celebrate our 'escape' from Campbeltown. The shipping forecast would have done nothing to gladden the hearts of sailing folk still on the pontoon waiting to round the Mull of Kintyre and warned of gale force 8 for sea area Malin, but that was for the open sea and in the sheltered waters of the sea lochs it was often much less severe.

During the night *Amulet* rolled gently in the swell, though by morning the swell had gone, the surface of the loch was like a mill pond and there was not so much as a zephyr of wind. It was 10am when we left the mooring and the hills were draped in a mantle of grey clouds and it was raining steadily, yet we could feel the heat of the sun, tantalisingly hidden behind the clouds, and sweated in our bulky waterproofs. We were making for one of the most delightful sailing passages in the Clyde area, the Kyles of Bute, a narrow seaway running round the top of the island of Bute and appropriately named East and West Kyle. There was no point in hoisting sail, and we went under engine from Loch Ranza, crossing the track we had taken when we had sailed from Arran to Ardrishaig, and up the West Kyle hoping to anchor in Caladh Harbour at a wooded point where the two Kyles met. I had forgotten that it was a popular destination, within easy sailing distance of the many marinas on the Clyde and, being a Sunday, the tiny harbour was chock full of day sailors who glared at us when I threaded *Amulet* between them looking for a patch of water that wasn't occupied. No one waved a friendly hand of greeting and, rather put off by the hostile reception, we went across to the Bute shore. Patricia was about to drop the CQR in Wreck Bay when she pointed excitedly to the shore and cried, "Look, there's an otter!" By the time I knocked the engine into neutral to glide along silently, all I saw was a tail slithering into the seaweed on the rocks. "Do you think we might see it if we went ashore?" she said, clearly disappointed that she had only caught a glimpse of it. Before we set off for the west I had assured her she would see lots of wildlife, including otters, but we hadn't seen a solitary whisker throughout the whole journey. I knew it was unlikely we would see it again, but said that when we had anchored we would go ashore and look. Though the name Wreck Bay was rather forbidding, it was an attractive anchorage protected by the Burnt Islands, a chunk of land mass that might have blocked off East Kyle from West Kyle and joined Bute to the mainland had not the architects of Scotland's glacial upheaval preferred islands and provided a couple of navigable channels. I inflated the dinghy and we landed on Bute, but Patricia's injured foot prevented her from walking very far and, giving up the search for otters, we returned to *Amulet*. The 6pm shipping forecast came as a shock with a warning that the gales raging out at sea were to back easterly and increase, and in the Coastguard's 'Clyde' forecast there was a strong wind warning; yet in the Kyles of Bute we were relaxing in *Amulet*'s cockpit basking in the evening sunshine and watching the convoy of day sailors leaving Caladh Harbour bound for the Clyde. Once the stern of the last boat had disappeared through the channel into East Kyle not a thing stirred, and even the sea birds seemed reluctant to disturb the peace. At dusk I went forward to let out a few extra fathoms of anchor chain and hoist the anchor light, and was concerned to see a large expanse of black cloud advancing from the east and shutting out the stars as if a sliding hatch was being pulled across the sky. Within minutes, torrential rain was drumming on the cabin top and vicious squalls were straining the anchor chain bar taut. After pounding us for an hour, the wind and the rain suddenly stopped and, hoping the storm had passed over, I climbed into my sleeping bag and tried to sleep. Apart from rain dripping off the boom onto the cabin top it was dead quiet; but then I heard a noise that, at first, I thought was a ship's siren in the distance, but as it got louder I realised it was the wind absolutely screeching through the trees on the far side of the bay. Within seconds it was on us, and bowled *Amulet* over on her starboard side as if she was a child's bathtub toy. It was the Ardmore Islands all over again and, grabbing the big torch, I shot into the cockpit to check that the anchor hadn't dragged. The squall had passed over but even so, when I stuck the wind speed indicator above the hatch, it measured 28 knots (force 7). The storm and the torrential rain raged all night and the din was so loud it was impossible to sleep, so Patricia made regular brews of tea and we tried to read. Unlike in the Ardmore Islands, this time I wasn't too worried. It was good holding ground, there was plenty of chain out and, if the unthinkable happened and the chain parted, at least we would be driven on to a gently shelving beach. It was nearly 5am before it was light enough to see across the bay, and the water was white with breaking waves. When I checked a transit I had taken on two trees on Bute when we anchored, I found *Amulet* had dragged anchor slightly, and I decided that if there was a lull in the wind we would make a dash for Caladh Harbour. By 9am there was no sign of a lull and, though the wind had moderated to force 6, the sky was so threatening it was obvious there were more nasties to come. With the engine pushing *Amulet* forward, Patricia managed to get the chain on board but, just as the anchor was coming in we were hit by a severe squall of white rain that flattened the seas, and for a moment it was not possible to determine which was sea and which was sky. It seemed to take an eternity to pass over but finally, far across the Kyle, I caught a glimpse of Eilean Dubh, the island that formed part of Caladh Harbour. Checking that Patricia was safe, I gave the engine full throttle and, after a ten minute trouncing by frenzied squalls of wind and rain, we reached the quiet serenity of Caladh and let go the anchor. The rain was still pouring in torrents but it was sheer bliss to be out of the wind and, changed into dry clothes, we pumped some warmth into the cabin with the galley stove and had a mug of hot soup. With no sign that the rain was going to ease off, it was a day for reading and catching up on sleep but, to confound all predictions, at around 3pm the rain stopped and the wind ceased moaning over the island. Taking advantage of what appeared to be a gap between vigorous areas of low pressure the shipping forecast had said was heading for Scotland, we hastily pulled up the anchor and, towing the dinghy behind us, motored in flat calm through the south channel of the Burnt Islands and emerged into East Kyle. Fortunately we had not hoisted the sails, for we had hardly covered the mile to Colintraive Point where a MacBrayne ferry plied back and forth to Bute, when a squall came raging down off the high hills above the Kyle and lashed into *Amulet* with such ferocity she was laid right over and water actually spilled over the coaming into the cockpit. The weight of the keel soon righted her but, almost immediately, another squall knocked her over again and the dinghy, flying like a kite at the full extent of the tow line, landed upside down in the water. "I think we ought to go back to Caladh, don't you?" I shouted to Patricia, but the shocked expression on her face and the arrival of another squall, this time accompanied by driving rain, was sufficient answer and, turning *Amulet* round, I headed back through the channel. In West Kyle, beyond Burnt Islands, hardly a ripple disturbed the water and there was only a light drizzle. It was quite uncanny.

Empty of boats and people, Caladh was an idyllic anchorage and when we went ashore Patricia thought the estate very lovely and wondered who owned it. "I'm not sure," I said. "I've got an old Forestry Commission leaflet that says the original Caladh Castle Estate was at one time owned by George Stephenson, a nephew of the railway pioneer, but I've also read that it was owned by the Stevenson family who built the lighthouses. I suppose that figures since there's a miniature lighthouse at the entrance to the harbour, but someone has obviously got his facts wrong. Anyway, whether they built trains or lighthouses, they sold it to a family called Ingham-Clark before the first World War. The Castle was knocked about by the military, who used it as a base during the 1939/45 war, and it was in such a bad way it was eventually blown up by the army. I'll bet that cheered the National Trust for Scotland no end; they might have been worried they would be lumbered with it. The Forestry Commission obviously owns some of the estate, and if the Ingham-Clarks still own the rest they must be heartily sick of visiting 'yotters' like us swarming all over it."

It rained heavily during the night, but the gale had blown itself out and at breakfast time it was flat calm and pleasantly warm. Reluctantly leaving Caladh just after 9am, Patricia steered *Amulet* through the Burnt Islands channel and, under a ceiling of low cloud, we motored down a benign and peaceful East Kyle to the noisy contrast of a pontoon mooring in the bustling harbour town of Rothesay, the capital of the Island of Bute. The warps were hardly secured before Patricia set off at a fast hobble in search of showers, and returned triumphant having discovered the ultimate in palaces of abdominal relief, a world-renowned Victorian gent's urinal with period closets and a shower room. A relic of the time when Rothesay was a fashionable Victorian seaside resort, the urinal was lavishly tiled and the polished wooden cubicles extravagantly furnished with elegant toilets complete with mahogany seats and brass flushing-chains. There was also a female annexe but, with Victorian male disregard for the status of women, not by any means as flamboyant as the 'gentlemen's facilities'. When I went for a shower I was shaken to discover that ladies, curious to see where the men hung out, could actually be taken on a guided tour of the urinal. I cowered under a layer of soap suds when, first making a quick check to see that no unsuspecting chap was standing in front of the flowery porcelain at the point of no return, the guide warned the hidden occupants by intoning, "Gentlemen, stay in your cubicles, there are ladies present," then led a wide-eyed group of blue-rinsed American ladies on a conducted tour of the last bastion of masculine privacy. "I aint never seen anythin' like it in mah 'ole life," exclaimed one of the blue rinses, snapping away at the urinal with a camera, "The Scots guys sure pamper their dongs." Later on, while sitting on the harbour wall waiting for Patricia to have a shower, I could recognise when a ladies tour was in progress by the queue of men standing cross-legged outside with pained expressions on their faces.

I have never been keen on visiting castles and stately homes, mainly because I object to paying the outlandish entry prices, but when the man who relieved us of the overnight charge for staying at the pontoon said that a bus left the harbour every day for Mount Stuart, the home of the Marquess of Bute, Patricia talked me into going. I expected to be bored out of my mind but it turned out to be an absolutely fascinating visit, and it was all down to the guide who took us round. All too often, tour guides sound like robots with a built in tape recorder, but our guide, Ian Gimlet, had a sense of fun, and was so lively and knowledgeable I felt he probably knew more about the Stuart family than the Marquess himself. A lineage that reached back into the 14th century must have ranked the Stuarts of Bute as one of Scotland's oldest families, and with a garden of 300 acres and a house with more rooms than a rabbit warren, the present Marquess had plenty of space to exercise his six children, but I felt no envy for his lifestyle. I enjoyed looking at his priceless collection of paintings and would have loved to have browsed through his enormous library, but after the tour we went 'below stairs' and had a very nice lunch in what had been the vast kitchens of his forebears before wandering through the grounds and catching the bus to Rothesay.

Back on board *Amulet*, we had a rather sombre discussion when the evening meal was over. We had set out from Cumbria in July and it was now well into September, and we were faced with a difficult decision. Apart from it becoming increasingly evident that Patricia needed treatment for her foot, she was urgently needed at home to attend to matters of business. To add to the complication, I had a writing commission that was pressing, but we were still a long way from Maryport and the weather outlook was very unsettled, with strong wind and even gale warnings for the Irish Sea and the North Channel. Neither of us wanted to face that sort of weather, nor did we want to make any decision that would bring our wonderful cruise to an end and we sat in silence, my mind buzzing with options. The obvious answer was to lay *Amulet* up for the winter in a yard on the Clyde, but then I realised I wouldn't be able to work on her in the winter as conveniently as if she were in Maryport Marina, and I scrapped the idea. "I suppose we could ask Nick Newby, at Nichol End Marine in Keswick, if he would come up with his trailer and take *Amulet* down by road," I ventured. Patricia thought about it for a moment or two and said, "Well it would solve lots of problems, but where would we meet him?" "Oh, there's any amount of marinas on the Clyde that have boat lifts. I'll make a list and ring them up tomorrow if you want." "Yes, do that," said Patricia. "Now let's talk about something else, it's too depressing!" Instead of talking, we went to the local cinema and watched an hilarious film that did wonders for our flagging morale.

On the phone the following day, Nick Newby said he would come up to the Clyde at any time, all I had to do was let him know when and where. I phoned several marinas and explained the urgency of our situation, but only Kip Marina at Inverkip, near Gourock, showed any interest in helping at short notice; the Manager said to arrive at any time and he would do his best to see that we were loaded as quickly as possible. I arranged with Nick and the marina that we would arrive at Kip in three days time and, casting off from the pontoon, we left Rothesay under full sail bound for Great Cumbrae island some ten miles to the south. The depressing, dull, grey day, with an overcast sky and a damp south-westerly wind driving *Amulet* through a listless sea, reflected our mood and it seemed that, since making the decision to end the cruise, the summer had turned to Autumn very rapidly. Even swathed in my waterproofs I felt cold. Clear of Rothesay Bay, a fresh wind against the tide built up steep seas that flung freezing water over us when *Amulet*'s bow cut through them, and I felt utterly miserable. I had a desperate urge to put about and head back to the Western Isles; but what was the point of going back without my indestructible and ever-cheerful crew? It just wouldn't be the same. Resigning myself to the inescapable fact that the cruise was almost at an end, I gripped the tiller and concentrated on the set of the sails.

The island of Great Cumbrae, about three miles long by two wide, and its neighbour Little Cumbrae, stand guard in a narrow channel between the southern tip of the island of Bute and the mainland, and there are many who consider this the true entrance to the Clyde. Millport, a small town at the southern end of Great Cumbrae, looked dark and deserted when Patricia doused the sails and I rounded up to a visitor's mooring close to the town pier, and after a quick mug of tea we went ashore and tied the dinghy to the slippery stone steps of the old harbour. Boasting the smallest cathedral in Britain, Millport claims 'city' status, but it would need more than a church spire for the claim to be taken seriously. Like the once flourishing resort of Rothesay, the town reached its heyday during Victorian times when cheap steamer fares enabled thousands of Glaswegians to go 'doon the watter' to escape the drudgery of work and have a rip-roaring holiday. But that era had long gone and, with it, the money that kept the town vibrant and alive. As much as Patricia's foot would allow, we walked along the promenade and window-gazed in the few shops, managing to find a yachting magazine in a newsagents, but there was little else of interest to us. Patricia dodged into a shop and came out with a couple of meat pies, and we ate them sitting by the harbour feeding bits to a rather sad-looking herring gull with a wing so badly damaged it could barely walk, let alone fly. But it was a true survivor and chased off other gulls attempting to move in on the feast, and it seemed to have been adopted by the locals. Occasionally a car would stop and the driver would get out and feed the invalid with bits of fish, and a group of passing schoolgirls shared their chips with it. Despite its incapacity, it was probably the best-fed gull on the Clyde and, while Millport may have lost its position in the resorts league, it was a sure sign that the island's reputation for kindness and hospitality lived on.

The south-westerly wind pushed a lot of swell into Millport Bay during the night and *Amulet* pitched and rolled, halliards flapped against the mast, blocks creaked, and twice I was forced outside into the damp, dark night to secure the mainsheet when it worked loose and allowed the boom to bang from side to side. I slept fitfully, and was pleased when it came light enough to get out of my sleeping bag and make tea. It was a murky morning, with the sea and the sky the same ugly grey and hardly a breath of wind, but the met. man on the radio said that further south the Irish Sea was being blasted by strong winds. After breakfast, we hoisted the sails in the hope that it would inspire the wind gods to give us a sporty final run up the Clyde to Inverkip, but they were in an unco-operative mood and we left Millport and made our way up the west side of Great Cumbrae with the aid of the Farymann.

A massive black submarine, escorted by a police launch, passed us heading for the open waters of the Lower Clyde and it left behind a wake that came at us in a wall of water like a tidal bore tearing up an estuary. *Amulet* lifted high into the air, paused for a second then nose-dived down the back of the bore and hit the trough with a tremendous crash that flung icy spray over the boat and us. Had it happened unexpectedly during a night passage, it would have been a terrifying experience. The submarine Commander may not have heard the words I called him, but they would certainly have clouded his periscope.

It was only ten miles from Great Cumbrae to Kip Marina and, as the huge chimney of Inverkip power station drew ever nearer, so did the end of our cruise; but a ferry charging out of Wemyss Bay heading for Rothesay was determined it shouldn't end without a reminder that MacBrayne ruled the western waves, and it ploughed across our bow leaving *Amulet* dancing in its wake. I used the same words for the captain as I had used for the submarine commander, but gave extra weight with a few choice words in Gaelic in case the MacBrayne man was from the Hebrides.

It was with a heavy heart that I steered *Amulet* through the channel leading to the marina and tied up alongside a pontoon, but I felt a lot better for meeting Brian Rowley, the yard manager. He was a man who obviously had a considerable knowledge of boats, and also had a fund of amusing stories that kept us yarning in the office for a couple of hours until he mentioned the word 'shower' and Patricia set off back to *Amulet* for her towel and wash bag. Brian said that as soon as Nick Newby arrived the next day, his team would take the mast off then lift *Amulet* out.

Returning from the shower looking immaculate, Patricia did her best to raise morale by suggesting we celebrated the end of our memorable cruise by dining out and, feeling somewhat conspicuous in a crumpled shirt and trousers, I was led into the marina's swish restaurant, lined with wonderful action photographs of old-time yachts racing on the Clyde, and enjoyed a superb meal. It was very pleasant to relax in welcoming surroundings with the best of company and enjoy a bottle of wine and a whisky or two, but through the panoramic windows I could see a little, blue, clinker-built yacht looking forlorn among the alien forest of masts and I wanted to be with her. I had helped her to live again, and she had helped me to fulfil an ambition. Together with Patricia we had sailed nearly a thousand miles, exploring a part of Scotland that has no equal anywhere in the world.

Shafts of sunlight streaming through the cabin windows woke me early in the morning, and I was furious when I climbed into the cockpit and saw a clear blue sky. It would have been perfect for sailing down the North Channel, and I roundly cursed the met. office for getting the shipping forecast wrong; but when the man reading Radio Scotland's weather forecast said that a ridge of high pressure was passing over the Clyde but the Solway Firth could expect continuing strong winds, Patricia said it confirmed we had made the right decision. We spent the morning slackening the bottle screws on the rigging and removing the boom ready for the mast to be lifted off. When Nick Newby drove into the compound with his Landrover and heavy boat trailer, I was instructed to motor *Amulet* over to the boat hoist. With impressive speed and professionalism, Brian and his cheerful team took the mast off, lifted *Amulet* out of the water, hosed her down and lowered her onto the trailer, then picked the mast up again with a crane and lashed it to the pulpits, and in a little over two hours *Amulet* was on her way back to Cumbria.

Later, when I took Patricia to the railway station to start her long journey home, I thought I detected tears in her eyes, but it might have been due to a rain shower passing over. "Thanks for a truly unforgettable trip," she cried, as the train pulled away, "Let's do it again some time!" "You bet," I shouted back, "How about the Outer Hebrides next year?" But the train had gone.

Amulet Goes Home

When the British Aluminium Company opened a plant in the West Highland town of Fort William, it was powered by hydro-electricity and in the course of laying pipes to tap the water in the hill lochs above the town, the company bought a considerable amount of land and property. Having acquired it, they needed an estates manager to run it and the man appointed was Jim Cameron, and enthusiastic dinghy sailor, who moved with his wife Jean and two sons, Graham and Ian, from Beattock in Dumfries-shire. The company owned the *Morag*, a large cabin launch with a permanent skipper and accommodation for twelve people, and one of the 'perks' of senior managers was that they could use the boat for weekend trips and holidays. The Cameron family spent as much time as they could exploring the Western Isles in the *Morag*, and it inspired Jim to consider building his own boat; but rather than have a power boat he wanted a sailing yacht.

He liked the design of the Folkboat, but wanted something a bit more spacious, and after a lot of head-scratching he decided to design his own boat based on traditional lines with a clinker planked hull. In the privileged position of estates manager he had access to surplus larch and oak, and the means of having it cut to size and kiln dried by a friend who owned a sawmill. Wherever he went he was constantly on the lookout for materials suitable for building his boat, and scoured the west of Scotland as far south as a ship breakers yard at Faslane on the Clyde – now a nuclear submarine base – and came home with a van load of superb mahogany that had once panelled the saloon of an ocean liner. It was perfect for building the cabin, the cockpit coamings and the gunwales; and in a derelict shooting lodge on the company's estate he found the ideal transom - only it wasn't a transom when he found it, it was large table that generations of deer- stalking gentry had sat round over dinner, and it was being thrown out. Scraping away layers of varnish with a penknife Jim was thrilled to discover it was made of solid teak, and it was promptly 'rescued' and stored in his garage at home. Hearing that a farmer in Glen Nevis, right at the foot of Scotland's highest mountain, had bought some long boards at an auction intending to cut them up for fencing rails, but having got them home said the wood was 'too hard for knocking nails in and was useless', Jim shot round to the farm in his van and came away loaded with 'useless' lengths of timber which, by means of a circular saw and planing machine, were converted into a superb teak deck.

With Jim always searching for lead for the keel, his friends joked that there wasn't a church roof in Fort William that had not developed a leak since he started to build his boat, but the timing of the building programme could not have been better. Concerned by the reports of the dangers of drinking water running through lead pipes, the British Aluminium Company embarked on a scheme to replace all the lead pipes in its properties. The result was a small mountain of scrap lead which the resourceful Jim quickly earmarked for a new life at sea and which was temporarily stored in the now bulging garage.

Never having built anything bigger than a GP14 dinghy, Jim felt he ought to have his design vetted, and with amazing cheek he parcelled up the plans and sent them to McGruers, at the time one of the foremost yacht builders and designers on the Clyde, with a note that simply said, "Would you mind checking these for me." Not only were the plans approved, but Ewing McGruer, one of the brothers who ran the business, called in to see Jim when he was driving through Fort William, giving him firsthand advice on building a clinker-built boat, and they became good friends. In 1960 the lines of the hull were lofted out in the attic of his house and the garage cleared out so he would be able to build the boat under cover, and with no experience of using a boatbuilder's adze, but wearing steel toecapped boots just in case he missed, Jim chopped the oak keel to shape and the dream began to come alive.

His only power tools were an electric drill and a small homemade circular saw table, but with young Graham and Ian helping whenever they could the hull began to take shape. Jim suffered severe 'tennis elbow' through constant nail knocking, and it was only through pleading with his sailing friend, Dr Murray Kirkwood, to give him painkillers to help him to keep going that the planking was eventually finished and the cabin and decks fitted. It was time to turn their attention to making the lead keel and Jim made a wooden mould, the shape of the keel, and pressed it into a pit of fine sand. Then in conditions that bordered on medieval and would have had today's Health and Safety gurus tearing their hair out, a ton and a half of scrap lead was melted down in three cast-iron washtubs taken out of company houses that had been modernised. The heat source was bonfires of coal packed round the vats, and as the scrap turned to liquid lead Jim and the boys were faced with the tricky job of opening the taps on the tubs and pouring the lead into the mould. The team came close to being annihilated when one of the taps broke off and the white-hot molten lead spewed out and formed a large pool over the garden. Undaunted, they waited until it had cooled then scraped the soil off and melted it down again. With the aid of rollers and a robust block and tackle, attached to a beam at one end and to his van at the other, Jim hauled the new lead keel under the hull and it was bolted into place. To help slide the finished boat out of the garage, planks of wood coated with goose grease were pushed under the keel, but it would not budge! More grease was applied, but still the boat wouldn't move and, in despair, Jim was on the point of 'phoning for a tractor with a winch when someone discovered the problem. While Jim and his helpers had been concentrating on steadying the hull, the family dog, 'Rusty', had rushed between their feet and licked the goose grease off the planks. Once outside in the open the last-minute jobs were completed, the mast bolted to the tabernacle and a marinised Austin 7 petrol engine fitted. It was now 1964 and the boat was ready for launching; but though several names were suggested, Jim decided on *Amulet* for no other reason than that it was the name of the colour of the paint he had chosen for the hull. How he had a brass plaque made with the builder's name, the date and the name of the boat on it is almost as improbable as the way he chose the name for the boat. Another of his sailing friends was Mike Carmichael, the local vet., and one of his jobs was to make routine visits to the islands of the west of Scotland to test the crofters' cattle. He told Jim about a man on the Island of Eigg who ran a brass foundry. Nowadays, you have as much chance of finding a brass foundry on a remote and sparsely-populated island in the Inner Hebrides as you have of discovering a steel works on the Isle of Wight: but in the 1960s island communities were thriving and there were all sorts of interesting enterprises.

With the aid a wooden template, and probably a bagful of old brass taps 'rescued' by Jim, the man on Eigg cast a brass plaque, and it was proudly in place on the main beam in the cabin the day Mrs Norman Goss, the wife of the Manager of the British Aluminium Company's Fort William plant, cracked a bottle of champagne over *Amulet*'s bow at the old Admiralty yard at Corpach, near the entrance to the Caledonian Canal. Very shortly after the launch, Jim, his wife and the boys took *Amulet* on a short cruise up the Sound of Mull and the boat became an inseparable part of the family.

Some time later, Jim took a job as estates manager with the Scottish National Trust and the family moved to Ayrshire. *Amulet* was moored in Troon harbour. But while driving to a meeting in Edinburgh, Jim was tragically killed in a car crash and, with his sons Graham and Ian barely out of university and unable to look after *Amulet*, his wife Jean was forced to put her up for sale. She was bought by someone in Troon, but when Graham tried to trace her a few years later she had been sold out of the area and the trail went cold. It seemed she was lost forever.

The summer after Patricia and I had returned from our cruise we sailed to Fort William in *Halcyon*, a gaff yawl, and tied up at Corpach Basin in the Caledonian Canal. I was keen to spend a few days trying to trace the J.M.Cameron whose name was on the builder's plate in *Amulet*, and Patricia wanted to meet a man called Alan she had corresponded with for years but had never met. She arranged for him to come on board with his wife for a meal and as we relaxed over a dram Alan said "Years ago my brother Jim built a boat in his garage in Fort William. I'd love to know what happened to it and try and get it back, but I don't suppose I ever will. It was sold after he was killed in a car crash and it seems to have disappeared without trace." "What sort of boat was it?" I asked. "Well, it was a wooden boat about twenty six feet long and clinker built. I remember it had a lead keel because they melted the lead in tubs in the garden." The hair stood up on the back of my neck and I saw Patricia go tense. I could feel my throat tightening but I managed to croak, "What was it called?" "*Amulet*," he said. "He named it after the colour of the paint he used for the hull."
I stared at him for a moment, hardly able to take in the way that fate had brought us together. "Well, your search is over," I said at last,

"you're looking at the man who owns *Amulet*, and she's in good condition." His eyes opened wide with amazement and he could hardly control his excitement. "You own *Amulet*?" he gasped. "This is truly remarkable, I must phone Jim's wife when we get home, she'll be overjoyed."

The following morning Alan came down to the boat with the news that Jim's son Graham was very keen to buy *Amulet* and keep her in the family, and he was going to drive to Maryport to look at her. When I talked to Graham later, he said that going on board for the first time since his youth had been a very emotional experience and it brought back many happy memories. He was very keen to get 'Dad's boat' back, and in the Autumn of 2001 I stood sadly in the yard of Maryport Marina and waved a last goodbye to *Amulet* as the transporter drove through the gates, carrying her home to the Cameron family, her rightful owners.

About the Author

Bob Orrell was born in Manchester in 1934. At the age of fifteen he ran away from home and lived on the Isle of Skye and worked on fishing boats out of the port of Mallaig. At the age of 18 and eligible for National Service he went to join the RAF Air Sea Rescue Service but someone got the forms mixed up and he found himself in the RAF Mountain Rescue Service, leaving after four years to become a lighthouse keeper at the Butt of Lewis in the Outer Hebrides and at Ardnamurchan Point on the mainland. Later he joined the Forestry Commission in Inverness-shire, then the staff of Brathay Hall Outdoor Centre in the Lake District as a sailing instructor, transferring to a Merchant Navy school as an instructor in seamanship. He has been an instructor at an Outward Bound School, was a partner in a sailing and mountaineering school and served as a mountain guide.

He worked for a spell as a yacht delivery skipper in the Mediterranean, then as a radio operator on a North Sea oil rig. When the rig blew up and the crew were rescued, he sailed on a container ship before taking up lobster fishing in the Irish Sea; but his boat was wrecked in a gale and, taking a break from the sea, he tried numerous occupations before joining BBC Radio as a producer. He also worked for BBC Television but, desperate to return to the sea and to Scotland, he bought a 40' steel ketch and with his partner Jean Thompson ran skippered charters in the Western Isles. Numerous financial setbacks, including a complete engine failure, eventually forced the sale of the boat and almost penniless he returned to Cumbria and journalism, but then fate brought him to *Amulet* and the start of another adventure.

Bob Orrell lives in the Lake District and devotes his time to writing and sailing a Laurent Giles designed gaff-rigged Keyhaven Yawl in Scottish waters.

Glossary of Terms

Like any strongly made frame built to withstand being squeezed or twisted, the hull of a wooden boat is a lattice work of lengths of timber fastened together in a traditional way that has stood the test of time. The boatbuilders of old gave the pieces of timber names which have been handed down through centuries, and I hope the following will help to explain some of the names used during the restoration of *Amulet*.

Ballast Keel	A lump of lead or iron cast to fit the shape of the hull. Usually bolted through the keel and the keelson.
Beam Shelves	Sometimes called the Shelf – are long pieces of wood fastened inside the hull along the top plank during the construction of the boat. Fastened to the stem and the transom with lodging knees they strengthen the hull and also support beams fitted across the hull to which the deck is attached and also the carlins.
Bulkhead	Dividing walls between cabins – mostly made from sheets of plywood but occasionally of solid timber.
Carlins	These are lengths of timber that run parallel to the beam shelves and form the part of the deck frame that supports the cabin sides and the sides of the cockpit.
Caulking	Filling the gap between two plank edges with lengths of round caulking cotton prior to sealing it in with water curing mastic. Being clinker built, the only seams that needed caulking on *Amulet* were the garboards, the deadwoods and the stem.
Coamings	Usually the name given to the deep sides of the cockpit which are a handy backrest when sitting on the cockpit seats.
Deadwood	Short lengths of wood, usually oak, that fit one on top of the other and build up the stern end of the keel.
Garboard	The first plank of a hull next to the keel and often difficult to reach for caulking. In the old days it was known as the 'Devil' and led to the expression 'There'll be the devil to pay (caulk).'

Keelson	Basically, the backbone of a wooden boat is a wooden keel to which is fastened the stem (bow) and the stern posts but often the keel is strengthened with a heavy piece of timber, the keelson, which is fitted on top of the keel and at either end forms part of the stern post and the stem.
Knees	Called lodging knees when fitted horizontally and hanging knees when fitted vertically, they are simply triangular pieces of wood, usually oak, used to strengthen joints e.g. where beamshelves are joined to the stem and transom. Rather than fitted as a plain triangle knees are usually shaped to give a professional look.
Lands	In clinker built boats the plank edges overlap each other and are permanently fastened with copper nails and roves (dish shaped copper washers). The area where the planks overlap is known as the land.
Limber Holes	Drain holes bored through the floor frames to allow any seepage of water to drain the whole length of the boat into the deepest bilge at the stern where a pump is normally fitted.
Ribs	Sometimes confusingly known as 'timbers' – strips of wood, often oak, bent round the inside of the hull, to which are fastened the planks.
Sacrificial Anode	To prevent sea water eating into vital metal fittings beneath the waterline of a boat e.g. the propeller, a piece of softer metal, called an anode, is bolted to the outside of the hull below the waterline and wired up to vulnerable fittings. The sea water attacks the softer metal in preference to the more expensive fittings, hence the term 'sacrificial'.
Skin Fittings	Bronze or nylon flanges which fit through a boat's hull (skin) to which are attached pipes for allowing water to come in e.g. for cooling the engine, or to drain water out e.g. the galley sink. Usually fitted with an on/off valve inside the boat.
Tabernacle	On some yachts the mast is fitted right through the deck and rests on the keel but for ease of fitting and removal the modern tendency is to fit the foot of the mast into a steel casing, a tabernacle, bolted to the deck or the cabin stop.

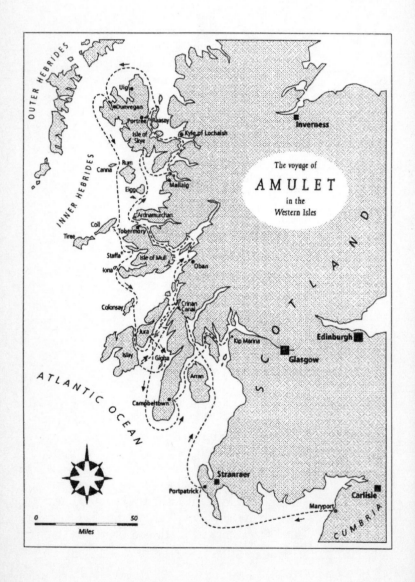

The voyage of

AMULET

in the
Western Isles